Kapitalizm

D0560710

Rose Brady

KAPIT

ALIZM

Russia's Struggle to Free Its Economy

YALE UNIVERSITY PRESS • NEW HAVEN AND LONDON

Designed by Nancy Ovedovitz and set in Simoncini
Garamond type by The Composing Room of Michigan, Inc.
Printed in the United States of America by R. R. Donnelley
and Sons Company, Harrisonburg, Virginia.

Library of Congress Cataloging-in-Publication Data

Brady, Rose, 1956–
Kapitalizm : Russia's struggle to free its economy / Rose Brady.
p.   cm.
Includes bibliographical references and index.
ISBN 0-300-07793-9 (cloth : alk. paper)
ISBN 0-300-08262-2 (pbk. : alk. paper)
1. Russia (Federation)—Economic conditions—1991–
2. Russia (Federation)—Social conditions—1991–
3. Capitalism—Russia (Federation)   I. Title.
HC340.12.B7   1999
338.947—dc21   98-38353

A catalogue record for this book is available from the British
Library.

The paper in this book meets the guidelines for permanence
and durability of the Committee on Production Guidelines
for Book Longevity of the Council on Library Resources.

10   9   8   7   6   5   4   3   2

To my parents, Jack and Rosemary Brady,
to John, Michael, and Ellen,
and to Jackie, Jennifer, and John

Contents

Photographs follow pages 62 and 154

Preface   *ix*

Chronology of Events, 1991–1997   *xvii*

1 Images, Voices   *1*

2 The Shock of Economic Freedom   *7*

3 The Rise of the New Russians   *44*

4 The Battle for Russia's Wealth   *63*

5 Capitalism Versus Communism   *155*

6 The Wary Westerners   *184*

7 Kapitalizm Reborn   *203*

Postscript   *244*

Appendix   *249*

Notes   *257*

Recommended Reading   *271*

Index   *275*

Preface

By eleven o'clock on the night of July 3, 1996, the worry and fear had passed. At Boris N. Yeltsin's campaign headquarters, his aides and followers were already tasting victory. Although only the initial returns were in, the incumbent Russian president was commanding a convincing lead over his rival, Russian Communist Party leader Gennady Zyuganov. Across the nation, as people turned on their television sets and watched the results, those that believed in political and economic freedom breathed a sigh of relief.

The official tally came out later: Yeltsin had defeated Zyuganov by a margin of 54 to 43 percent; more than two-thirds of the electorate had taken part in the ballot. The first presidential election in post-Soviet Russia had produced a victory for democracy, despite the expectations of many Russians and westerners alike. Two days after the poll, reformer and Yeltsin aide Anatoly Chubais drew a bold conclusion from the results. "Russia has proved to the whole world its right to be considered a democratic country," he told a packed press conference. "Russian democracy is irreversible, private ownership in Russia is irreversible, market reforms in the Russian state are irreversible. Nobody will ever succeed in reversing this in my country. . . . Never."[1]

Not everyone agreed with Chubais. No sooner was the election over than observers began worrying about the health of Yeltsin, who was sixty-five years old, had a history of heart trouble, and had looked frail on election day. Others wondered about a possible power struggle in the Kremlin. Only a week after the ballot, two Moscow trolleybuses were bombed, raising fears of a campaign of political terrorism by Chechen separatists. It was as if Russia could never be without crisis.

Yet there was no doubt that the country and its people had reached a watershed. Russia had come a long way since the summer of 1991, when a failed coup against then–Soviet president Mikhail S. Gorbachev had led to the disbanding of the Communist Party and, by December, to the breakup of the Soviet Union and Gorbachev's resignation. The coup had catapulted Yeltsin into the most powerful position in the country and given him the opportunity both to defend democracy and to accelerate the Soviet Union's demise. It had also placed in his hands the burden of launching desperately needed economic reforms. These measures, begun on January 2, 1992, had transformed Russia from a centrally planned economy owned and controlled by the government to the post-Communist world's wildest, potentially most lucrative, and possibly most dangerous democratic capitalist state.

The face of the Russian economy had changed from one of product shortages and consumer lines to one of plentifully stocked store shelves, colorful shop fronts, and ravenous consumerism. Supermarkets, cafés, beauty salons, clothing stores, sex shops, restaurants, furniture warehouses, auto showrooms, casinos, electronics outlets, and informal retail markets offered goods and services to those who could pay. Entrepreneurs, factory directors, bureaucrats, mafia groups, and foreign investors had joined a mad scramble to grab a piece of the state's wealth—and sometimes resorted to violence to acquire or defend their property.

Russia had taken a rocky, winding road from socialism to capitalism. Many Russians felt injured and confused by the journey, which had caused their living standards to plunge and upset the stolid predictability they had taken for granted all their lives. Others flourished. They were able to adapt quickly to the ever-changing situation, whether simply to survive or to build new lives for themselves. Between the haves and the have-nots, a middle class was also taking shape. They were the most important of Yeltsin's backers—the ones who had not necessarily benefited from reform but who could recognize that capitalism held out better opportunities for their children than did a return to the Communist past.

This book is an account of Russia's difficult economic and social transition from 1992 to 1997. I had the privilege of covering Russia as a correspondent for *Business Week* magazine from 1989 to 1993, and I returned for lengthy visits to chronicle changes from 1994 to 1997. Russia's transformation to democratic capitalism is a story of how the people at the grassroots of the economy and society reacted when their government imposed yet another experiment on them. This time, the state's goal was to grant economic freedom and privatize property rather than to build socialism, nationalize industrial property, or collectivize agriculture. Still, the people had little choice in the matter.

The story of Russia's transition embraces human endurance, ingenuity, guile, greed, corruption, violence, and determination. For many westerners, it is a surprising story, because many of us doubted that Russia would change much at all. We seemed to think that seventy-four years of Communism had wiped out all human initiative in Russian minds and souls. How many times did westerners write that Russians were not ready for price reform, democracy, privatization? And yet they pressed ahead. They turned the majority of the economy over to private hands, curbed inflation, and made the ruble function as a real currency. And they democratically reelected the president who had set them on their revolutionary path.

But the history of Russia's shift from socialism to capitalism is also one of mistakes. In the euphoric period after the Communist Party disbanded and the Soviet Union fell apart, both Russian reformers and their Western aides developed unreal expectations about what they could achieve. Yeltsin promised Russians that they would suffer for six months but that within a year their lives would begin to improve. The liberalization of prices shocked the economy more severely than anyone had predicted. By April 1992, Yeltsin's opponents were already trying to impeach him, forcing a slowdown of the liberalization effort.

Widespread corruption also marred the process. It didn't take long for Russians to understand that the new democrats were no less corrupt than the Communists had been. Although Yeltsin himself seemed to be above petty graft, the poison was widely assumed to have spread through the government bureaucracy and the presidential administration. Meanwhile, the militia and other security forces failed to protect citizens and businesses from the rising influence of mafia criminal groups. Even the army, once the proudest institution in the land, lost face through a series of corruption scandals that prompted one newspaper to dub Defense Minister Pavel Grachev "Pasha Mercedes."[2]

For westerners, understanding this dramatic, unprecedented transformation in Russia proved just as difficult as understanding the Soviet Union during the Communist era. If statistics on the centrally planned system were suspect, statistics on the private sector in the early years of reform simply weren't available.[3] Given the rise of the mafia and the government's heavy taxes, entrepreneurs and enterprises had strong incentives to lie about their incomes.

Moreover, the extraordinary shift from socialist to free-market ideology involved the development of new attitudes toward money, property, and entrepreneurship. It was about changing habits and lifestyles, the clash between new values and old traditions. All these things were inexact, and difficult to describe objectively.

Finally, many Russians and westerners (especially Americans) have found it hard to shake the remnants of Cold War mentality. Some Russians despise what they call "the Americanization" of their society. They can't bring themselves to trust prospective foreign investors, whom they assume are out to rob them. For their part, some westerners, deep inside, just don't want Russia to succeed in building a vibrant, market-oriented economy.

For all these reasons, I think it's impossible to be objective about Russia. Instead, like an artist trying to capture the essence of a scene, we must look at the country from various angles and do our best to piece together the elements of a constantly changing picture.

In the following pages and chapters, I endeavor to create, in words, just such a mosaic. We listen to the voices of Russians—well known reformers and entrepreneurs as well as ordinary people. To the extent possible, the Russians tell their own tale.

Inevitably, a reporter faces difficulties in Russia, especially in unearthing information about business. What to do when one entrepreneur advises you to interview another because "he hires killers to solve business disputes?" For a Russian businessman, there's no incentive to admit openly that he pays bribes or avoids taxes. Generally, in these pages, I allow businesspeople, reformers, and ordinary people to speak for themselves, leaving the judgment to the reader.

If journalism is the rough draft of history, this book is an attempt at perhaps a second draft. I hope the picture that emerges begins to offer answers to some of the key questions about Russia's economy.

For instance, what changed most in Russia's economic life, both positively and negatively, and in Russia's own terms, from 1992 to 1997? What still remained to be done? Could Russians enjoy economic freedom and create their own prosperity?

How did this era of tumult compare to previous transition periods in Russia? What can history tell us about the nature of Russia's emerging capitalism?

As Russia continues to change, so will the answers to these questions. There are few definitive answers.

The mosaic that emerges from my journalistic work may contrast sharply with that of a professional economist or historian. Nonetheless,

I offer it as a product of my deep interest in a perplexing country and my respect for its enduring people.

I could not have written this book without the help of many people, and I am very grateful to each of them. I owe deep thanks to all those in Russia and other countries who granted me interviews on the complicated subject of Russian capitalism. My editors and colleagues at *Business Week* magazine were extremely generous in giving me time off to work on this project. (And they were kind enough to send me to Russia, during the most exciting period of its history, in the first instance.) Special thanks go to editor-in-chief Steve Shepard, assistant managing editor Bob Dowling, and senior editor Frank Comes—my bosses—for their patience. I also very much appreciated the help and insights of my colleagues Patricia Kranz, currently *Business Week*'s Moscow bureau chief, and Deborah Stead and Rosemarie Boyle, who worked as *Business Week* correspondents in Moscow when I was bureau chief there in the early 1990s. Thanks also to Karen Pennar, a senior writer at *Business Week*, for her help and insights on the history of Russian entrepreneurship.

I did research while serving as Edward R. Murrow fellow at the Council on Foreign Relations. Historian and council member Daniel Yergin and then-director of studies Nick Rizopolous were particularly helpful. Columbia University in New York, where I was a visiting scholar, also assisted me. Simon Johnson, an expert on Russia and Central Europe at Massachusetts Institute of Technology, offered important and helpful suggestions on the manuscript. The Working Centre for Economic Reform of the Russian government and the Russian European Centre for Economic Policy kindly offered full access to their archives of *Russian Economic Trends*. Lelia Ruckenstein, my friend and agent, encouraged me to write the book in the first place, while Jonathan Brent of Yale University Press was bold enough to take it on. Manuscript editor Brenda W. Kolb made important suggestions to improve the text. Thank you.

I must also offer my appreciation to Alexei Rogov and Vladimir Sumovsky, photographers and founders of the Russkoye Polye Gallery in Moscow, for accompanying me on many assignments and providing many of the photographs for this book. Warm thanks also go to Natasha Verkhovskaya, who assisted me for several years in arranging interviews in Russia.

Of all the many people who helped me in Moscow, I am especially grateful to Elena Antonenko, a Moscow actress and my friend. She arranged and accompanied me on numerous interviews, devoted years to explaining the quirks of the Russian character to me, and provided encouragement and a place for me to stay on many visits to Moscow. Her family became my second family when I was there. Many of the human parts of this book—the real people as opposed to the officials—would have been impossible without their assistance.

Finally, I am deeply grateful to my family for all the love and support they have given me over the years: my parents, Jack and Rosemary Brady; my siblings, John, Michael, and Ellen; my sister-in-law, Jackie, and my niece and nephew, Jennifer and John. This book is dedicated to all of them.

Chronology of Events, 1991–1997

1991

August   Communist hard-liners mount short-lived coup against Soviet president Mikhail Gorbachev. Coup collapses in face of resistance by Russian president Boris Yeltsin and other reformers, but Gorbachev's position is weakened.

October   Yeltsin addresses Russian Congress of People's Deputies, proposing radical reforms. He goes on to win Congress's approval of special powers allowing him to rule economy by decree. He will run the government himself.

November   Reform government is appointed and begins work. Advisers from the West fly in to assist First Deputy Prime Minister Yegor Gaidar, architect of the reforms.

December   On December 8, leaders of Russia, Ukraine, and Belarus sign treaty abolishing the USSR and creating a

Commonwealth of Independent States. Shortages mount as public hoards goods.

On December 25, Gorbachev resigns as president of the Soviet Union. The hammer and sickle flag is lowered over the Kremlin and the Russian tricolor hoisted.

1992

January   On January 2, prices are liberalized, quickly soaring from eight to twenty times on most goods. Program of radical reforms gets under way.

On January 29, Yeltsin signs decree liberalizing trade. Russians head to the streets to trade goods.

February   Russia and International Monetary Fund (IMF) sign memorandum of understanding on economic policy.

April   Russia misses first target set in memorandum: freeing prices for fuel and eliminating special exchange rates. Gaidar government threatens to resign under pressure from Russian Congress of People's Deputies.

Russia wins pledge of $24 billion in aid from the West. First auction of stores in small-scale privatization program takes place in Nizhny Novgorod. Privatization minister Anatoly Chubais is helped by advisers from World Bank's International Finance Corporation and by financing from U.S. AID.

June   Yeltsin reshuffles cabinet, appointing three industrialists to top posts, including Gazprom chairman Viktor Chernomyrdin as minister of fuel and energy. Yeltsin also names Gaidar as acting prime minister.

July   Viktor Geraschenko is appointed Central Bank chairman after resignation of Georgy Matyukhin, who is blamed for interenterprise debt problem and other bank inefficiencies. Interenterprise debts continue to mount.

Russia establishes one unified market rate for the ruble, an important step in making the ruble internally convertible and freely tradable for hard currency inside the country.

Russia becomes a member of the IMF, which issues its first $1 billion loan to Russia.

August   On anniversary of 1991 coup, Yeltsin announces mass privatization program, promising each citizen a chance to participate in auctions with a voucher worth ten thousand rubles.

September   Industrial production continues to fall, but enterprises generally do not lay off workers.

October   First vouchers are distributed. Opposition to economic reform mounts.

December   First privatization auctions are held.

Congress of People's Deputies meets. Gaidar is ousted as acting prime minister, and Chernomyrdin is appointed prime minister. Yeltsin loses his special economic powers to rule by decree. Boris Fyodorov is appointed deputy prime minister for economy and finance.

1993

January   The year begins with inflation running close to 30 percent per month, raising fears of hyperinflation.

Privatization auctions pick up in regions across the country.

March   Congress of People's Deputies debates resolution to curb president's powers and stop reform.

Yeltsin announces special rule and calls for an April referendum on his presidency and on economic and political reforms. Outraged, opposition politicians demand Yeltsin's impeachment, but resolution fails to win enough votes in Congress.

April   April 25 referendum supports Yeltsin and his economic
             policy, calling for early elections for members of the
             Congress but not for the president.
             Government launches sale of Treasury bills, or GKOs.
July   Geraschenko introduces controversial monetary re-
             form.
             Yeltsin fails to utilize momentum from referendum win.
             Parliament tries to stymie reform. Talks over new con-
             stitution end in deadlock.
September   Gaidar rejoins government as first deputy prime minis-
             ter.
             Yeltsin dissolves parliament and calls for parliamentary
             elections in December. Incensed, parliament names
             Vice President Alexander Rutskoi as president. Tension
             grows as deputies refuse to leave the White House, the
             parliament building.
October   On October 3, Rutskoi calls for an armed attack on
             Russian television tower and Moscow mayor's office.
             On October 4, army shells the White House after in-
             tense meeting between Yeltsin and defense ministers
             the night before.
November   Yeltsin remains virtually silent as election campaign
             revs up.
December   In elections, voters approve new constitution by a slim
             margin, thus awarding the president broad powers, but
             they also elect a majority of Communist and nationalist
             deputies.

             1994

January   Gaidar and Fyodorov resign from government, raising
             fears in the West that reform is over.
February   Surprising period of relative political stability begins, as

new constitution takes effect and Chernomyrdin's government and parliament find ways to work together.

Money frenzy breaks out as inflation continues to rise and ordinary citizens fall for pyramid schemes like the "investment fund" MMM.

The gap between rich and poor grows, as some become wealthy while most struggle to get by. "New Russians" begin stashing wealth in Cyprus and Switzerland.

May	Foreign investors begin rushing into still tiny, illiquid stock market, causing a huge run-up in prices.
July	Tax authorities crack down on MMM. Millions of investors lose their money.
October	Ruble crashes on Black Tuesday, October 12. Geraschenko and Finance Minister Sergei Dubinin are asked to resign. Tatiana Paramonova is named acting governor of Central Bank.
December	Bankers grow concerned as Kremlin security guard attacks security force at Most Bank (located in Moscow mayor's building), Rossisky Kredit Bank is attacked, and mafia threats against bankers also rise.

Russia attacks Chechnya. Supposed "lightning strike" against Chechen rebels will become prolonged war.

1995

January	Central Bank raises reserve requirements for commercial banks and takes other actions to prop up ruble, as reserves dwindle dangerously.
March	Ruble begins to stabilize as monthly inflation rate falls below 10 percent.
May	Central Bank raises reserve requirements again.
June	The Duma places a vote of no confidence in the government.

July   Second vote of no confidence fails.

Paramonova and Chubais, now first deputy prime minister in charge of the economy, announce temporary "ruble corridor," setting currency's trading range between 4,300 and 4,900 rubles to the dollar.

Yeltsin hospitalized with a heart complaint later described as a mild heart attack.

August   Government announces that enforcement of ruble corridor will be extended until at least December 31, 1995.

Crisis hits banking system. Central Bank is forced to take action to keep major banks from failing.

Yeltsin signs decree laying out loans-for-shares privatization program. Vladimir Potanin, chairman of UnExim Bank, is architect of controversial program.

October Government announces that foreigners will be excluded from loans-for-shares program.

Yeltsin suffers another heart attack.

November Paramonova is removed from position as acting governor of Central Bank after she fails to gain support of parliament. Dubinin is appointed Central Bank governor.

First loans-for-shares auctions take place as UnExim Bank buys 38 percent of Norilsk Nickel.

Ruble corridor extended once again, at a range of 4,550 to 5,150 rubles to the dollar.

December Menatep Bank wins control of Russian oil giant Yukos through loans-for-shares auction.

On December 17, elections of the Duma overwhelmingly favor Communists. Communist leader Gennady Zyuganov appears to be front-runner for presidential elections scheduled for June 1996.

Law on joint-stock companies signed, protecting shareholders' rights. Law on oil and gas production sharing signed.

1996

January	Chubais resigns from government as parliament launches an inquiry into loans-for-shares privatization, a thinly veiled attack on the program. Policy-making essentially stops as the country gears up for presidential elections.
February	Miners strike to protest arrears in wages. Government promises extra subsidies to industry. Foreigners are allowed to take part in GKO market. Yeltsin officially announces his candidacy for president. He trails in the polls. IMF agrees to $10.2 billion loan for Russia, on the condition that the country control its budget deficit and inflation. Zyuganov, Chubais, and Russian bankers and businesspeople like Boris Berezovsky and Vladimir Gusinsky attend World Economic Forum in Davos, Switzerland. Alarmed that the West is taking Zyuganov seriously as a future Russian president, Berezovsky recruits Chubais as election analyst. Chubais soon becomes Yeltsin's campaign manager.
March	Yeltsin signs land decree, making it easier for farmers to buy and sell land. The Duma passes a resolution reversing 1991 decision to dissolve the Soviet Union.
April	Group of thirteen businessmen, led by Berezovsky, publishes appeal asking Yeltsin and Zyuganov to seek compromise in the interests of peace and stability in Russia. They later drop their plea and throw their support behind Yeltsin.
May	Presidential campaign officially begins, and television advertisements are allowed. Yeltsin wins major support

from media outlets controlled by Berezovsky and Gusinsky as well as huge financial support from Russia's most powerful businesses.

Russia and Chechnya agree to a cease-fire.

June   World Bank approves loan to support development of Russia's securities market and its regulatory agency, the Federal Securities Commission.

Yeltsin wins first round of presidential elections with 35 percent of the vote. Zyuganov comes in a close second with 32 percent. Other major candidates' results are Alexander Lebed, 14.7 percent; Grigory Yavlinsky, 7.4 percent; and Vladimir Zhirinovsky, 5.8 percent. Yuri Luzhkov is reelected Moscow's mayor with close to 90 percent support.

Lebed is appointed Yeltsin's chief national security adviser. He throws his support to Yeltsin.

Yeltsin fires bodyguard Alexander Korzhakov, head of the presidential security guard and a longtime friend, after Korzhakov clashes with Chubais over the arrest of aides who allegedly spirited campaign funds from the White House.

July   On July 3, with 68.9 percent of Russian voters going to the polls, Yeltsin is reelected president in the second round of voting. Yeltsin garners 53.8 percent of the vote, Zyuganov, 40.3 percent.

Fighting begins again in Chechnya.

On July 15, Yeltsin appoints Chubais as chief of staff. Yeltsin, apparently in poor health, keeps a low profile.

August   Yeltsin, looking frail, is sworn in as president for his second term, set to end in 2000.

Chernomyrdin is again named prime minister. He creates a government that includes Potanin as first deputy prime minister in charge of the economy.

Lebed brokers peace in Chechnya.

September   Yeltsin reveals that he will undergo coronary bypass surgery, admitting that he had suffered another heart attack between the two rounds of elections. As Yeltsin prepares for surgery, a battle for influence breaks out in and around the Kremlin. Chubais wields enormous power as conduit to the president and as signer of presidential decrees.

Potanin and Lebed ensure that loans-for-shares privatizations are not reversed.

October   Yeltsin fires Lebed from his position as secretary of the National Security Council and national security adviser, after Lebed attempts to increase his power inside the Kremlin.

IMF delays loan, citing Russia's poor record of tax collection and other problems.

November   Yeltsin survives heart surgery.

Russia successfully issues its first Eurobond.

Ruble corridor is continued.

December   Yeltsin returns to work after surgery.

By year-end, *Moscow Times* stock market index has risen a total of 138 percent, making Russia one of the world's most attractive emerging markets.

1997

January   Yeltsin is again hospitalized, this time with double pneumonia.

February   The Duma passes law giving the same rights to both foreign and domestic investors in Russia.

March   Yeltsin, looking healthy and reinvigorated, delivers state of the nation address to the Duma, calling for new wave of reforms.

In government shake-up, Chubais is appointed first deputy prime minister in charge of the economy and finance, as Potanin leaves the post. Boris Nemtsov, reformer from Nizhny Novgorod, is also appointed first deputy prime minister.

April Nemtsov launches attack on the power of such monopolies as Gazprom and Unified Energy System. Both Nemtsov and Chubais begin crackdown on enterprises that owe taxes to the government.

Interest rates continue to fall, increasing prospects that enterprises can at last borrow money from banks.

Berezovsky claims that seven bankers control more than half of Russia's wealth.

July Russian government sells 25 percent of telecommunications giant Svyazinvest for $1.875 billion to consortium led by UnExim Bank. The sale sparks controversy among bankers who claim that Chubais favored UnExim Bank. Its chairman, Potanin, rejects that view, claiming his bid was highest. International financier George Soros takes part in the deal.

In other auctions, Yukos obtains Eastern Oil, and Alfa Capital buys Tyumen Oil.

Yeltsin announces that industrial depression has ended and that production is now growing.

August Currency crisis spreading throughout Asia has little effect on Russia until August 7, when stock market reaches its peak and begins downward slide.

October–November Continued currency and economic crisis in Asia hits Russia harder, as investors from South Korea and Brazil withdraw funds from the Treasury-bill market. The Central Bank is forced to sharply raise interest rates, hurting prospects for industrial growth. But a ruble devaluation is avoided.

December Government struggles to meet deadline, set by the president, for paying off all arrears in wages owed to state employees.

Year ends with economy having grown 0.4 percent, while industrial production is up 1.9 percent. Consumer spending is on the rise (up 6 percent in the last quarter), showing greater confidence in the economy and the future, in spite of continuing problems.

Russia prepares for ruble redenomination, a measure that will effectively knock three zeros off the rubles-to-dollar exchange rate, effective January 1, 1998.

Kapitalizm

1
Images, Voices

Babushki. Grandmothers. A conga line of babushki stood shoulder to shoulder outside the railway station.[1] Their feet stamped in the slush and mud. Their blank eyes gazed into the distance. Their rough hands held out bottles of vodka, loaves of bread, Ukrainian sausages, Chinese-made handkerchiefs, T-shirts, used boots, old cameras . . . all for sale.

Hundreds of grandmothers stood at a makeshift market at the Kiev Railway Station on the south side of Moscow. Or a few miles away at Belorusski Vokzal. Near metro stations on the outskirts of town. At Luzhniki Stadium. And at train stations and stadiums in St. Petersburg, Yekaterinburg, Vladivostok, Nizhny Novgorod, Perm, and all across Russia.

Hundreds and thousands of Russian traders were doing what just a few years ago had been against the law—exercising their freedom to buy and sell goods or to sell their old belongings, for a profit. *Dengi.* Money. They needed money to supplement miserly pensions or salaries.

Not to buy sausage or bread, which they could still afford, but to replace eyeglasses that had been lost or to buy medicine or to pay the huge telephone bill (which used to be so low) or to buy a birthday present for a friend . . . In other words, to survive Russia's transition to capitalism more or less as human beings.

Antonina Grigorievna had worked for decades at a lightbulb plant. Nadezhda Petrovna had guarded a factory during the siege of Leningrad. Vera Nikiferovna, orphaned at birth, had raised four children on her own after her husband died of a heart attack.

"Milaya, moya . . . my darling . . . what would you like?" Dressed in a big brown wool coat, with a brown wool hat, Vera Nikiferovna was selling lemons, milk, and cottage cheese.

"We are pensioners. We don't have enough money. We have to work a little bit—what can you do? We buy these goods in the store and sell them for a little bit more—whatever we can get. I come here at about five in the afternoon and leave at nine. During the day I buy, and at night I trade—that's my work."

Vera's husband had died twenty-two years ago. "I have two daughters and two sons, and I raised them all myself. It was easier then. Everything was much cheaper. I had seven thousand rubles in the bank. At that time I could buy both a dacha and a car with that money. Now you can't buy anything. We planned and planned and then everything was lost. We were lied to."

They enjoyed life more before, these babushki. Life was hard but more predictable. "We were just beginning to live when it was Brezhnev's time. With him, it was good, very good. We were paid very little, but we ate well," said a woman combing through the garbage bins near my office. She wouldn't give her name. "Before we could buy meat, clothes, boots. Now I can't buy boots. It's impossible. You have to save, save, save. That means don't eat anything, don't drink anything. What to do?"

She didn't search the garbage bins for food, though. "I look for children's toys, pretty containers, empty wine bottles, sometimes pens. I want to buy something for my grandchildren, maybe some fruit, maybe some bananas. . . . I come here—it's far away from my own neighborhood—so no one there will see me. *Mne stydno,* after all. I'm ashamed. Maybe someone will tell my children, . . . 'Your mother is picking in the garbage.' Even sometimes my grandson asks, *'Babka,* where did you get this?' And I say, 'I bought it.'"

"I worked in a sewing factory for forty-one years," she recalled. "I started when I was fourteen years old. I got married young, lived with my husband, gave birth to children, raised them, and that's it. I don't have beautiful furniture. I don't have a beautiful apartment. I don't have a dacha or a car. I didn't earn anything in life. Now my children tell me I raised them the wrong way. All that honesty and fairness, no one needs it now. If you are honest you are a fool.

"They say we are going to live better but I don't know."

Viktor knew. "I live better, much better," he said. He had come to my apartment at the invitation of a friend. A young man in his thirties, tense, he leaned forward in his chair and smoked Camels fiercely. He was big across the chest and in the arms. He spoke in a matter-of-fact voice—without emotion. "We live as we like. I am not dependent on anyone. Everything is perfect. But for every job, I always am prepared for the worst—that I won't come back. That's it. It's pressure, constant tension."

A robbery conviction had landed Viktor in prison at the age of fourteen. After his release, he had wandered for a while, looking for a job. When Gorbachev's perestroika allowed new private businesses to open, Viktor had joined a Moscow gang.

"What can I say? People with higher educations are being cut back from work every day. There's nothing to do, nowhere to go. You have to live somehow, so we steal, we kill. There was one businessman in recent days, the director of a firm. He didn't want to pay us. So we took him, tied him up, brought him into the forest, and beat sense into him.

After that, everything was fine. As soon as he gave us our money, we arranged for him to be kicked out of his company and we put our own man in. We invested our money into it."

"There's a street here in Moscow—Tverskaya Ulitsa. Just look at it," Viktor urged. "All those buildings, all that land. All those new stores. It's almost all owned by people who at some time were involved in the *raket*. My life today is such that I can get for myself anything I want. But one perfect day maybe it won't be like that anymore."

"I go to church every week. I light a candle. I give the bums there money for something to eat. Everything is fine."

At a Moscow school, I met Julia. She was an attractive young woman, dressed in a short black skirt, high heels, a vest. She was in her last year, planning to enter the Institute of Foreign Languages. Her best friend had just been killed. "He was a bodyguard for a businessman, and he was shot. He was the only person who had the kind of life I respect. He worked, he brought money home to his family. He lived for something and for someone. I haven't met many people like that."

Julia spoke with a great deal of irony for one so young. "This is the kind of country that makes you tired," she explained. "It's that kind of life, impossible to predict. You go along and suddenly *bonk*—a new reform. Yesterday you had ten thousand rubles, and today it's only worth a ruble. And in our country now if you don't have money, you will not succeed. Whether you are a genius or a fool, you need money. All around, you have to give bribes."

But she did not want to go back to the way it was before. "I think Russia should be a capitalistic country. We shouldn't have the situation when a stupid, cruel, immoral person should have as much as an intelligent person. It's not moral. If people behave differently, work differently, why should they be paid the same?"

On the assembly line of the huge tractor plant in the ancient city of Vladimir, Alexander Martisyanov missed the old socialist egalitarianism. A spark plug of a man, short and tough, Martisyanov was hoisting a half-built engine onto a hook. He had worked at the factory for forty-four years. "Look at these hands," he declared, holding them up. The right hand was covered by a thick, grease-stained blue mitten. The left hand was bare except for the grease working its way into his pores. "Before, they gave us two. Now I only get one. I switch it from hand to hand. One hand gets dirty, the other gets a rest. Our conditions have worsened in every way. We produce one-half of what we used to. Our wages are never paid on time. Socially, we are poorly defended. The minimum amount you can live on is seventy thousand. We get paid forty thousand or fifty thousand a month."

"Look at the assembly line," he gestured. "It's shut down. Today isn't a holiday. It's a normal working day. But we didn't get the right parts so we cannot work."

"Whose fault is this?" he asked rhetorically. "It doesn't depend on us, the working class. The bosses dictate everything. They say there are no parts, but there always used to be parts. The parts came from all over the union—from everywhere. Now we are all disintegrated. Everything is ruined."

Poverty, crime, industrial collapse. These were images of Russia's lurch toward capitalism. Yet there were also images and voices of abundance, optimism, hope. In his newly remodeled office in a prerevolutionary mansion in downtown Moscow, Sergei Solodov leaned back in his plush leather chair. As vice chairman of Rossisky Kredit, one of Russia's largest commercial banks, he felt the burden of his responsibilities. "I spend about twelve or thirteen hours a day at work. Saturday I usually work—either meeting with the collective or on business trips. I have almost no personal life. Once a month I rest, and the rest of the time I work. I am the kind of person who decides to live and die at work."

Solodov was in his early twenties. Not long before, he had received his diploma from the economics faculty of the automotive construction institute. An average student, he had spent one week on the assembly line, the next week in the classroom. Then his life changed. His sister started working for Rossisky Kredit, and he soon applied for a job there. He worked part-time while finishing his diploma, then full-time. In two years, he rose from analyst to vice chairman. "Now is the time for young entrepreneurs," said Solodov. "We are playing. We are playing football. And the more we play, the better. As we go up, the country will go up." He wanted to help his bank grow throughout Russia and the world, and he was not modest in his objectives. "Empire. To create an empire. That is our goal, to become a transnational corporation. Our goal is to develop while there is the possibility in Russia."

"I very much like the climate that we now have in Russia," Solodov said. "Whether we say it is good or bad, at least it gives you the freedom to work. If a person has energy, initiative, and a strong mind, that person is able to work."

Solodov predicted, "In Russia today, there are those who are satisfied with their lives and those that are not satisfied. The new formation will be those that are not satisfied. It will be those that will take the initiative to push forward for the nearest fifteen to twenty years at a minimum. Everything depends on the intellectual potential of the young people. I am by nature an optimist, and I believe that in Russia everything will be fine."

The Shock of Economic Freedom

The economic situation is catastrophic. . . . I
cannot overstate how utterly desperate, utterly
bankrupt, the Communist regime left Russia.

Jeffrey Sachs, economist

"There is no meat and there won't be any!"

Propped on the counter in a Moscow *gastronom,* the sign captured
the dire mood perfectly. No meat, no hope. It was the fall of 1991, and
Russians were in a panic over food shortages. At stores across the country, long lines formed by seven o'clock in the morning, and there people stood, sometimes for five hours, before receiving their piece of subsidized beef or sausage. Although the stores set limits on purchases of
beef (two kilos), sausage (one kilo), cheese (three hundred grams), and
cooking oil (one liter), the shelves and refrigerated compartments were
usually bare by the afternoon. "This is the tensest period I've seen in all
my thirty-two years of work," said Lyudmila Rukova, director of Dieta,
a state-owned food store on Moscow's Tverskaya Ulitsa.[1] Fistfights
erupted when supplies ran out. Hoarding reached unprecedented proportions, as Russians stashed huge supplies of macaroni, flour, preserved vegetables, and potatoes on their balconies and filled their freez-
ers with meat and other perishable goods.

It was as if they were preparing for war. Indeed, hardly a day passed without rumors of a new military-inspired coup popping up in press reports or in conversations among ordinary people. The Soviet Union was reeling from its most tumultuous autumn in decades. After hard-line Communists failed to topple President Mikhail Gorbachev in an attempted putsch in August 1991, the pace of political events had taken on an unreal momentum. The Moscow and Russian governments seized all Communist Party property. A reformer was put in charge of the KGB, which was split into two parts and renamed. The Communist Party of the Soviet Union was disbanded. One by one, the Soviet Union's fourteen other republics declared independence, leaving Russia without its vast empire. The Soviet State Bank for Foreign Economic Affairs, which held the country's hard-currency reserves, closed its doors, effectively bankrupt. And, in the ultimate act of political chutzpah, the leaders of Russia, Ukraine, and Belorussia met in a hunting lodge not far from Minsk on December 8, 1991, and signed a treaty creating the new Commonwealth of Independent States. It marked the end of the Soviet Union. Gorbachev wasn't even invited to the meeting.

The political tension fueled people's worries about the supply of food and other goods. Not only were families hoarding, but stores, state trading organizations, and collective farms were, too. Everyone anticipated that prices would soon soar. Why sell now, farmers figured, if they could make much more money in a few months? In Moscow, St. Petersburg, and other cities, grocers posted signs declaring *sanitarny dyen*—sanitary or cleanup day. There was little food to be sold.

Yet even as extraordinary political events unfolded, a team of Russian and Western economists worked furiously behind the scenes on a plan of shock therapy for the economy. For them, it was a turning point in economic history. Russia, the centerpiece of the world's oldest and largest socialist, centrally planned economy, was preparing to embrace capitalism. From both Europe and the United States, economists flew to Moscow to join Russian president Boris Yeltsin's remarkably youthful economic team, led by thirty-five-year-old Yegor Gaidar. The grand-son of a famous Red Army regiment commander and popular Stalin-era children's author, and son of a top-ranking journalist for the Communist Party daily, *Pravda,* Gaidar had become known in his own right as a writer for a Communist publication—the journal *Kommunist.* But his specialty was economics.

For a child of the Communist elite, Gaidar held unorthodox views. He was one of a small group of Soviet economists who maintained that their country desperately needed free prices, free trade, a freely convertible currency, and private property. As a boy, he had witnessed Castro's revolution in Cuba and the 1968 Prague spring, which his father had covered for *Pravda.* As a student at Moscow State University, he had studied with the dissident economist Stanislav Shatalin, analyzing market reforms in Eastern European countries. It had been a dangerous time for intellectuals, the height of Leonid Brezhnev's crackdown on dissidents. Shatalin had been dismissed from the mathematics department of Moscow State University, but he had been able to find work at a small institute. Gaidar had worked with him, as the ideology department of the party suspiciously eyed them both.

When Gorbachev launched his glasnost and perestroika reforms, Gaidar joined *Kommunist* as economics editor. It became easier to write boldly about economics without running into trouble. The first step that Gaidar took as economics editor was to legalize the term "inflation" for the Soviet economy. Until then, discussing inflation had been forbidden; instead, economists had hinted broadly at the problem by writing awkwardly about such phenomena as "financial economical equilibrium." Soon Gaidar was airing views on the renegade topics of private property and price reform.

In 1990, after a brief stint at *Pravda,* Gaidar became director of the new Institute for the Study of the Economy in Transition. The institute's backers included Abel Aganbegyan, a key economic adviser to Gorbachev. By that time, the Soviet economy was dissolving into chaos. The Baltics had demanded economic sovereignty, and republics like Kazakhstan were assuming greater control over their own resources. Gaidar began studying ways for the Russian republic to reform its own economy, independent of the Soviet Union. His institute churned out in-depth policy analyses every month.

With the coup and the collapse of the Soviet Union, Gaidar gained the chance to put his ideas into action. He had gone to the White House during the August events. Even before that, his studies had caught the eye of Gennady Burbulis, Yeltsin's adviser and state secretary. Although there were better-known economists to choose from, Burbulis asked Gaidar to join the Yeltsin team. Gaidar had one clear advantage: he wanted to reform Russia's economy, while other economists were still struggling to preserve the Soviet Union as a whole.

Through September and October 1991, Gaidar's group of bright thirty- and forty-year-old Russian economists huddled with such Western experts as Harvard University's Jeffrey Sachs and Swedish economist Anders Åslund. Sachs had written economic-reform plans for Bolivia and Poland. Åslund was known for his insightful writings on Gorbachev's "struggle for economic reform."[2] Working long hours inside the somber, gray former headquarters of the Communist Party on Staraya Ploshad, they put together an economic strategy more radical than anything Gorbachev had ever considered.

It was modeled after Poland's successful shock-therapy reforms of January 1990. The aim: to liberalize the economy by stabilizing its precarious finances and privatizing state property. The first stage would involve freeing most retail and wholesale prices, which the state had controlled since the 1920s; drastically slashing government spending; and shrinking the money supply by soaking up the vast pools of rubles that flooded the country.

That last step was crucial because the Russian currency had lost nearly all its value. By 1991, enterprises preferred to pay each other in goods rather than rubles. (Indeed, the cleverest factory managers struck domestic and international barter deals that enabled them to pay their employees, not with rubles, but with food, clothing, consumer goods, even Cuban rum.) Russians who could get their hands on dollars lived much better than their neighbors did; at least dollars could buy goods at special *beriozka* stores set up for foreigners. Meanwhile, Russians stored thousands of rubles in accounts at the state savings bank or, more often, at home. Newspapers cited incidents of citizens using rubles for wallpaper or toilet paper, both in short supply.

On October 28, 1991, Yeltsin stood before a special session of Russia's parliamentary assembly, the Congress of People's Deputies, and presented his economic plan. Gaidar had written most of the speech. "I appeal to you at one of the most critical moments in Russian history," Yeltsin declared. "Right now it will be decided what kind of country Russia will be in the coming years and decades. . . . A big reformist breakthrough is necessary." He continued: "We have defended political freedom. Now we have to give economic [freedom], to remove all barriers to the freedom of enterprises and entrepreneurship, to give people possibilities to work and receive as much as they earn."[3]

Yeltsin asked for, and won, the Congress's approval of his acting as his own prime minister—a gesture demonstrating that he wanted to devote full attention to the economy. He made Gaidar deputy prime minister in charge of economics and finance. The Congress also granted Yeltsin's request for special powers to issue economic decrees without parliamentary approval. Such powers were needed, the president argued, to implement reforms quickly.

But Yeltsin made one serious mistake. He pledged that after a rough, six-month transition, Russians would begin to see their lives improve. That prognosis turned out to be wrong. Economic reform would prove to be a far harsher and far longer process than Yeltsin and the reformers envisioned.

On December 25, 1991, Gorbachev resigned as Soviet president. The red hammer-and-sickle flag was lowered at the Kremlin—a precise and poignant end to the Communist era. As Russia's tricolor was hoisted, Russians nervously awaited the New Year, when a new economic upheaval would begin.

The Russians weren't the only nervous ones. Westerners in Moscow in the fall of 1991 rushed around the city with expressions at once excited and dazed. We all understood that we were living in a historic moment, but no one knew what to expect. Had cranes really dismantled the statue of KGB founder Felix Dzerzhinsky and removed it from its pride of place in the center of Moscow? Had Ukraine truly declared independence? Would the demoralized Red Army bow to the breakup of the Soviet empire? With food so scarce, would Russians be able to survive the winter?

For those of us who had followed Gorbachev's agonizing struggle to reform his socialist economy, there was a sense of disbelief that Yeltsin was finally taking serious steps. We had seen so many halfhearted moves, so many economic programs written, debated, and discarded. (My office was cluttered with them: Leonid Abalkin's anticrisis program of 1989; Nikolai Ryzhkov's 1990 proposals for a regulated-market economy; Shatalin's and Grigory Yavlinsky's Five Hundred Days program of the summer of 1990; Valentin Pavlov's anticrisis program, released just before the coup in 1991 . . .) Gaidar, by contrast, made a point of not publishing a program. His plan was to act first and talk later.

Around the city, visiting Western economists spoke highly of Gaidar and his team. They were "the best macroeconomists in the Soviet Union," Åslund told me. But westerners also spoke in apocalyptic terms about the imminent price liberalization. "We are holding our breaths," acknowledged Jean Foglizzo, the newly arrived Moscow representative of the International Monetary Fund, practically whispering the words as he sat among unopened boxes in his makeshift office at the Metropol Hotel. (Despite its pricey rooms, the Metropol had become a temporary command central for representatives of the IMF, World Bank, and other international organizations; office space in

Moscow was nearly impossible to find on short notice.) Foglizzo expressed the hope that Russia would avoid the worst—which, for him, meant civil unrest or even civil war. Åslund echoed his dire warnings. "This is a real powder keg," he told me. "The expectations should be kept very low. Anything that is less than complete chaos must be considered a success."[4]

Both Western advisers and journalists had absorbed the fears and threats of Yeltsin's Communist opponents. We were all afraid of the *tolpa*—the unruly masses—and what they might do when food prices soared. This quiet terror gripped us even though nothing disastrous had occurred the previous spring, when Gorbachev's government had raised (but not freed) state prices on food, clothing, and consumer goods by as much as 1,000 percent. Now, however, the mood of the country seemed darker, the situation more desperate. And the reforms were intended to be far more sweeping.

Russia was experiencing three revolutions all at once. It was attempting to lock in a new democratic political system (and sorely needed to replace its old Communist-era constitution). It was trying to launch a new capitalist economy. And it was coping with its postimperial status: within a few short years, Russia had lost the Cold War and its superpower position in the world, and it had given up its influence over Central Europe and neighboring republics that had been part of its empire for centuries. All this was incomprehensible to most Russians, from high-level officials to simple souls who had defended the country against the Nazis or answered their Communist leaders' call to sacrifice themselves for the sake of a better future, a better state. "We lived for an idea. You Americans live just for money," the elderly father of a friend told me bitterly one May Day, as we sat around drinking vodka and champagne. "We spent our whole lives working for an idea. Now it turns out you were right."[5]

The Communist ideology had lost its power. But Russians had not united around a new cause. True, they had backed Yeltsin when he faced outright treason during the August 1991 coup. But after the excitement had died down, they weren't sure whom they supported and what they believed in. They only knew that they wanted to live better. But what to do? How to get there? No one really wanted to sacrifice more than they already had.

So the question hung over the government and its advisers ominously: would the people support Yeltsin as he pushed them into even more economic hardship, or would they revolt?

Not long before the launch of the reforms, I called on Alexander Shokhin, minister of labor and a key member of Gaidar's team. Before entering the government, he had studied with Gaidar at Moscow State University, then worked as an economic adviser to Soviet foreign minister Eduard Shevardnadze. Behind his thick glasses, Shokhin's eyes looked tired. His modest office at the Labor Ministry was overflowing with papers. "We are kamikazes," he told me. "Nobody expects us to last more than a few months."

By Shokhin's scenario, the government would launch the reforms, then be driven out of office by riots or political opposition. Already, Yeltsin's vice president, former general Alexander Rutskoi, had called the government program "economic genocide" and dubbed Gaidar and his team "the boys in pink pants." Shokhin didn't care. "As long as we are in power, we will push the process as far and as fast as we can," he said. Over the next weeks, the kamikaze theme would be repeated again. (Government officials later came to regret that they had referred to themselves thus.)[6]

On New Year's Day, I strolled to a gastronom near my apartment to check out the food supply. The shelves had never looked barer. Four wrinkled sausages lay forlornly in one of the refrigerated display cases. Otherwise, the store was empty. Had management made any special preparations for the price reform? Of course not. The bored cashier told me to come back in a few days. "We don't know what to do. We don't know what will happen," she said.

Later that afternoon, at a party, Igor, a still-loyal Communist, warned me to expect chaos. "In a few weeks," he predicted darkly, "people will simply start stealing from the shops, from depots, and from anywhere else they can get their hands on food." He forecast a social explosion. The result, he said, would be a return to Communist power, or perhaps fascist rule. He almost smiled at the notion. Hardly cheered, I was nevertheless looking forward to January 2—the start, at last, of truly radical economic reform in Russia.

It turned out to be a beautiful morning. A heavy snow blanketed Moscow. At nine o'clock the streets were hushed, as if Muscovites had decided to stay home and extend their holiday rather than face the weather. Walking the block separating my apartment from my office, I reassured myself that it was not a day for mass riots. At noon, I headed to a small commercial bank outlet to exchange money—ninety-six rubles to the dollar. Then I went out to survey Moscow's reaction to the first day of shock therapy.

Over at a small Produkti store on Aleksei Tolstoy street, shoppers were snapping up sugar for seven rubles a kilo—without ration coupons. Days before, sugar had cost just two rubles a kilo, but shoppers had to present a coupon, and supplies were strictly limited. Near the exit, a woman in her fifties or so carefully placed several packets of sugar into a suitcase. Her adult son, probably in his twenties, helped her. "I'm for the reforms," he said. "It will be better. We will have to work, but it will be better." Still, he admitted that life would be tough because he earned only four hundred rubles a month—just over four dollars—as a computer technician at a government institute. "I am not in favor of this new policy because it will be very difficult," his mother disagreed, adding that she earned three hundred rubles a month as a clerical worker. "How will they feed their little daughter?" She nodded toward the young man's wife, who was rocking a baby carriage outside. A stocky woman with gray hair and big circles under her eyes nodded. "It's awful, of course, a nightmare. How will we live with prices like these and pensions of two hundred rubles a month?"

Yet most shoppers seemed more resigned than angry. At the Smolensk Supermarket, on the Ring Road near the Foreign Ministry, I chatted to a man visiting Moscow from the Urals, where he worked on a collective farm. He was in town for a funeral and smelled of vodka. "Nado vizhit," he said. "We just have to survive." But he assured me that he would and that the Russian people would and that Russia would. "It's better for the country people than the city people. I have my own chickens and garden and can feed myself."

Late in the day, I decided to stop by one last store—the Arbat Gastronom. It was newly redecorated as part of a joint venture with an Irish group, which ran the adjacent hard-currency store, Irish House. As I approached the building on busy New Arbat Street (formerly Kalininsky Prospekt, after Mikhail Kalinin, a Bolshevik hero), close to one hundred people, both foreigners and Russians, lined up outside Irish House. They were waiting to join the crowd snapping up the store's imported food, clothing, and electronic equipment. Business at the Arbat Gastronom was brisk, too. Bright new red-and-white awnings gave the place a far more cheerful atmosphere than that of the typical gastronom. Shoppers bought chicken for forty-eight rubles a kilo, eggs at ten eggs for twelve rubles, and smoked fish for forty rubles.

A small woman in a plaid coat leaned against an empty counter, carefully adding figures on scrap paper. Her name was Raya Yuroshova. She informed me that she worked as an engineer at an institute in Moscow, had a seventeen-year-old daughter, and believed in God. "I was born in 1936 and lived in Moscow through the war. I remember what it was like. I remember standing in line with my mother for hours. This is not bad. We are not living badly," she said. "We will survive this period."

Her main concern was feeding and dressing her daughter. "I don't need much, but I want to provide for my daughter. She is in her first year at an institute, studying historical archives." She and her husband, who was also an engineer, had saved up six thousand rubles. "In today's conditions that's a miserly sum. Still, it will help for a while." She paused and added, "The Russian people are very patient."

On that day, no one could disagree.

Going back to my office, I swung by the gastronom where I had seen the scrawny sausages the day before. There still was no food, but the store's management had placed bottles of Georgian wine (at forty-two rubles each) in the display cases meant for meat and eggs.

How long would it take for goods to start filling the shelves? Would prices eventually dip after the initial inflationary shock? How long could Russians' patience last? On the television news later that night, there were reports of shoppers breaking the windows of a meat store in Stavropol. But most people reacted calmly to the first day of shock therapy. Once again, they had defied the worst expectations of Western and Russian commentators alike.

Within days of the start of the reforms, however, the demonstrations began. They were largely peaceful "meetings," as the Russians called them, both against and in favor of reform. Judging from the numbers willing to stand out in the cold and chant, the population seemed split down the middle. On February 9, 1992, a crowd of more than ten thousand workers, pensioners, and hard-line Communists rallied near the Kremlin. "Pozor! Pozor!" (Shame! Shame!), they screamed, calling for Gaidar's resignation. Not a mile away, outside the Russian parliament, just as many demonstrators waved placards begging for speedier reforms: "Yeltsin and Gaidar—don't retreat. Take more radical steps now!"

Yet as people grappled with the day-by-day inflationary shock, more meat, butter, cheese, vegetables, and wine began to fill the shelves of state-owned stores. Prices were leveling off and even falling in some stores as managers unloaded surpluses of perishable foods—sour cream, butter, cheese. Most surprising of all, the ruble was gaining strength. The rate fixed by the Central Bank for purchase at "exchange points" and commercial banks hovered around 110. On the black market—where Russians bought and sold rubles and hard currency privately—it had soared from 135 to 65 to the dollar. And at the weekly interbank currency auctions, which set the ruble rate for commercial transactions, the currency had firmed from 230 to a dollar to 170 by mid-February.[7]

At press conferences and other public settings for the first two months of 1992, Gaidar was upbeat. He promised that the monthly inflation rate, nearly 250 percent in January 1992, would already begin to drop in February and March. Because the government had printed one-third less money in January, he said, the ruble was stabilizing. But the opposition forced him to compromise on his new value-added tax, cutting it from 28 percent to 20 percent on some goods.

Overnight, Gaidar had become Russia's most controversial figure. Communist newspapers satirized him. Old people complained bitterly that he had stolen their savings. Appearing in parliament, the determined economist seemed to talk right over the heads of deputies—speaking quickly and using economic jargon liberally. (He also had an unfortunate habit of smacking his lips when he spoke.) Gaidar came across as a technocrat—smart, a little arrogant. People who worked with him called him "a nice man," but he did not appear that way to the ordinary Russian. He obviously had little concern for his political fate.

Just after the demonstrations calling for Gaidar's resignation, I paid a visit to his office at Staraya Ploshad. I had not yet met him face to face, and I felt it was time to get a sense of the direction of the country. It felt odd to be simply walking up to the main entrance of the former Communist Party headquarters, where I had previously been escorted to interviews with party bigwigs. The day after the August coup ended, the Moscow government had seized the building, placing a huge seal over the door to prevent anyone from entering. Now, the security was more relaxed. I had to show my identification, but the atmosphere seemed looser, less rigid.

I was led to Gaidar's office, where he greeted me before sitting in a big leather armchair. Short, pudgy, he reminded me of a teddy bear. But he spoke fast, fluent English—a smart bear in a hurry.

"I hope to create the conditions for stable economic growth in Russia," he said, ticking off his goals. "Macroeconomic stability, liberal prices. A more or less system of the market, an open economy with limited obstacles on the way of resource flows between this country and the outside world.

"I want not a terrible amount of budgetary expenditure as a percentage of gross domestic product, and distribution of the goods in a way that can be regarded as just. Not because I adore equality for itself, but because otherwise it will be very unstable."[8]

How long would it take to achieve his goals? He didn't hesitate for a second. "It will take about five years, maybe a little bit less. I hope that this policy for which I fight now will be promoted for at least five years."

Five years! Yeltsin had told the parliament—and the people—that things would look up in six months. I wondered what Russia's economy would look like in half a decade. "Let's say," I ventured, "that you stay in your job for five years. What would the economy look like then?" Turning red, he laughed and shook his head: "It will be an economy with a lot of potential for growth. There will be a few sectors of the economy that will be rapidly incorporating into the world economy, especially those previously connected to the military industrial complex that can also make civilian goods. It will not be the economy of a rich country. It will be a developing country with a lot of unsolved social problems. And it will be a country with a lot of serious problems because structural transformation will require a lot more time than five years. There will be serious problems with different branches of the economy. And the problems of unemployment will be serious."

But Gaidar clearly felt that he was performing an important civic mission by launching the reforms, however unpopular. "I do not have political ambitions. But I see that this country is in a very dangerous situation. I think that all of the citizens who can do anything sensible for the country should do it. Of course it sounds a little pathetic but all the same it is true. When your country gets in this situation, even without being pathetic, you have to try to take the necessary action."

Although raised according to Communist ideology, Gaidar firmly believed that Russia had to escape totalitarianism. He vehemently disagreed with those who said the country needed an "iron fist" or dictator to prevent chaos. "I don't believe in a reformist dictatorship in this country. I am very much afraid that a dictatorship in this country would not be a dictatorship of the type that creates the conditions of market economic transformation, but just another bloody dictatorship that really tries to establish the military industrial complex." Gaidar made it clear that he would do all he could to prevent that. And, indeed, he was to do just that—whether in government or outside it.

All that winter, people coped with the shock of economic freedom. Yeltsin's gift of economic freedom was far more demanding than was the political freedom Gorbachev had granted through glasnost five years before. Gorbachev's glasnost had given Russians the opportunity to discover the truth about their past and to criticize their present. Political freedom meant the freedom to learn, to analyze, and to express an opinion different from that of the government. For some loyal Communists, the revelations of glasnost had proven psychologically difficult to accept. But for the majority of people, glasnost had allowed them to shake off the fear that had become second nature. They no longer had to wear a public face different from their private one—to have "two souls," as short-story writer Svetlana Vasilenko once described it to me.[9]

Political freedom allowed Russians to reject their past. But economic freedom forced them to take action now in order to determine their futures. When prices soared five, ten, twenty times, people had to find ways to carry on, feeding and clothing themselves. The government was no longer willing to subsidize the entire population.

Hardest of all for many Russians to accept was the new unpredictability of life. People had grown accustomed to the certitudes of central planning—to waiting for the foreman, the factory manager, the Communist Party boss, or the Politburo to pass down orders for not just what to do but how to do it. There was no need for personal initiative. Russians had taken comfort in knowing that the state would provide a minimum wage—enough to get bread, sausage, and vodka on the table—no matter how hard they worked. There had been comfort in knowing that the price of bread was thirteen kopeks, that it had been that way for decades and would likely be that way for many years more.

Money had not been important in the Soviet era—certainly not as important as in a capitalist society. Soviet citizens had lived their lives and improved their lots by engaging in endless informal barter deals. People gave "gifts" to get anything from a nice cut of meat to a driver's license. These gifts usually weren't monetary. They ranged from theater tickets to supplies of scarce goods (sometimes stolen from state stores or enterprises). In the Soviet era, Russians rarely talked about what they "bought" or "paid for"; instead, they managed to *dostat,* to "obtain" or "get" goods—to get their hands on something. Although money often didn't change hands, the distortions and inadequacies of socialist central planning had turned Russia into a great trading society.[10]

But now people needed money—desperately. Salaries, especially at state institutions and enterprises, lagged far behind the rising prices. Teachers, doctors, lawyers, factory workers, and pensioners suddenly found themselves in dire poverty. The shock was hardest on older people. Savings accounts built up over decades—enough to buy cars or dachas—became the equivalent of a week's worth of groceries. Some called it the government's *grabyozh,* or "robbery." Others began to worry about how they would pay for their funerals.

The worthless ruble had become a scarce commodity. Indeed, while Gaidar bragged about the ruble's strengthening exchange rate against the dollar, on some days exchange points in Moscow actually ran out of the currency. The situation was worse in provincial cities. The government's tight money policy had created a physical deficit of rubles. Some days, exchange points simply hung out signs declaring "No rubles."

Meanwhile, across the country, people scrambled to find new ways to earn, and money took on a whole new importance in their lives. On January 29, Yeltsin signed a decree that provided a crucial safety valve for the impoverished population. He essentially granted permission for anyone to sell virtually anything (except for drugs, guns, and a few other restricted materials) and to sell it anywhere.

Overnight, makeshift markets sprang up all over Moscow and other cities: thousands of petty traders gathered around train stations, outside farmers' markets, in the entranceways of food stores and on major thoroughfares. In the center of Moscow, a long line of traders stretched from the sidewalk opposite the Bolshoi Theater, near the TSUM department store, up the hill several blocks to the Detski Mir (Children's World) store, just opposite the KGB headquarters. From there, it snaked around the block, encircling the huge concrete edifice.

To me it was an incredible sight—the very image of an economy unbound. Thousands of traders stood opposite the mound, now empty, where Dzerzhinsky's statue had so recently towered. Only a few years before, these traders could have been thrown into a KGB prison for hawking Bic pens, brassieres, coats, shoes, teakettles, liquor, and food, as they were doing now—and all for profit. Some of the goods were new, some used. Many of the traders were pensioners earning a few rubles' profit to supplement their pensions. But there were younger people, too—housewives, students, and factory workers moonlighting from their regular jobs.

I liked to walk among these traders, elbowing my way through the crowd, inspecting the prices, sometimes chatting with a friendly merchant. Like other westerners, I had worried about Russians taking to the streets and rioting. Now I was intrigued, bemused, and relieved that they had taken to the streets—by the tens of thousands—to trade instead.

Some of these traders would become known as *chelnoki,* "shuttlers," because they made frequent trips to places like Turkey and China, filling their suitcases with inexpensive goods to sell back home. Andrei and Vera were young traders—in their twenties, and in love. Andrei had worked at a factory producing electrical equipment on the outskirts of Moscow. Vera came from Irkutsk in Siberia, where she had worked for Komsomol, the Young Communists, organizing a group of young women who entertained visiting party chiefs. ("Basically they were prostitutes. We called them the *razvlekaiuschy* contingent [the entertainment group], and they got a certain amount of money for that. I myself didn't take part, but I was in charge. I didn't like it," she told me, explaining that eventually she ran away.)

The couple had met in Moscow, where Vera had come on holiday to visit a friend and simply stayed on. She married Andrei and they began working together. Andrei bought and sold all kinds of goods. "Why did I leave the factory? I didn't like that type of work," Andrei told me one evening. He and Vera had invited me to their apartment, which they shared with Andrei's mother. "You had to be there every day from six o'clock in the morning, five days a week. I wanted to set my own schedule."

Andrei managed to adjust quickly to the shock of economic freedom. For a short while, he stayed on at the factory, skipping out from his job to stand near the metro a few miles away, selling whatever he was able to get his hands on. He sold scrap from the factory (which he simply took; it would have been discarded anyway, he claimed). Then he began buying other goods: clothes, food, business diaries. "I buy something and I sell it for more money. I make money on the difference."

It was hard work. "I stand near the entrance to the metro. It is difficult to stand there. Before I was working in an official job. It didn't matter what you did and you got money. Now I stand near the metro and I have to sell. Will they buy something from me or not? Will I make money or not? There are moments when I make almost nothing and there are times when I do very well. That's the way it is."

Vera was philosophical. "We should be happy about what we have. If you have it, that's good. If you don't have it, don't worry about it." They were saving money to buy furniture. Andrei was planning to travel to Ukraine to find cheaper goods to buy so that he could earn a bigger profit. She wanted to get pregnant.

They were like any young couple trying to build a life together. They simply were doing it in the midst of an economic revolution in their country. But I felt they would succeed. Eventually, Andrei said, they wanted to start up their own business. Maybe they would run their own kiosk.[11]

Such glass-and-aluminum kiosks were springing up all over Moscow, St. Petersburg, Yekaterinburg, Vladivostok, and other cities. While most stores were still in state hands, these privately owned retail huts had names like "All for You" and "All Night Shop," and they lived up to their billing. They sold an astonishing array of imported goods, often twenty-four hours a day: vodka, beer, wines, and other liquors; Japanese and Korean electronics, Danish hams, French cheese, Korean-made "I Love You" condoms; and much, much more.

American products flowed in, too: toys like Ninja Turtles and Barbie dolls, health products from Johnson & Johnson, detergent and household goods from Procter & Gamble, candy bars with brand names like Snickers, Mars, and Bounty. Their prices were beyond the reach of many people, but the kiosks thrived all the same. Russia was on its way to becoming a consumer society.

The new economic freedom smashed the uniformity of Russian life, the grayness and sameness dictated by the (false) equality of the Communist era. Despite years of ideological conditioning, many Russians soon lost their fear of setting up businesses, of becoming openly wealthy, of standing out from the crowd. And those who were capable of moving shrewdly in the freer economic climate could make more money than they had ever dreamed. They could buy foreign cars, build expensive houses, and attain a lifestyle unimaginable in Soviet times. Money became both the key to survival and the measure of success. Some people thrived; many people struggled. But for others, the shock of economic freedom was profoundly demoralizing. That is one reason why in the 1990s alcoholism soared and life expectancy fell—to fifty-seven years for men and seventy-five for women.

Many people over fifty years old—those who had come into their own at the height of socialism—found the new life psychologically as well as economically tough. Workers in defense factories whose skills were no longer needed after the government slashed orders practically to nil, economists and engineers at state institutes suffering from budget cutbacks: they once held prestigious jobs, but now they were among the poorest in the country. Many lacked the desire, drive, or skills to hit the streets to trade. "People aren't experiencing inflation only in the form of prices," my friend Elena Antonenko, an actress, explained. "They're experiencing inflation of conscience, happiness, love. With shock therapy, the value of all these things is falling. Now it's either money or death. It says something about the collapse in people's morality."[12]

Sociologist Natalia Tikhonova studied this crisis of both morals and morale as well as this change in values. Russians' notion of economic and political freedom contrasted sharply with that of westerners: "If in the West political freedom means realizing your possibilities within certain laws, in Russia freedom means *volya*—will. It is to do what you want, to be your own boss, to be freed up from the authorities that you always hated." But in the early months of reform Russians had only a vague understanding of freedom. "When we understood that we were rejecting the kind of society in which we lived, our vision of how to live further was very idealized. We knew it would be better to live in a different kind of society, but we did not understand how it would be. After the price reforms, when we met the new situation, it was of course a shock for the whole society." People had to learn how to solve their own problems, Tikhonova continued. Many came to think that "to be your own boss—a free boss—is more important than material success."[13]

Unfortunately, economic freedom in Russia did not mean equal economic opportunity. In the new era, the path for hardworking people intent on shaping their own fortunes was wider and more open than at any time under Communism. But not everyone started at the same point. Those with former contacts in the Communist Party, KGB, government bureaucracy, or factories had better chances of getting ahead. Contacts became their starting capital. Government officials openly used their positions for their personal benefit. The triumph of Yeltsin's democrats did not bring an end to government corruption. Said Tikhonova: "Those who had been in the state organs, Komsomol, the party, in trade—they all had a better position because the capital was churning in these places. These people could better use their economic freedom." By contrast, "the possibilities for the ordinary person to use his economic freedom were much more limited. At the most, they could collect a loan from acquaintances, some starting capital, and become a shuttle trader. But it was hard to move beyond that stage."

If under socialist ideology the government had focused too much on promoting the common good, now the tide had completely reversed. The era of economic freedom turned into a free-for-all, a mad scramble for the spoils of the state. At its root, the transition to a market economy in Russia meant the redistribution of state assets—the privatization of state industry and the rechanneling of the government budget to different uses. The race was on to grab a chunk. As necessity, opportunity, or greed propelled nearly everyone to look out for themselves, government officials, state factory directors, customs agents, and police brazenly lined their pockets—or diverted funds to offshore bank accounts. The state only minimally fulfilled its basic functions: it barely enacted laws and rarely enforced them when it did, and it often failed to protect its citizens. The vacuum of power and collapse of values made it easy for hundreds of criminal gangs to infiltrate businesses, banks, privatized factories, and, many believed, the government itself.

One day, at a demonstration on Manezhnaya Ploshad, near the Kremlin, I met a Russian truly fed up with the country's transformation. A small woman with dark hair and horn-rimmed glasses, she hardly looked a representative of the angry masses. But she held a white placard with blue letters: "Da, CCCP. Yankee, go home!"[14]

Her words were sharp. "I lived happily under Soviet power,"

Nadezhda Yakovleva Kojikova, forty-eight years old, told me. "I consider that there is no alternative to Soviet power. I am an economist and I used to work in a school. Now I work as a cleaner. I was not a member of the party, but I believed in the Communist idea. The Communist idea was always the best idea."

"Now, we live very poorly," she continued. "My salary is two thousand rubles a month. My son and I live on that." The exchange rate at that time was about four hundred rubles to the dollar. She was making just five dollars a month. "We don't eat meat. How can you eat meat when it costs two hundred rubles a kilo?" Her son was standing next to her, decorated in badges and buttons of Lenin.

I asked why her sign said, "Yankee, go home." She smiled under her white knit hat. "There are different kinds of Americans. But I am against the Americans who want to come here and influence our policy. I am against the Americans who have an anti-socialist policy. I don't accept the market. The market can't bring anything to the Russian people. And I don't accept the International Monetary Fund. That's why I am against this government."

Although the IMF had helped shape Russian economic policy, the United States and other Western nations were holding back from granting Russia much economic aid. Gaidar had asked for a $6 billion fund to help stabilize the ruble. Economists like Jeffrey Sachs had pleaded for a modern-day Marshall Plan of tens of billions for Russia. But U.S. president George Bush was hesitating. He feared pouring money down a black hole.

Did Kojikova think that the United States should help more? "We are a great people. We will settle things ourselves, with our state and our government," she said. "I think that if there won't be changes, people will take up arms so that they can clean the Kremlin of this anti-people government. We don't accept it. They are anti-people and anti-Russian. We are for the Communist idea. But these people, they really are ruining the country."

At the time, I didn't believe that Russians would take up arms against Yeltsin. I would later be proven wrong.

Outside Moscow, the picture varied widely from city to city during that first winter of shock therapy. In Yaroslavl, a few hours' drive from Moscow, goods began to fill the shelves. The market was working. In Naberezhnye Chelny, home of Kamaz, the world's largest truck and engine plant, people still stood in line with ration coupons to buy food. Here the regional government was subsidizing food prices out of its own local budget. Naberezhnye Chelny was located in the autonomous republic of Tatarstan, which had called a referendum on independence. The government was buying votes by keeping prices for chicken, eggs, meat, bread, butter, vodka, and milk down at about half their Moscow prices. The enormous Kamaz factory also distributed food to its workers.

I found Naberezhnye Chelny a tough town when I visited there in the winter of 1992. For starters, I couldn't find a local person willing to drive me around, as I often did in other cities (for money, of course). Officials at city hall wouldn't find time to talk with me. They had seen many foreigners over the years because Kamaz was located there. They were jaded. Even the directors of the truck plant denied my request for a visit, claiming that I had not given them enough notice. I did manage a walk along the nearly one-mile-long assembly line, thanks to a joint-venture manager there, an acquaintance, who gave me a blue work jacket and allowed me to sneak in. (The line seemed to be going at full tilt. In the section where workers tested trucks, exhaust fumes filled the air. Price reform obviously hadn't affected Kamaz yet.)

Later, as I trudged along in the snow, I asked directions from a woman who was walking briskly toward the town center. We began to chat. How did she find the economic situation in the town? "Nichevo," she answered, meaning "nothing" special. "I work in the engine factory and they give us food. We get a chicken almost every day." Before we made it to the food store near my hotel, she had reached into her big bag and pulled out a can of herring.

"No, no," I protested. "I was only asking about the condition of the town." I didn't need food.

"I am giving it to you *ot dushy*—from my soul," she replied, holding out the can. So I took it. She disappeared into the food store, heading for the sugar line. I bought two loaves of bread for forty-five kopeks each (twice the old Soviet price, but a third less than the current price in Moscow). I saved the herring as a souvenir.

Whereas Russian people adapted to the price shock better than most reformers and observers had expected, Russian enterprises reacted far worse. As the ruble strengthened and the prices of most raw materials and parts soared in the late winter and early spring of 1992, Gaidar warned that industrial production would plunge by about 20 percent and that a painful restructuring of industry would begin.[15] Bankruptcies and unemployment would rise. The freeing of energy prices, which had remained controlled in January, would partly precipitate the shakeout.

But it didn't happen. At first, most factories hardly changed their behavior. Many had hoarded and stockpiled supplies, so they just kept producing and shipping as they always had, not worrying about whether their goods were still wanted or whether the customer would pay. With prices on raw materials rising, enterprises hiked prices on finished goods, too. But they made no effort to cut costs. For weeks and months, they kept turning out ventilators, machine tools, autos, or tractors—with or without orders—until their warehouses and parking lots were overflowing with unneeded and unwanted output.

The result: astonishing debt between enterprises. By March 1992, enterprises owed one another 800 billion rubles—the equivalent of about $4 billion. (By July, the debts would total a stunning 3.2 trillion rubles, or 24 percent of gross domestic product.)[16] These debts built up in accounts left over from central planning days. Often factories owed about as much as they were owed. By Western standards, 90 percent of Russian industry was bankrupt. But by Russian standards, enterprises managed to continue functioning in a kind of virtual industrial economy. They were in essence creating their own noncash money. (Indeed, *beznalichniye dengi,* "noncash money," had been a feature of the Soviet economy.) Enterprises needed cash mainly to pay workers their monthly or semimonthly wages.

The massive interenterprise debt was a disaster for Gaidar. It made a laughingstock of his efforts to control the money supply and cut the budget deficit. "How can you run a tight monetary policy when money has lost its meaning?" the IMF's Foglizzo once demanded. Looking at Russia from a Western perspective, I assumed that the debts could not keep mounting for long. Surely enterprises would have to either shed labor or close down because they were insolvent or produced nothing that people wanted to buy. The crisis, I figured, would come to a head after Gaidar began freeing up energy prices.

He had originally planned to do that in February 1992. But an outcry from the industrial lobby—led by longtime apparatchik Arkady Volsky, head of the Union of Industrialists and Entrepreneurs—gave him pause. Gaidar decided to delay until April the liberalization of energy prices. Later he would tell me—and other analysts would agree—that this delay was one of his biggest mistakes. The political climate and opposition to reforms, especially from the industrial lobby, only grew worse as time went on.

Even with the delay until April 1992, I felt that Russia must be on the verge of a great industrial depression, comparable to or even worse than the 1930s collapse in the United States. I figured that, with their debts building up, factories would soon start closing their doors and putting millions out of work, as Gaidar had predicted. So I headed to the Russian Rust Belt—the Ural Mountains industrial region, Russia's center of heavy industry, where Stalin had built dozens of steel factories, machine-tool manufacturers, and tank producers in time to churn out the weapons needed to defend the Soviets from the Nazis. I wanted to see how the industrial heartland was reacting to reform. Until the demise of the Soviet Union, much of this region had been off limits to foreigners because of its strategic importance. Even in 1992, some cities were still closed. But one of the key centers, Yekaterinburg, formerly Sverdlovsk, had opened up. It was Yeltsin's hometown and also home for Uralmash, one of the Soviet era's showcase factories.

Stalin's political prisoners had built Uralmash in the 1930s. During the Great Patriotic War (as World War II was called in Russia), the factory produced the famous T-34 tank that beat Hitler's army. Now it manufactured oil drilling equipment, excavators, machine tools, and tank cannons. It employed thirty-nine thousand workers and, like most Soviet plants, owned apartments, day care centers, recreation halls, cultural centers, and sanatoria—for workers, their families, and others in the community. Several top political leaders had risen to power thanks to Uralmash. Nikolai Ryzhkov, Soviet prime minister under Gorbachev, had previously run the giant enterprise.

Uralmash had recently chosen a new general director after the previous boss had died of a heart attack. Thirty-eight-year-old Viktor Korovin had defeated four other candidates in what was the factory's first such election. Surprisingly, Korovin had beat out his opponents with a tough platform that called for major restructuring at the giant plant. How had he persuaded workers to vote for him on a platform that called for cost-cutting and possible layoffs as well as modernization?

The short, wiry man greeted me in his general director's office and was serious from the start. "The crisis is hitting us in the face," he said bluntly. "The volume of production has fallen 10 percent so far but it will be 20 to 25 percent by the end of the year." The reason, he explained, was that supplies of raw materials from Chechnya, a breakaway part of Russia, and other former Soviet republics weren't arriving on time. But rising prices were also behind the slump. "Our customers are saying, 'At these prices I will not buy this equipment.' Since the prices we pay [for supplies] are going up, we are forced to increase our prices.

The price of our excavators grew eleven or twelve times last month," he declared.[17]

Korovin had worked in the West and knew something about market economics. A native of Yekaterinburg, he had taken a special course for Soviet managers in Frankfurt, Germany, and had worked at Uralmash's joint venture with the Austrian engineering company Voest-Alpine. He had clear ideas about what he wanted to do with his factory and workers.

But he had to face short-term crises first. Above all, he needed cash. "We don't have a kopek—hardly enough to pay workers their wages. We stopped the financing of apartments, which we always did. We stopped project finance, which means we are forgetting about investment. We have started to sell equipment that isn't needed in the factory—old machine tools. Anything to get rubles."

To keep his workers occupied, Korovin had also started manufacturing new types of equipment—agricultural machines, small motors, even safes. "We are taking any order from anywhere. It's not real work, but it's a way not to lose people."

He planned to put some of his workers on short-term, unpaid vacation for two or three months. If the factory was still in crisis, he figured he might have to lay off several thousand. That was a bold statement for the director of a state-owned enterprise, even in 1992. Most managers refused to countenance layoffs. Indeed, while the state technically owned the factories, many socialist factory directors ruled their plants like fiefdoms and treated their workers as children. In many towns in the Urals, Siberia, and the Far North, only one or two plants employed and supported entire communities. That's why the prospect of layoffs and unemployment was truly dangerous.

But Korovin was something of a renegade. Though he had run the Young Communist unit in Yekaterinburg several years before, he had abandoned most of his Communist principles. "I was a very convinced Communist. But my ideas changed a lot," he told me. "Now I believe that workers should work and make a good wage. It's not up to the enterprise to keep people just as people. Everyone should fend for themselves."

To put that philosophy into action, he planned to charge money for the enterprise's services to the community—managing the apartments and running the day care centers. And he would slash subsidies to the local police force. "We will not lose money any more on financing local militia. Socially it will bring very serious consequences because crime is growing catastrophically. But understand me—I came here to manage a factory," Korovin declared. He was right. "The state should find money for the militia. The government takes 50 percent of my profits to finance the budget."

More than most enterprise directors at that time, Korovin understood that municipalities would have to take on the burden of the "social" assets long supplied by state-owned enterprises. But it would take years. Russian city and town governments didn't have the wherewithal and skills to manage apartments, day care centers, and recreation halls. It was unusual that Uralmash paid for the police, but Korovin's decision to cut that budget would have serious consequences. As I walked around the neighborhood surrounding the Uralmash factory, locals expressed terror of rising crime. One man's apartment had been broken into while he was at work, the food stolen from his refrigerator. Another man was killed in a fight over his fur hat. Sales of steel doors were soaring. Later, Yekaterinburg—and, in particular, the Uralmash neighborhood—would become known as a major center for organized crime in Russia.[18]

Korovin agreed with the principles of Gaidar's reforms, but not with all the details. "Not many factory directors think that way. Many think that what's going on is a big mistake," he said. Korovin backed Gaidar's efforts to bring about "the return of money" to the economy. "Gaidar considers that the financial situation in the majority of enterprises today is very bad. But it will allow a return of money. Let it be inflationary, worthless, but money.

"No more barter. Today that is fair. I am starting first of all to have business with those customers who are able to pay money. I need money so that I can pay my workers, so I can pay bills to my suppliers, so I can pay whatever I think I need in the social sphere. I need money. In that sense, the government is rightly evaluating the situation. But whether the government controls the situation after [the energy prices rise in] April, it is hard to say."

This was refreshing stuff. Many enterprise directors would prefer to do exactly what they had always done and not worry about finding money. I wondered, did Korovin expect an industrial collapse?

"What does 'collapse' mean?" he retorted. "There will be big instability in industry—the industry that we had yesterday. It is a very serious situation. But if the government manages to protect the situation from inflation, then a process of stabilization will start. Those enterprises that survive will be forced to restructure themselves and work anew—if the government manages to control inflation."

Korovin's words were prescient. Inflation would prove to be the government's biggest calamity.

"The government shouldn't issue new credits," Korovin warned. "There is no possibility of issuing new credits unless the government prints more money. But if they print more money, the whole thing loses sense. Issuing more money means the collapse of everything again. If they are firmly intending to maintain their policy, they won't give credit resources to industry.

"What is credit for industry? It is a good thing. It happens everywhere when it is necessary. But that credit is found by the state. When the government prints money to give out credit, then it gives something to industry but it doesn't bring any overall result. If Uralmash received credit, Uralmash would start to live better. I would be delighted to get some credits, I'll tell you honestly. But for reform as a whole, it would be very bad. It will mean a new possibility for hyperinflation." He added, somewhat ominously: "There is a very dangerous border. Up to the border, it is reform. After the border, it is chaos. So the government should be very competent."

Korovin was one of a handful of managers in Russia who understood exactly what was going on. He was willing to sacrifice the short-term gain for long-term success.

He faced an enormous job. I could see that while walking around Uralmash's many different plants. In some sections of the enterprise, imported machine tools cleanly and quickly formed and shaved metal parts for Uralmash equipment. But in other parts of the plant, conditions seemed out of the last century. Women stood before hot molten metal, banging it into shape with hammers. Sparks sprayed from furnaces, endangering workers. In the defense section of the plant, which I visited accompanied by a KGB representative (things hadn't changed that much), workers stood idly around greasy, antiquated equipment that had once ground out guns for tanks.

"We never expected that things could change so fast," said Valery Vasyukov, who had worked in the plant for seventeen years. Two years before, he said, 3,800 people were assigned to the military part. Now just 347 remained. As I walked through another cavernous building where the equipment stood idle, two workers approached me. One asked, not in jest: "You are from America, right? Maybe you are thinking of buying our factory?"

Despite all the problems, Korovin was optimistic that he could steer Uralmash through price liberalization and privatization toward a stable future. "We want to save our basic assortment of production and compete in the world—in the metallurgical, oil equipment, and mining equipment industries. I see a chance for us to be among the world's leading companies. It should be a company with better technology and fewer people. But the same is true of all the factories that I see surviving as independent enterprises."

Korovin was a real standout. He had vision. When I talked to other managers and politicians in the Urals region, however, I was surprised at their insistence that the region's factories would survive and that Russia would avoid unemployment. Weren't they hiding their heads in the sand? "There cannot be mass unemployment. It is not in our tradition," Arkady Chernadski, Yekaterinburg's mayor, informed me.

It couldn't be as simple as that.

In the end, Gaidar's prediction that bankruptcies and layoffs would accelerate in 1992 proved to be wrong. The reason: state enterprise managers began fighting for their jobs, privileges, and lifestyles. They wanted to halt Russia's economic transformation. On one hand, they hated the pain of rising prices. Secondly, they feared privatization, planned as the next phase of reform. Many, unlike Korovin, did not understand how to operate in a market economy. For them, it was much easier to beg the government for support—just as they always had—and to use the threat of mass unemployment and social chaos as leverage. Although ordinary Russians had defied expectations and reacted calmly to rising prices, no one could predict the breaking point of Russian patience. Perhaps mass unemployment would indeed spark riots. The industrial lobby strove to take advantage of that unknown.

As pressure intensified on Yeltsin and Gaidar, the economics minister caved in on crucial reforms. These were the first blunders on the slippery slope toward failure of the reform's first phase—the effort to stabilize Russia's finances. Gaidar had already compromised by slashing the planned value-added tax on some goods in January and by delaying the planned liberalization of energy prices in February. That wavering only spurred his opposition. By April, not only were industrial lobbies and Yeltsin's opponents pushing for a further delay in deregulating energy prices; they wanted Gaidar to resign.

The clash came to a head at the Congress of People's Deputies in April 1992. The Congress wanted the government to open up the money tap, granting huge subsidies to industry and agriculture, and to authorize wage indexation. The total cost: a huge 1.2 trillion rubles. Passions ran high as pro- and anti-reform delegates debated the issue. Suddenly, Gaidar and his entire cabinet stood up and walked out of the session in the Kremlin. They offered their resignations to the president.

It was political drama, Russian-style. But Gaidar's bold gesture spurred talks with industrialists and other opposition figures in the Congress. The result was a "declaration on economic reform" between the Congress and the government. At a press conference on April 16,

1992, Gaidar discussed its contents: "The Congress clearly expressed its support for the policy of the government and that is why it agreed to share responsibility not only for the reform but for the likely negative consequences. All social programs should be commensurate with available economic resources." He added, "The government is functioning, working, and will continue to solve problems of structural changes in our economy."[19]

Gaidar had struck a tough pose, implying that the opposition had given in to him. But that wasn't the case. As part of the compromise, the government agreed to issue 200 billion rubles in credits to industry. That was far less than the Congress demanded, but enough to blow a hole in the government's budget. Gaidar forecast a budget deficit of 5 percent of gross domestic product. That was far more than the 1 percent deficit he had wanted but much better than the previous year's 18 percent deficit. And if the government had implemented the Congress's proposals, the budget deficit would have been 23 percent of GDP. Once again Gaidar pledged to liberalize energy prices, but again it would not happen. The industrialists had won the ear of Yeltsin and persuaded him that freeing energy prices would damage their enterprises and the economy.

In late May 1992, Yeltsin appointed three industrialists to the cabinet, essentially turning the government into a coalition. Although Gaidar remained the leading economic figure, he would now have to consult with Vladimir Shumeiko, former head of a Krasnoyarsk defense plant; Georgy Khisa, a former factory director from St. Petersburg; and Viktor Chernomyrdin, former chairman of the state gas monopoly Gazprom. They all became deputy prime ministers—a signal to the opposition that the period of shock therapy was over.

Once again, Gaidar met me at his office at Staraya Ploshad. He spoke the same confident, fluent English, but this time he sounded chastened. "When our government was formed, the situation was very critical. It was absolutely necessary to take some unpopular but unavoidable steps—budget corrections and price liberalization," he began.[20]

"In this situation it was absolutely critical to have a government that works like a team, that does not have to lose time on internal discussions and discussions with social groups. The task was to accomplish things in which it was impossible to create a consensus in society. That's why it was necessary to include the president in the government [as prime minister] to base the government on his authority."

"But of course it cannot be a stable situation," Gaidar conceded. "It can be done in the situation of urgency. If you want anything like a stable government, you need at least some amount of consensus and cooperation. You can't govern if you are not basing your government on a rather broad coalition of social groups that are influential in society."

The time had come for such a broad coalition. At least that was the president's reasoning. Gaidar apparently disagreed, but he didn't say so outright. "Now the president is trying to include the influential segment of society represented by the industrial pressure groups and to find ways of gaining the understanding of managers of the previous socialist industry. That of course broadens the social and political basis of the government. But of course it also creates problems because it means the possibilities of maneuver in a situation of emergency are decreasing.

"But I hope that this government will be in a position to proceed with reforms and to elaborate workable compromises that will get us farther in the direction of liberalizing and opening the economy. There will be a greater accent on industrial policy and an increased role of the industrial interest groups."

Gaidar had made some serious mistakes. I asked him to analyze them. He was frank. "The big mistake of this government was that we didn't resolve to raise energy prices in February, which was probably the best possible time. As to other mistakes, probably we did not stress enough attention from the beginning on the propaganda of the new norms of behavior of the state enterprise. Of course, you do understand that it is impossible to persuade a socialist enterprise director that the world to which he adapted himself for decades will be changed drastically and new ways of behavior and attitudes are now both efficient and necessary. He will not believe you until he is confronted with it. But probably even in this situation, we did not make enough effort to explain to them the necessary changes." Gaidar added: "The biggest problems now are the interenterprise debts. And a very highly socially explosive problem is the cash crisis."

The period of radical reform had ended. I was reluctant to believe it, but it was true. Like many Western observers who had hoped that economic reform would succeed, I didn't want to see the effort unravel. The hopes and expectations had been so high—much too high. The dynamics of Russian politics would make reform in that complex country a zigzag process. It would require at least one step backward for every two steps forward.

Gaidar had managed to liberalize prices without a social explosion, but he had not succeeded in stabilizing Russia's finances. After declining for four months, monthly inflation began picking up again in June 1992, as a result of the loosening up of the money supply and of all the subsidies that he had approved. And the problem of interenterprise debt was still unsettled. Gaidar himself was already relaxing the reins on Russia's money supply, submitting to the pressure on him from all sides.

But in July came another political earthquake. Central Bank chief Georgy Matyukhin suddenly resigned. He was blamed for failing to fix the problem of interenterprise debt and to reform the country's payment system, which suffered from such enormous bottlenecks that money transfers took months to move from one bank to another. (Both the Central Bank and commercial banks made big money on this lengthy "float.")

In Matyukhin's place, Gaidar backed the nomination of Viktor Geraschenko, the former head of the State Bank of the USSR. This would prove to be Gaidar's biggest mistake of all. Geraschenko was a true believer in state regulation of the economy. He felt that the government should control prices. He also felt that it was criminal to leave enterprises and people to struggle for themselves with soaring prices.

"There are two ways to teach a child to swim," Geraschenko told me much later, justifying his position. "You can take him to school at three years old, support him, teach him how to swim, maybe he will even become a sportsman. Or you can do it like it is done in the village. If he swims, he swims, if not . . . That's a cruel way to learn how to swim. In my view, the liberalization of prices by Gaidar was teaching a person to swim in that way."[21]

I was surprised that Gaidar wanted Geraschenko as Central Bank chief. He had been close to Valentin Pavlov, the former Soviet prime minister who had helped lead the 1991 coup. Many believed that Geraschenko had quietly backed the coup. At the same time, although he believed in state regulation, Geraschenko had been the first to push the start of commercial banks in 1988 and 1989. He understood that if private business were allowed, the Soviet state banking system—in which one bank, the Soviet State Bank, controlled nearly everything—wouldn't work. After Matyukhin was pushed out, sources told me, Gaidar didn't know where to turn. He looked around for a qualified central banker and all he could see was Geraschenko. In the end, it wasn't the best choice, but few bankers in Russia then had any experience whatsoever at steering monetary policy.

With the government being pressured from all sides to print more money, Geraschenko was not about to resist. Between July and September 1992, he ordered that the printing presses crank out 350 billion more rubles—credits to be passed on to agriculture and industry. That was exactly what Uralmash general director Korovin had warned would lead to hyperinflation and chaos. And it nearly did.

Geraschenko later insisted that every credit disbursed was at the behest of either the government or the Supreme Soviet. The Central Bank hadn't yet grown accustomed to the notion that its job was not to serve the government but to defend the currency. But in 1992 Geraschenko also believed that issuing credits was necessary for Russia's industry and agriculture. Both the Western and the pro-reform Russian press began portraying Geraschenko as the destroyer of reform. Jeffrey Sachs was even widely quoted as calling him "the worst central banker in the world."[22]

In the fall of 1992, I met with Peter Derby, a smart, young American banker of Russian descent who was working in Moscow. He had come to Russia a few years before to set up Dialog Bank, a Russian commercial bank that began as part of a U.S.-Soviet joint venture called Dialog. Foreigners ran to his bank in droves when the Soviet State Bank for Foreign Economic Affairs collapsed at the end of 1991. Derby had a keen sense of Russia's financial development, though he sometimes mixed his metaphors in explaining it. "We have been through a stress test this year," he told me.[23] "The stress test has been that Gaidar took the first three months of the year and cut off the river and drained the lake. The industrial complex is at the bottom of the lake. That was not easy to do, to cut off the financial support of these factories, because people were unemployed [and] without salaries for months. . . . So that was a real significant thing and they did it."

"But by far the majority of industrial companies are not market efficient," he continued. "They had to make a decision. The parliament's decision was to flood the lake with water, which is rubles, and that will make a nice clean top and a sunset and we don't need to know what's going on down there. Gaidar [at first] said no. There had to be monetary restraint. Hyperinflation will lead to depression anyway. Gaidar said, 'We are going to sit down and open the rivers to help those enterprises that have a chance to be prosperous and for the others we will give them some support so that they have time to rechannel their employees to other productive areas.'"

"But the parliament says, let's flood the thing and make sure everyone is happy," Derby said. "The parliament has betrayed the Russian people even more by devaluing the currency in which their labor is monetized—the ruble—to a price in which their labor is meaningless. The worst thing to do is to give the people a piece of paper for their sweat which is worth nothing."

Derby was right. Whoever was to blame, the government or Geraschenko, the result was that inflation was rising and the ruble's value was collapsing; soon that would only hurt Russians more. But as a politician Geraschenko was cleverer than Gaidar, and the economics minister ended up bearing the responsibility. "Mr. Geraschenko organized the very high inflation and destroyed the possibility for financial stability in 1992," Andrei Illarionov, a pro-reform economist, told me. "In July and August 1992, we had 7 to 9 percent inflation per month. It was possible to wait another four to five months to December and we would have had 3- to 4-percent-a-month inflation. It would have been the situation that Mr. Gaidar and Mr. Yeltsin had promised to the people. They promised in late 1991, 'We shall liberalize prices and we shall come to financial stabilization, to the stable exchange rate to the stable prices.' But they did not do this. And that's why all the blame fell on them." Geraschenko, he added, was "opposed not only to Mr. Gaidar but to Mr. Yeltsin as well."[24]

By the late autumn of 1992, monthly inflation was running at 25 percent a month. Gaidar had to admit that financial stabilization had failed. The country was again growing politically uneasy. Although they had previously supported the president, coal miners, oil workers, and doctors—disgruntled with their delayed wages—turned against Yeltsin and threatened to strike. Communists and nationalists formed a united opposition, calling themselves the National Salvation Front. Democratic politicians like Foreign Minister Andrei Kozyrev began fretting publicly that Russia could tilt to the right, turn fascist, and adopt a xenophobic foreign policy.

On December 1, 1992, the Congress of People's Deputies gathered again. Volsky's Union of Industrialists and Entrepreneurs was out for Gaidar's head. They wanted to ensure a continued, loose monetary policy to protect industry. The Congress stripped Yeltsin of his powers to issue economic decrees without parliamentary approval. And it forced Gaidar's resignation. This time, Yeltsin agreed. The kamikaze deputy prime minister had done his duty and met his fate—at least for now. Yeltsin appointed the gray apparatchik Viktor Chernomyrdin as prime minister. That would prove to be a turning point in Russia's route to *kapitalizm.*

The Rise of the New Russians

For seventy years, we have been taught that
business in Russia is mafia. If you were in business
involving more than ten thousand rubles you
could be shot. The rules of the game in the West
were formed over one hundred years or more. We
are going along that way much quicker. *Sergei
Zverev,* Most Group

The liberalization of prices shocked most ordinary people. But one
group of Russians was poised to take advantage of it. For them, economic freedom represented the chance to start or expand businesses,
to make and spend money, to break away from the sullen, gray monot-
ony of Soviet life.

These were Russia's early entrepreneurs.

They were an odd collection of former black-marketeers, intellectuals, and Communists. Some were renegades who rushed to set up cooperatives—small private companies—when Mikhail Gorbachev allowed them to do so in the late 1980s. Others were students and
researchers who got their start through Komsomol, the organization for
young Communists. Still others were shrewd Communists who saw the
tide turning and rushed to get into business as the Soviet economy de-
teriorated and the country fell apart.

What they had in common was the ability to *krutit dengi,* to "roll" or "turn around" money, as the Russians put it—to make it grow by taking advantage of the distortions that accompanied the transition from a centrally planned to a market economic system. For a price, they would ease the pain of chronic shortages of everything from vodka to computers. They played the fledgling debt and foreign exchange markets—borrowing money and lucratively trading rubles and dollars. They bought goods or resources at subsidized state prices and resold them at vastly higher market rates.

Yet this group, representing a tiny slice of the economy in 1992, was living proof that seven decades of Communism had failed to obliterate the innate human drive that some people possess to take risks, to accumulate capital, to create new organizations, to strive to do better for themselves. Initially they sparked the ire and envy of their fellow citizens, who had been persuaded by decades of indoctrination that private business was evil. But over time, the entrepreneurs would become the driving force for change in Russia—even though their business methods were sometimes ruthless and often stirred controversy. Whether they responded to government reforms or built businesses despite political and economic instability, they spurred Russia's economic and social transformation at the grassroots—at the level of factories and stores, cities and towns, across the country. From the ranks of this fledgling entrepreneurial class would come the Rockefellers, Morgans, Oppenheimers, Macys, and Fords of the new Russia.

Their heritage stretched back more than a century to the early years of Russia's industrialization. As far back as 1855, Moscow boasted at least a dozen millionaires, compared to about twenty in New York at the time. Their numbers grew sharply after 1890, when the finance minister Sergei Witte actively promoted Russia's industrial development. Early Russian capitalists made their fortunes manufacturing textiles and heavy machinery, building railroads, and producing vodka, chocolate, and other products. Although some came from the nobility, a great number clawed their way up from the lower classes.

Many were serfs who bought their freedom before the emancipation of 1861 or who began trading to accumulate capital after they were freed. Many were non-Russians, mostly Jews and Poles, who fought to get ahead despite their disadvantageous position in czarist society. And many of Russia's prerevolutionary entrepreneurs were religious dissidents—followers of the Old Believer faith, with which the Russian Orthodox church had broken.[1]

These early serf-capitalists often started with only the knapsacks on their backs. Their pattern of accumulating capital, as described by nineteenth-century Russian economist Heinrich Storch, would later be echoed by post-Soviet entrepreneurs.

He usually begins as a *rasnoschtsik,* a seller of things in the streets; the profits arising from this ambulatory trade and his parsimony soon enable him to hire a *lavka* or shop: where, by lending of small sums at high interest, by taking advantage of the course of exchange, and by employing little artifices of grade, he in a short time becomes a pretty substantial man. He now buys and builds houses and shops, which he either lets to others or furnishes with goods himself, putting in persons to manage them for small wages; begins to launch out into extensive trade, undertakes contracts with the crown for deliveries of merchandise, etc. The numerous instances of the rapid success of such people almost exceed description. By these methods, a Russian merchant named Iakovlev, who died not many years ago, from a hawker in the streets became a capitalist of several millions.[2]

But prerevolutionary entrepreneurs like these did face public attacks. The landed gentry, the bureaucracy, such professionals as lawyers and doctors, and the intelligentsia all ridiculed, satirized, and castigated Russia's merchants and industrialists. Dramatists like Alexander Ostrovsky portrayed merchants as dishonest, tricky despots. "God save us from the bourgeoisie," wrote the philosopher Alexander Herzen. Anton Chekhov, too, displayed his dislike for businessmen in his short stories and through his portrait of the merchant in *The Cherry Orchard.* Even the literary critic Vissarion Belinsky, a prominent nineteenth-century proponent of westernization who argued that Russia needed a bourgeois class, described a merchant as "a base, despicable, vulgar creature who serves Plutus and Plutus alone."[3]

Partly in response to this barrage of negativity, and partly to save their souls and consciences, some Russian entrepreneurs aggressively promoted charitable and cultural causes. In industrial cities and towns, from the textile center around Ivanovo to Irkutsk in Siberia to Moscow itself, they built hospitals, schools, orphanages, theaters, and ornate public baths. Konstantin Stanislavsky, a successful international trader, founded the Moscow Arts Theater. Pavel Tretiakov channeled profits from his textile empire into a vast art collection that became the Tretiakov Gallery in Moscow. Near the end of his life, he wrote his daughter: "My idea from my earliest years was to make money so that what had been accumulated by society should be returned to society, to the people in some sort of beneficial institutions. This thought never deserted me throughout my life."[4]

But, by and large, the prerevolutionary Russian capitalists were a rough, unsophisticated lot. In doing business they followed instinct rather than logic. They counted on the help of friends and relatives. Most were poorly educated. Visiting foreign industrialists were appalled by the ethical standards of their Russian partners. As one British merchant noted, "A disastrous theft . . . is regarded by them as the very triumph of their genius."[5]

And, in what would become a familiar refrain, Russia's late nineteenth-century capitalists often clashed with the government, which was constantly changing signals. On one hand, the bureaucracy financed projects to promote the expansion of the steel industry, weapons producers, and the railroad. It pushed the creation of banks, stock exchanges, and consulting organizations to help business throughout the country. On the other hand, it interfered with successful businesses by banning Jews from owning property or by arbitrarily imposing taxes. The bureaucrats were ready to encourage industry— as long as they could control it.

On the eve of the 1917 revolution, Russia was still an economically backward country. The early capitalists had gained in influence, but they were never united enough to become a true middle class. Regional, ethnic, and economic differences divided them. So when Lenin came to power in 1917, the entrepreneurs had no power base from which to resist his attack. Tens of thousands of private businesses—from giant factories to small handicraft workshops—were nationalized. Scores of entrepreneurs fled or were killed.

So, it seemed, ended the development of Russian capitalism. Yet even after the revolution, entrepreneurship did not totally disappear in Russia. For a few years after the devastation of the civil war, Lenin himself called on Russians to once again trade food and other goods privately. It was the New Economic Policy (NEP), a renewed flirtation with private enterprise and foreign investment aimed at saving Russia from total economic collapse. For a while, especially in 1924 and 1925, NEP led to a boom in trade as small-scale traders known as "bagmen" and "NEP-men" hit the streets and market squares to sell bread, butter, tobacco, furs, and other goods from bags they carried with them or from small stalls or kiosks.[6]

Few of these NEP-men had been leading merchants or industrialists before the revolution. Most of the strongest prerevolutionary capitalists had disappeared under the harsh years of war Communism. By contrast, most NEP-men had previously been petty traders or employees of private stores. Although NEP encouraged exiled industrialists to return and work in their factories, now run by the state, few did. Industrial production slumped and then remained stagnant. And while foreign concessions were allowed—some Western capitalists, such as Armand Hammer, did take advantage of them—their overall economic impact was minimal.

But in trade, NEP-men dominated retail and often wholesale sales of goods like grain, textiles, bread, butter, tobacco, furs—representing as much as 60 percent of all purchases of these items.[7] The influence of these capitalists and their money alarmed Stalin, who throughout the

1920s was positioning himself to succeed Lenin. Even though Lenin had proclaimed that NEP was "serious and for a long time," it was already over by 1929, when Stalin began forcibly procuring grain from peasants and restricting the NEP-men. Soon he nationalized joint ventures and introduced strict central planning of the economy.

From then until 1985, when Gorbachev became general secretary of the Soviet Communist Party, private business was officially banned in the Soviet Union, and it was severely punished. *Spekulanty,* people who bought and resold goods for their own profit, or *tyeneviki,* those engaged in the *tyen* or "shadow" economy, were thrown into prison for anywhere from five to fifteen years. Even babushki caught with a suspiciously large amount of salt or other goods in the war years, the height of Stalin's terror, were harshly punished. In these years state factory directors who stole part of their production and sold it privately were simply shot.

Stalin put the Communist Party and the State Planning Committee firmly in control of the economy. They dictated everything: what plants would be built, which products would be manufactured, how industries would be developed, and, not least, what price each product would be sold for. The propaganda machine whirred nonstop. "Forward to the Victory of Communism!" "Exceed the Five-Year Plan!"

Even under strict central planning, however, the Russians' trading instincts did not die. A trading mentality was a matter of survival even under a socialist dictatorship. Throughout most of the Communist period a black market flourished. It reached its height in the Brezhnev era, when food, gas, cement, and other goods could be acquired *na levo*—on the left.[8] Thievery and bribery mounted, exacerbating the stagnation of Soviet industry. Underground traders—the precursors to perestroika entrepreneurs—kept the black market growing.

By the time Gorbachev came to power, the underground market provided anything from clothing to weapons to theater tickets. True, only a tiny minority of the population actually risked imprisonment to do secret black-market deals. But Russia in the Communist era was nonetheless a trading society. To deal with the inefficiencies of the centrally planned economy, managers of state enterprises had learned how to trade, too. Factory directors had grown accustomed to going to one another or to contacts in the industrial ministries for favors ranging from supplies to approvals or exemptions from rules. Russian economist Vitaly Naishul called it the "bureaucratic market" or "the economy of getting approval," a trading system that had helped to breed corruption and dishonesty throughout the economy. ("An academician in our country is not necessarily a scholar, while a physician with a degree may not know how to treat his patients," Naishul wrote.)[9]

Still, Gorbachev tried to tap Russians' hidden entrepreneurial skills. He wanted to stimulate initiative rather than stifle or punish it. He wanted to bring it out into the open, to encourage the creation of new stores and service businesses, to boost competition with the sluggish state sector. In 1986, he legalized "individual labor" by craftsmen, artists, sportsmen, and other solitary workers who wanted to sell their talents. The following year, he won Communist Party support for allowing groups of people to form "cooperatives"—an ideologically safe euphemism for small private companies. He also permitted the creation of Western-Soviet joint ventures, all for the first time since NEP in the 1920s.

No one uttered the evil word at the time, but these moves marked the Soviet Union's first efforts to recreate *kapitalizm* in Russia. After spending decades trying to stifle initiative, the Communist Party finally gave the country's ambitious, frustrated, materialistic, creative, energetic people the chance to channel their talents into productive ventures—and to benefit directly from their work.

Who were they?

Some did come from the black market, as one would expect. But the majority, surprisingly, were highly educated professors, scientists, artists, and successful managers—representatives, in other words, of the intellectual elite.

By and large, though, they weren't the satisfied people, the bosses with the best privileges. They were the restless ones, those banging up against the limitations of the Soviet system.

Andrei Fedorov had had a top job in Moscow's Intourist Hotel. He wanted to live better than he could on his state salary, so he gave up everything to start Moscow's first cooperative restaurant.

Ilya Baskin had been second in command at the sprawling Volno Sewing Amalgamation in what was then called Leningrad. "The general director told me I would never be able to replace him because I was Jewish and not a Communist Party member," Baskin told me. "So I quit." With four sewing machines, he set up a cooperative, sewing children's clothes in a Leningrad basement. Within a few years, he had built his own factory on the city's outskirts.[10]

Konstantin Borovoi had been a mathematics professor at Moscow State University. At thirty-five years of age, he had grown bored with his job, so he created the Russian Raw Materials and Commodities Exchange, a bustling and highly lucrative floor for trading everything from oil to cigarettes in the old Moscow post office.

Vladimir Gusinsky had organized musical festivals for Komsomol before he and a playwright friend set up a construction cooperative. (The Komsomol job had been a compromise after Gusinsky quit Moscow's state theatrical studies institute, in protest against the Communist Party's declaring two of the plays that he directed "anti-Soviet.") Gusinsky's company, Most Group, would grow into a leading Moscow property developer, bank, and media company.

Other early cooperators were doctors, scientists, and journalists. Many were young university graduates who felt disillusioned by the world around them. They had been born too late to experience the ideological fervor of the early years of socialism, when Stalin industrialized the country and defeated Hitler or when Khrushchev sent cosmonaut Yuri Gagarin into space. Instead, they looked around and saw stagnation, corruption, futility, drunkenness.

They were looking for ways to start their working lives. "I didn't want to have a gray life like the people who seemed satisfied. Why were they satisfied? They were born drunk and they died drunk. There was no society," Andrei Chuguevsky told me. An intense young man from the remote province of Chita, near the Chinese border, he averred, "Simple people lived a frightening life. I felt that if I would be like others, it would be death—the death of my morale, the death of my soul."[11]

Chuguevsky was the son of a history professor and a schoolteacher. To please his parents, he studied for a Ph.D. in history at a local pedagogical institute after finishing school in the late 1970s. But he knew that he didn't want a career in academia, the military, or the Communist Party. "I felt I was capable of so much more," he said. So in 1983, he asked local party officials to allow him and a few friends to sell a kind of walkie-talkie that they had invented to local state enterprises. Even though private business was banned at the time, punishable by fifteen-year jail terms, the party officials agreed.

Chuguevsky's communications devices sold fantastically. Factories snapped them up because telephone communications were so poor in Chita. But the success was too good to be true. Local party officials decided Chuguevsky was charging too much. He was arrested for speculation and given a three-year prison sentence.

Fortunately for Chuguevsky, Gorbachev came to power a year later. When the Communist general secretary legalized cooperatives, Chuguevsky was released from prison. He headed straight to Moscow, where he set up a business importing personal computers from Asia and selling them for huge profits to Soviet enterprises and individuals. Chuguevsky built up a business with revenues of 11 billion rubles a year—an astounding sum at a time when the average Soviet salary was two hundred rubles a month.

The Soviet Union was starved for computers. It had faced Western strategic embargoes for decades, and the government had tightly controlled the distribution of domestically produced computers for fear of political consequences. The computer boom of the late 1980s provided the starting capital for several major companies and banks. By buying computers for two thousand dollars and selling them for four thousand dollars, for example, programmer Oleg Boiko built up capital that he then used to create a network of retail stores called OLBI (for Oleg Boiko Investments) and the first debit card for Russian consumers. Entrepreneur Ivan Kivelidi, a former journalist, raised capital for his bank by trading computers. "We could make profits of 1,000 percent on computers," he told me.[12]

Kivelidi explained how the business worked: "We bought computers for *valuta*—hard currency—overseas. There was a very primitive way to convert rubles into dollars. You had to appeal to an agency that had the right to buy valuta. There were possibilities for barter deals, such as exporting some kind of equipment in exchange for computers. It was extremely profitable because of the wild difference between prices on the internal and external markets." Oil, for example, cost 50 rubles a ton domestically, whereas the world market price was $120, he said. Even at the old artificial exchange rate of $1.60 to the ruble, such barter deals were profitable.

In those days, Kivelidi noted, many Soviet factories had built up surpluses. "Some factories had collected a huge amount of copper. It just lay there. Or fuel oil. No one needed it, so they would trade it. Back then, oil refineries had to throw out gasoline so they could take in more oil to process. By using these kinds of imperfections of the Soviet system, we were able to make big profits."

That was the trick: using the distortions of the economy. As Gorbachev struggled unsuccessfully to reform the economy, the opportunities to make money by selling scarce goods and services exploded. From Vilnius to Moscow to Vladivostok, cooperators set up new restaurants, bars, food stores, trading companies, clothing manufacturers, retail chains, newspapers, and radio stations in the late 1980s and early 1990s.

But the challenges for the entrepreneurs were tremendous, too. Although the state officially sanctioned such private ventures, the entire system was predisposed against them. The state controlled nearly 100 percent of the economy, from building supplies to distribution networks. Bureaucrats opposed to Gorbachev—and competition—frequently changed regulations governing cooperatives' activities and often blocked licenses and other permits. Often all the officials wanted was a bribe, but that was dangerous for the cooperators, too, because they were under the constant scrutiny of the KGB. As Gorbachev pursued his reforms, entrepreneurs became the object of ideological battles between the Soviet leader and his enemies. From time to time, the KGB targeted an entrepreneur, finding irregularities for which he could be arrested.

All through the Gorbachev years, the Soviet media fueled public hatred of the fledgling entrepreneurial class. "They are sucking the people's blood. They are crippling young people's souls," complained a letter to the newspaper *Sovietskaya Kultura* in 1988.[13] The Communist Party newspaper, *Pravda,* and others regularly accused cooperatives of buying goods for low state prices and reselling them for much more. They blasted entrepreneurs for being *zhuliky* and *bandity*—thieves and bandits.

Nevertheless, by the early 1990s, as many as 200,000 cooperatives were already operating. They employed about 5 million people and were producing 10 percent of the country's economic output.[14] Gorbachev, his prime minister, Nikolai Ryzhkov, and other leading officials began talking about *rynochnaya reforma*—market reform. Everyone was for the market, even though everyone had a different idea of what market reform meant.

The Ryzhkov government, despite its reluctance to free prices and wholeheartedly endorse the concept of private property, opened the door to the creation of commercial banks (with the backing of then–State Bank chief Viktor Geraschenko), to leasing, to the expansion of ownership stakes that could be held by joint ventures, and eventually to the creation of shareholding companies. The key seemed to be government control: Ryzhkov was determined to ensure a role for the state bureaucracy, for the planners. It was as if the Soviets were willing to introduce a market economy, but only if they could rein it in.

Even the Communist Party had begun promoting entrepreneurship. In 1987, under a special decree of the Central Committee of the Communist Party, Komsomol was allowed to sponsor the creation of so-called scientific-technical-creative centers for youths—NTTMs, according to the Russian acronym. They were small units that offered, for a fee, research, consulting, and other assistance to larger state enterprises.

Mikhail Khodorkovsky, an engineering graduate of the Mendeleev Chemical-Technological Institute in Moscow, created one of the most successful NTTMs. Khodorkovsky was deputy secretary of the institute's Komsomol organization and director of student research. With seven thousand rubles from Komsomol and the Moscow City Council, he hired students to do research for the Moscow Institute of High Temperature. The job pulled in 169,000 rubles. Soon Khodorkovsky had hundreds of students researching projects for enterprises all over Moscow. "We started to get involved in serious work. We needed to invest money into equipment and materials. We tried to get a credit from the bank, but the bank refused us," he told me.[15]

So Khodorkovsky, who was then twenty-six years old, decided to set up his own bank. The Soviet State Bank was just beginning to license the first few commercial banks, which were to be allowed to compete, albeit under tight regulations, with the system of state banks. Khodorkovsky approached a state bank, Zhilsotsbank, and the State Committee for Science and Technology. They agreed to become cofounders of the new bank, to be called Menatep, along with the Mendeleev scientific center. "It was envisaged that we would invest 5 million rubles. The cofounders put their stamps on the document, but they said to us they wouldn't really pay. So the only real founder was our center," Khodorkovsky said. Apparently none the wiser, the State Bank granted Menatep a license to operate. It opened for business in 1989 and quickly became a leading commercial bank.

Khodorkovsky represented another type of early Soviet-era entrepreneur. He was not a renegade. In fact, he called himself "a loyal Communist Party member" until the August 1991 putsch. But Khodorkovsky was a visionary. He saw the tide turning in the country and caught the wave very early on. Because he was working inside party organizations, it was easier for him to cut through red tape than it was for other *kooperatory*, who were constantly under the scrutiny of KGB and bureaucrats. "We ran into almost no obstacles founding Menatep, which was unusual," he admitted.

Almost from the beginning, the Soviet press and other observers speculated that Menatep had been created by the Communist Party and the KGB, partly to serve as a conduit for channeling party funds to the West. Khodorkovsky always denied that the party propped up his bank or used it to export capital. "We have no money of the Communist Party and never had it," he insisted to me. Nevertheless, years later, after Menatep had grown by hundreds of times, some Western banks still hesitated to work with Menatep because of the mystery surrounding its origins.

Khodorkovsky represented a movement that would gain momentum as the Soviet Union fell apart: party, government, militia, and KGB officials on all levels went into business, using their contacts as starting capital. By 1991, the Communist Party had set up some 100 joint ventures and cooperatives, ranging from hotels to trading companies to security companies staffed by ex-KGB generals. Khodorkovsky put it succinctly: "Many people don't understand that you can make big money from nothing here in Russia—only here, because this is a turning point. Those who get in on time can do it."

Vagit Alikperov was another entrepreneur who got in "on time." Like Khodorkovsky, he was a shrewd, farsighted individual from inside the establishment. But he was further up the ranks. Alikperov was a deputy minister in the Ministry of Oil when he asked the government for the right to set up an independent oil company, Lukoil, in 1991. The Soviet oil minister refused because he feared it could lead to the breakup of the oil ministry. "So we set up Lukoil ourselves as a nongovernmental organization," Alikperov told me. When the Soviet Union collapsed, he had a foundation that he could build on.[16]

An Azerbaijanian, Alikperov had begun his oil career as an oil rig operator in the Caspian Sea. But he had honed his management skills in the frigid climate of western Siberia, where the oil ministry sent him in 1976. "I had never been outside of Azerbaijan. I was asked to go there as a specialist to help for three months and then I stayed. It was the school of western Siberia. There was nothing there . . . no houses, no facilities. We lived not in apartments but in wagons. People who went there were adventurers," he told me.

Alikperov helped to develop the oil town of Kogalym in the far north. Oil was discovered there in 1978, when Alikperov worked for Bashneft, the oil company in the nearby ethnic republic of Bashkir. Kogalym is Alikperov's town. He built its rows of five-story, concrete apartment buildings, the tidy day care centers, the arts school. Even though Alikperov had to take orders from the oil ministry, Kogalym was far from Moscow, and Alikperov could make many of his own decisions. "You could make good money and build a career in western Siberia," he recalled. "If you look at the oil towns of western Siberia, they are all different. You got the chance there to make your own decisions about how to build the housing and the kindergartens, about everything. A lot of people in power were trained in the school of western Siberia— people who went there when they were very young."

Alikperov was a legend in Kogalym. People talked about how he worked sixteen hours a day when he first arrived in the region, about how they fired shots at him from the wagon at a drilling site because he had taken a tough line against drinking on the job. They talked about Alikperov and his wife sharing a wagon with other men and how her hair froze to the side of the wagon.

In 1989, the Soviet government appointed Alikperov deputy minister of oil. He was partly responsible for negotiations with Chevron on its joint venture in Kazakhstan. That's how he got the idea to set up a vertically integrated oil company in Russia. "In 1989, Chevron invited us to go look at their operations in the United States. The idea grew in my head that we should do the same." So Kogalym, two neighboring oil fields, and two oil refineries connected to those fields decided to team up under Alikperov. "When the ministry didn't support us, we set it up on a goodwill basis. We just joined together ourselves. I received a lot of criticism for breaking up the oil ministry, but we turned out to be right," he said.

When the Soviet Union collapsed, Alikperov became the full-time president of Lukoil. It already extracted one-sixth of Russia's annual oil output. His goal was to make it a serious oil multinational and a global competitor.

In some ways, Russia's early *biznesmen* resembled entrepreneurs the world over. They stood out as driven individualists. They expressed many of the same ambitions as did their counterparts in the West. They wanted to achieve greatness, make a mark, get rich, conquer their opponents. "I always had the desire to do some kind of big deal, something serious. I looked for a way to realize myself," Chuguevsky told me. "I want to build one of the largest companies in the world," Baskin declared.

And yet Russia's entrepreneurs operated in an environment that could not contrast more with the West's. Confronted by constantly changing official rules of the game, they based decisions more on instinct than on economic rationality. To survive the vagaries of the hostile business climate, entrepreneurs gathered around them a "collective" of their closest and most trustworthy relatives and friends, rather as the czarist-era entrepreneurs had. Many took what they considered, at least at the time, to be necessary steps to protect themselves and their businesses. "Factually and morally, we broke the law," Chuguevsky acknowledged.

Many Russian entrepreneurs paid bribes, broke contracts, evaded taxes, and avoided the bureaucracy whenever possible. In the chaos of the collapsing Soviet Union, it wasn't difficult to take liberties. "We didn't ask. We just did it," said entrepreneur Alexander Panikin, who, remarkably, had built his small clothing factory on an empty lot in the center of Moscow and had his operations well under way before any bureaucrats noticed. The authorities later demanded that Panikin lease the land, but they didn't close down the factory, which provided much-needed employment to Muscovites. "If we didn't [take advantage of] the freedom, the first bureaucrat would have strangled us," Panikin told me.[17]

Russian entrepreneurs also approached deal-making in their own ways. This maddened Western partners accustomed to rational decision-making based on economic laws. For Russians, developing a personal relationship with the partner was crucial. Serious discussion might not begin until the second or third bottle of vodka had been consumed. Many biznesmen also tended to take verbal agreements much less seriously than they did written documents. In Russian there's a difference between the words *obeschaniye,* "promise," and *soglasheniye,* "agreement." Explained Alexander Minkov, a Russian attorney with long experience negotiating Western-Russian deals: many Russians "don't believe in promises. If I promise with no paper, it's only a promise. There's no commitment."[18] In Russia, unlike in the West, spoken words are just words, but written words are more serious, he noted. That's why Russians wanted to sign "protocols of intention" and other tentative agreements with Western partners.

For westerners, it was hard to know when the lying ended and the truth began. Russian *biznes* was much more art than science. Another frustrating problem was that Russians often tended to hint at, rather than state directly, what they wanted from a negotiation. And they could walk away in disappointment when the Western partner didn't get it. "It will be a long time before our economy and the economy of America start to greet each other in a common language," Baskin warned.

To the Russians, it was natural that their "rules of the game" contrast sharply with Western, and especially American, rules. "The rules of the game in the West were formed over one hundred years or more. We are going along that way much quicker . . . so of course the rules of the game are different," observed Sergei Zverev, deputy general director of the property and media conglomerate Most Group, in 1993.[19]

For many entrepreneurs, there was a sense of haste. Deep inside, they couldn't believe that the economic freedom gained under Gorbachev and expanded by Yeltsin would last long. Perhaps they consciously remembered the harsh treatment of entrepreneurs in 1917 or Stalin's sudden ending of NEP. Or perhaps it was just a subconscious instinct for survival. In any case, that deep fear of change spurred many Russian entrepreneurs to rush to make as much money as they could while the getting was good. They didn't worry too much about their long-term reputation until they began to think that they and their firms might be able to last.

Zverev explained the mentality: "We have harsher rules. We have fewer moral limitations. In the first place, it affects companies that are either just starting or are [of] medium size. When a company gets big, the problem of losing its face becomes more significant."

"There are three stages," Zverev continued. "Firms can go through all these stages or they can rest on one or another stage. The first stage is when they earn their first money. The second is when they must decide whether they want to hide their money by sending it abroad or invest it into business. This is the moment of choice. If they choose the first way, the money is put in the West and the person usually goes to the West, too."

"But if the money is put back into the business," Zverev concluded, "then there is the creation of a serious infrastructure [the third stage]. And one begins to think of one's name, one's goal, of following a moral-ethical form, about the idea that it's easier to pay some hundreds of millions of rubles of taxes than to hide one's money. When the company becomes big, there is a different process."

"What about bribes and official corruption?" I asked Zverev.

Size helped here, too. The bigger a company became, the easier it was to avoid paying bribes. "Kiosks might have to pay bribes to local officials in the region where they set up. A larger company opening a store might have to pay a bribe to city officials. But when a person is already beyond the city and his sales can be compared to a city budget, then it's already a different situation," Zverev explained.

"These companies do serious, useful things for society, and here it is not always necessary to give a bribe. They can logically show the usefulness of what they do. They can explain and show their contacts with the government. Then there is the political problem, the political choice. If a company does something useful for the city and it is to the benefit of someone [in the leadership], many assume that the person can count on help in the future. So the bribe is not necessary." In the early 1990s, Zverev's company, Most, became known for its close ties to Moscow mayor Yuri Luzhkov.

Dealing with the mob posed similar challenges for entrepreneurs. Smaller, cash-driven companies were easier targets than were giants like Most. It and Menatep were among the first Moscow companies to gain government permission to form their own security forces. Armed and dressed in khakis, Most's private army guarded the entrance to the company's headquarters in the City of Moscow skyscraper overlooking the Moscow River. "It helps to have a serious security service. But the first principle in dealing with the *raket* is that you have to act within the framework of the law. If you break the law, you fall into risk. But if you work completely legally, there's no basis for them influencing you," Zverev said.

Most had chosen to invest its money in Russia and become one of Moscow's biggest real estate investors as well as a leading bank. The larger a company grew in post-Communist Russia, the more it began worrying about its reputation. And the more dealings it had with Western companies, the more it began to play by Western rules. Russia's new private businesses started out in the late 1980s trading goods and providing such services as construction and repair. They grew as they began trading resources and earning money from ruble-dollar arbitrage. When Yeltsin freed prices, these entrepreneurs had already built up capital and gained experience in the tumult of the market.

Banks like Most and Menatep were in a position to earn even bigger profits by taking advantage of rising inflation and the falling ruble. Banks, traders, and simple speculators really were making money from practically nothing. But the real chance to grow would come when the government started selling industrial assets through its privatization program. That would give Russia's new entrepreneurs the opportunity to invest the capital that they had amassed and to become real owners of the country's vast wealth.

Boris Yeltsin stands with two generals, Yevgeny Shaposhnikov (left) and
Konstantin Kobets, who crucially supported him against hard-liners in
the 1991 attempted coup against Gorbachev, at the Russian White House.
Photograph by Vladimir Sumovsky.

Russia was a country of queues as food ran desperately short in the weeks
leading up to radical reforms in 1992. *Photograph by Alexei Rogov.*

Yegor Gaidar, newly appointed deputy prime minister of economics and finance, was the architect of Russia's shock-therapy program, launched on January 2, 1992. *Photograph by V. Kuzmin, Itar-Tass.*

Anatoly Chubais, chairman of the State Committee on Privatization, designed and oversaw Russia's sweeping privatization program. *Photograph by A. Chumichev, Itar-Tass.*

As foreign goods poured into Russia in 1992, small-scale entrepreneurs opened millions of glass-and-aluminum kiosks to sell mainly imported goods. *Photograph by Alexei Rogov.*

After the government liberalized prices, it had to give Russians a chance to earn extra money. Yeltsin signed a decree liberalizing trade in late January 1992, and millions of Russians headed to the streets to buy and sell goods. In downtown Moscow and around subway and railway stations in other cities, impromptu markets sprang up as novice merchants sold both new and used goods. *Photographs by V. Kristoforov, Itar-Tass (opposite, top), S. Kalinin and O. Sizov, Itar-Tass (bottom), and Alexei Rogov (above).*

Enterprises reacted slowly to liberalization but faced a battle all the same. Yekaterinburg-based Uralmash, the giant heavy-equipment producer, was a star of the central planning system, but it struggled to adapt as it experienced a shortage of raw materials and cash to pay workers in early 1992. *Photograph by Alexei Rogov.*

The author interviews two Uralmash workers. Many women were engaged in dirty, difficult manual labor at the plant. *Photograph by Alexei Rogov.*

Viktor Korovin, general director of Uralmash, understood better than most the problems facing his plant and the country. *Photograph by Alexei Rogov.*

Some of Uralmash's production was up-to-date and competitive. But the adjustment to the new environment was still tough on workers. *Photograph by Alexei Rogov.*

Although Russians reacted generally better than expected to reforms, many Communist supporters nonetheless deplored the shift to a market economy and capitalism in Russia. Holding anti-Yeltsin placards and photos of Lenin and Stalin, Communist backers demonstrate near Red Square in Moscow in March 1993. *Photographs by Alexei Rogov.*

4
The Battle for Russia's Wealth

We had two choices—to try to destroy the elite by
force, or to compromise. The first strategy risked
civil war. That's why we were prepared to
compromise. We allowed the elite to exchange
their power for property. *Yegor Gaidar*

Freeing prices was just the first step. Just as important for Yeltsin and
his reformers was rolling back the state's control of property. In early
1992 the state owned nearly everything in Russia, from diamond mines
and oil fields to food stores and hairdressing salons. No modern country had experienced such comprehensive state control of its economy
for so long. And even though the system had begun to break down under Gorbachev's rule, federal ministries and bureaucrats as well as local politicians across the country still actively interfered in the economy.
Property and power had been tightly intertwined; inevitably, selling off
state property unleashed a fierce and even bloody battle for the country's wealth.

The man chosen to lead the privatization campaign was Anatoly
Chubais. Just thirty-four years old, the chairman of the State Committee on Privatization (known by its Russian acronym GKI) was tall and
thin, with blue eyes and a tendency to blush when his opponents criti-

cized him. An economist and former deputy mayor of St. Petersburg, Chubais had worked on initial attempts to build a private sector in his home city in 1991, the year after a reform candidate, lawyer Anatoly Sobchak, was elected mayor; Yeltsin's architect of economic reforms, Gaidar, had asked Chubais to join his team when he pulled it together in late 1991. Beneath Chubais's boyish exterior was a shrewd and tough politician. He became the most resilient and successful of Yeltsin's radical reformers.

Chubais's task was huge and ideologically charged. Backed by Yeltsin, he was determined to create an army of Russian shareholders. "The main goal of privatization is to have owners in Russia. We want to create a new social structure," he declared time and again in the early months of 1992. "Privatization will make the whole economic-reform process irreversible because to reverse economic reform will mean for millions of people to say farewell to their profit."[1]

But in order to move ahead with such a program, Chubais first had to win over privatization's opponents and skeptics, who were legion. Private property had been banned for so long that many people were instinctively suspicious of it. Indeed, even when Russia had debated market economic reforms under Gorbachev, economists and politicians had been afraid to publicly utter the very word *privatizatsia*. Instead, they spoke of the politically safer *razgosudarstvleniye,* or "destatification" (a horrible term underscoring how Soviets tried to deceive themselves through language). Bit by bit, as Gorbachev allowed cooperatives, joint ventures, and leasing—all partial steps toward full-fledged private ownership—the political elite grew more accustomed to the notion of private property. But it wasn't until 1990, when economist Grigory Yavlinsky boldly proposed privatization in his ill-fated five hundred days' economic-reform program, that privatizatsia became a subject for serious, open discussion.

Following that, in 1991, the Russian and Soviet parliaments approved laws that allowed state enterprises to turn themselves into shareholding societies. Through such *nomenklatura* privatization, some factory directors and bureaucrats managed to hand over state assets—enterprises or parts of industrial ministries—to themselves. At the same time, some enterprises turned themselves into 100 percent worker-controlled entities. On the fringes of Moscow, the Red Proletariat Machine Tool Factory became one of the earliest worker-owned enterprises. The Fyodorov Eye Institute and Moscow Taxi Park also privatized themselves by giving shares to the workers. But the managers in effect ruled.

Using the 1991 law as a starting point, Chubais began laying the groundwork for his own privatization program. His goal was to come up with a program that quickly pushed huge swaths of state property into private hands but that was politically achievable. Polls showed that Russians favored the sell-off of stores, service businesses, and apartments. Moreover, despite the strong opposition of state and collective farms, 60 percent of Russians favored private land ownership. But Russians still voiced reservations about privatizing industry. More than 40 percent thought that the "labor collective," or workforce, should own the means of production—an echo of the Soviet concept of collective property. Only 25 percent supported allowing private individuals to buy a state enterprise. But most people didn't know what privatization meant, Yuri Levada, a prominent sociologist, told me. When his Russian Center for Public Opinion and Market Research polled citizens in mid-1992, 40 percent thought privatization would lead to a more equal distribution of property, whereas 27 percent thought the opposite. "The most dramatic problem is who will win and who will lose," Levada explained; 22 percent thought ordinary people would win, but 43 percent thought they would lose.[2]

"More than half the people are in general for privatization, but when we ask who will be the owner, who will be the winner, the answer is unclear," Levada continued. "There is a great influence of populist ideas, the role of so-called collectives, some remnant of class struggle in the mass consciousness. It's more or less natural but it's painful for people. We ask the question 'What do you think about people who will be millionaires?' Year by year, the attitude is improving. Two years ago, more than half the people found millionaires unusual. Now 40 percent of the people find that those who possess millions is a natural thing. Step by step, people are coming to understand that differences in incomes are not tragic. It is more normal." Levada concluded, "Only 10 percent of the people understand what is a share. Even so, about 10 to 15 percent say they will be owners of shares. Our young capitalism is growing."

Popular resistance wasn't the big problem. The biggest obstacle was opposition from factory directors, particularly those in the military-industrial complex. They had strong backers in the Russian parliament. Even though the state owned the enterprises and government ministries tightly controlled them, factory directors enjoyed tremendous local power and privileges. Often they were the sole employer in cities or towns far away from Moscow. Many ruled their enterprises like kings or dictators. Naturally, they feared change. And just as they had with price reform, opponents of property reform tried to delay it by warning that "the people" weren't ready. Civic Union, a political group backed by the Russian Union of Industrialists and Entrepreneurs, was one of the organizations that argued for slow privatization. Its chairman, Alexander Vladislavlev, called on the government to privatize only a few selected enterprises as pilot projects. "If we privatize 50 percent of industry in fifty years, that already will be a big achievement. In Russia, we have few entrepreneurs. The spirit of entrepreneurship has been wiped out," Vladimir Shumeiko told me.[3] Ironically, Yeltsin tapped him, as the former director of a military enterprise in Krasnoyarsk, and two other industrialists to join Gaidar's government in the spring of 1992. Chubais was fighting skeptics from within the government itself.

Huddling with Western advisers, Chubais developed a program that relied on three main principles. First, the program aimed to depoliticize the economy—to get politicians and government officials out of economic decision-making. Second, the program assumed that Russians would respond to financial incentives just as actors in any capitalist economy would. (In other words, they were *homo economicus* as opposed to *homo sovieticus,* as Chubais's advisers wrote.)[4] Finally, the program endeavored to take into account the interests of various "stakeholders" in enterprises, including employees, managers, and the public.

It sounded good on paper. In reality, GKI was an epicenter of both dynamism and chaos in early 1992. Chubais was racing against time, rushing to do all he could before his opponents closed him down. Unlike Gaidar, Chubais understood clearly the importance of public relations, of getting his message out. In frequent press conferences at GKI headquarters a few blocks from the Kremlin, he or his deputy, Dmitri Vasiliev, spent hours explaining their plans to Russian and Western journalists. Like a chess player, Chubais tried to anticipate his opponents' moves, calculating his countermoves in advance. But he was also able to improvise in a pinch. That's why Chubais launched major privatization initiatives around the times of controversial Congresses of People's Deputies, when opponents viciously attacked Yeltsin. And that's why the privatization program turned out as it did—not fulfilling, in the end, all the reformers' earliest dreams.

Chubais and his team started with small-scale privatization of stores and service businesses. With the help of the World Bank's International Finance Corporation (IFC), he worked out a plan for auctioning stores and service businesses to the public for cash. They targeted Nizhny Novgorod, a city on the Volga River and a trading center in prerevolutionary days, as the site of the pilot auction. The city had been called Gor'kiy during the Soviet years, and the physicist and dissident Andrei Sakharov and his wife, Yelena Bonner, had been internally exiled there until Gorbachev released them in late 1986. In 1991, Yeltsin had asked a backer of Sakharov's, the thirty-two-year-old, bushy-haired physicist Boris Nemtsov, to be governor of the Nizhny Novgorod region. The irreverent Nemtsov was eager to make his region a pioneer, a showcase of experiments in Russia's free-market reforms.

The first auction of stores and service businesses took place in April

1992. Gaidar and Chubais flew to Nizhny Novgorod to witness the auction, which was held in the city's Palace of Culture. Before 1917 Nizhny Novgorod had been the site of one of Europe's leading industrial fairs; now a fast-talking auctioneer, gavel in hand, stood before a nervous crowd. To make their bids, the potential buyers held up numbered cards. By the end of the day, twenty-two state-owned stores had been sold. Some new owners represented the management and workers of the stores. Others were outsiders. Russia's sweeping state sell-off had begun.

Soon GKI offices in cities and towns across the country were holding similar auctions. Each region was allowed to decide for itself how it would conduct the sell-offs, but many followed the Nizhny Novgorod model. Indeed, the IFC prepared and distributed to municipalities around the country booklets describing how to set up the auctions. It was one of the best early examples of Western technical assistance to Russia. By the end of 1992, the government had sold off some 46,000 stores and service businesses throughout Russia.

A few months after Nizhny Novgorod's first privatization auction, I visited the region to see how some of the privatized stores were faring. The local GKI gave me the names and addresses of a few stores in the center of the ancient town, which boasted cobblestone streets and its own kremlin. A freshly painted sign hung over a formerly state-owned cheese shop. Inside, shoppers were examining—and buying—both domestic cheeses and imports from France and Holland. Local shoppers hadn't enjoyed such variety, for rubles, in years. A few blocks away, a newly privatized electronics shop looked shabby, and the choice of products wasn't that impressive compared to the array of Japanese- and Korean-made boom boxes and players available in Moscow. But the manager seemed pleased nonetheless.

Later that day, I met Nemtsov briefly in his office in the kremlin. It was a warm afternoon in early June, a Friday, and he was casually dressed. He propped his sneakered feet on his desk. He insisted on conducting the interview in English, which he spoke slowly but clearly. "Why are we doing all this? Because it is more effective than state ownership. People work hard when they understand in their minds that they are the owners, that the property belongs to them and not to the state. We have good results with private shops. And we have good results with private farms in the Nizhny Novgorod region. So it shows that we are moving in the right direction."[5]

He continued: "When we started privatization, we had very big opposition. But now the situation is stable. We have overcome the resistance from managers of state stores because they recognize the possibility of becoming owners themselves of these shops. More than 40 percent of the shops belong to the people who worked there before."

Nemtsov spoke of his plans to move ahead with the privatization of the region's transport monopoly. At that time all cargo was trucked by a local, government-owned company. He wanted to sell off the trucks, which the newly privatized stores could then use if they wished. He also planned to sell off state wholesale organizations, spurring the creation of local and regional distribution companies. He told me that he wanted to sell 60 percent of all state stores and half of all state-owned wholesale organizations as well as 15 percent of the region's transport assets by the end of 1992. He laughed at the ambitiousness of his goal, but in the end he would come close to achieving it.

But he voiced doubts about the government's plans to sell off industrial enterprises. "Right now, we are meeting very strong resistance to privatization from the heads of big plants. It is a very complicated process. It may take us five years to achieve some results in this area."

How had Nemtsov become so market-oriented? "I am thirty-two years old. I have never been a Communist. And I have never even been interested in Communist philosophy and sociology."

Determined, the radical young governor would continue to innovate in Nizhny Novgorod. The region was the first to carry out a comprehensive program of land privatization and one of the first to offer mortgages to local citizens and issue municipal bonds. As he experimented,

Nemtsov gained a reputation as a doer—a reformer, yes, but one who knew what it was like to carry something out on the local level. That would serve him well in the future, when he would move on to Moscow to take a position in the Russian government.

Chubais paid no heed to predictions, such as Nemtsov's, that privatizing state industry would be difficult, if not impossible. He simply kept working. His team tried to create a program that would satisfy not only factory managers and employees but also citizens who didn't work in industry, be they professionals or pensioners. The plan was called "voucher privatization." The state would give each citizen a voucher, which he or she could either sell for cash or invest in enterprises that were to be auctioned. Meanwhile, enterprises would be given a choice of different privatization plans. Employees would be given 25 percent of the shares of their enterprises for free and allowed to purchase 10 percent more at a discount; managers would receive 5 percent of the shares for a nominal price; the public would be able to buy the rest. If employees and managers wanted more shares, they would have to buy more in the voucher auctions.

But the parliament rejected the plan. The proposal did not give enough "rights" to the workers, Yeltsin's opponents declared. What they really meant was that Chubais's plan did not ensure that factory directors would retain control of their factories. By guaranteeing them only 5 percent of the shares, Chubais left room for new outside investors to gain controlling stakes in enterprises. As a fight broke out in parliament in the spring of 1992, it seemed that the entire privatization program would go down. "We were twitching with worries that the whole thing would collapse," recalled Tony Doran, who was heading the privatization project for the IFC. Declared Chubais at one angry press conference: "Those that say they want 'all priorities to the working collective' aren't interested in defending the working collective. They want to stop the process of privatization. And that would mean to put the cross on privatization checks, [on] large-scale privatization and reform as a whole."[6]

But Chubais was not to be stopped. He came forward with a compromise that saved the program, although it also significantly altered the course of Russia's reforms. He agreed to allow factory directors and workers to jointly acquire up to 51 percent of their enterprise, at favorable terms. This plan virtually guaranteed entrenched factory directors an opportunity to retain control of their plants, and in the end it was the plan chosen by nearly three-quarters of all enterprises going on the block. It meant that socialist-era factory directors were able to stay in their jobs much longer than they might have otherwise. It also slowed down the pace of industrial restructuring.

Gaidar later admitted that the course of privatization chosen was not the best. "It was not optimal. But the approach to privatization that we had to accept was the only possible one for Russia," he told me. "We were unable to push our preferred program through the Supreme Soviet. So there was a tight and very difficult compromise between the government and the parliamentary majority. It was not a matter of optimal solutions but of possible solutions and socially acceptable solutions. Of course, it created long-term problems. But, all the same, the possibility to move forward was much more important."[7]

The parliament approved the privatization program on June 11, 1992. Despite the compromise, it was an important victory for Gaidar and Chubais.

On August 19, 1992, on the first anniversary of the coup that led to the Soviet Union's downfall, President Yeltsin announced that the government would grant every citizen—from newborn babies to grandparents—a privatization check, or "voucher," valued at ten thousand rubles so that they could take part in the great state sell-off. The checks pictured the Russian "White House"—the parliament building on the banks of the Moscow River, which had become a symbol of democracy in the 1991 putsch. Russians greeted the vouchers with jokes and ridicule. Before January 2, 1992, ten thousand rubles could have bought a car or a dacha; by the summer of 1992, it was worth less than forty dollars. "The government robbed the people with rocketing inflation and is now trying to tip them with a voucher worth a pair of shoes," said the conservative newspaper *Dyen*. "This illegal scheme will not hand out property to the people but will rob them and lead to the laundering of mafia money," *Pravda* wrote.[8]

Nevertheless, Yeltsin had decreed that citizens could sell their vouchers for cash, invest them in the enterprise of their choice, or put them in one of the new voucher investment funds that were springing up to take part in privatization. On October 1, Sberbank, the state savings bank, began distributing vouchers to citizens. The Russian Raw Materials and Commodities Exchange, where everything from oil to cigarettes was already traded, opened up daily trading in vouchers. Located in the old Moscow Post Office, the commodities exchange operated under a huge bust of Lenin that peered down over the floor as deals were struck. The exchange invited journalists for the first day of trading, but there were more of us than potential traders. "This is the start!" Chubais enthused. Only five trades were completed, valuing the voucher at about 7,800 rubles. Ominously, on that same day, the ruble fell by 20 percent to a record low of 309 rubles to the dollar.

Despite that inauspicious beginning, Russians began collecting their vouchers within a few days. Soon other voucher exchanges opened up around the country. Kiosk owners posted cardboard signs reading, "Kuplyu voucher" (I will buy a voucher), and people stood at metro stations holding up similar signs or dangling them around their necks. Buying and selling vouchers became a business. To make extra money, ordinary citizens would try to arbitrage between the purchase price on the street and the selling price at the commodities exchange.

The voucher price on the market swung widely. Within a few months, the value of vouchers on the exchanges had plummeted from ten thousand rubles to five thousand. Nevertheless, 96 percent of Russians collected their vouchers. Every night on television, advertisements featuring the slogan "PrivitizAtsia" exhorted Russians to prepare to invest their vouchers in enterprises soon to be sold. (*Za* means to be "for," or in favor of, something.) Yet inside GKI, the sense of panic was growing.

Chubais was hustling to get the privatization auctions under way before factory directors—Red Directors, as they were called—stopped him. Their power was on the rise, helped by the appointment of industrialists Viktor Chernomyrdin, Vladimir Shumeiko, and Georgy Khisa to the government. In early December, another session of the Congress of People's Deputies would meet. It was expected to push for Gaidar's ouster. Chubais wasn't sure he would survive, either. He was determined to hold the first auctions before that meeting.

He needed help. With important assistance from the IFC and U.S. government–financed advisers (such as Harvard's Andrei Shleifer and Jonathan Hay), Chubais's team had sketched out the basic framework for privatization auctions. But with so much in the balance and time so short, Chubais decided to contact the European Bank for Reconstruction and Development to ask for further assistance. Its president, Jacques Attali, called up his friend Hans George Rudloff, the head of European operations for Credit Suisse First Boston (CSFB), and urged him to come to Chubais's aid. Against the will of many of his colleagues, Rudloff had pioneered the bank's expansion into Eastern Europe. Just a few months before, he had sent an American of Russian descent, Boris Jordan, to set up CSFB's Moscow office.

Jordan was a fresh-faced, blue-eyed twenty-six-year-old. Born into a family whose older members had been military officers and civil servants in the czarist era, he had grown up in New York on Long Island, attending summer camps to learn Russian language and culture. Upon graduating from New York University in 1988, he wanted to become an American diplomat and in particular to work in Russia. But he was told that, precisely because of his Russian background, he probably wouldn't get a posting to the Soviet Union. So Jordan went into business, joining a Wall Street brokerage house as an analyst and later working in Europe for Ireland's GPA, an aviation leasing company. When the Soviet Union fell apart in 1991, Jordan began looking for work in Russia. After contacting a number of investment banks and brokerage houses, he joined CSFB.

Jordan's first big job there was helping Chubais hold his first privatization auction. Although other major banks bid for the job, Rudloff offered CSFB's services for free. That pleased the Russians, as did the fact that Jordan and his CSFB colleague, Stephen Jennings, didn't try to tell them what to do. "We said, 'Tell us what you want to do, and we will tell you if we can do it,'" Jordan recalled. "We were frankly a little naive. We said we could do it. We didn't have an idea how we could do it but we wanted to get our name established and so we took a risk."[9]

Thus started a frenzied two months of work to prepare for Russia's first privatization auctions. Working day and night in CSFB's tiny representative office and at the GKI office, Jordan and Jennings, a New Zealander and expert on Central European markets, put together Russia's privatization mechanism with the Harvard team and Chubais's aides. "We went around the clock. We wrote public relations programs, wrote computer programs, trained hundreds of people, helped establish the laws," Jordan said. Sometimes Jordan, Jennings, and Chubais's aides stayed up all night writing a presidential decree needed to implement some part of the auction system. In the morning Yeltsin would sign it, and they would move on to the next step. "We all came together, and we did what we could to get it done," Jordan said.

Despite strict deadlines set by GKI, only eleven companies in all of Russia had done the preparatory work needed to turn themselves into joint-stock companies by the fall of 1992. Jordan and Jennings visited all eleven, asking the directors if they would allow their enterprises to be sold in a privatization auction. "We had to ask. Chubais wasn't prepared to force them. But none of the companies were excited about doing it," Jordan recalled. "It was a nightmare."

After all, these were still politically uncertain days in Russia. Opposition to Yeltsin and his reforms had grown more vociferous. Some former Communist factory directors and apparatchiki no doubt hoped that somehow the tide could be turned back and the reforms stopped. Even those who more or less backed the shift to a market economy were afraid that they could be attacked later if the Communists returned to power. Recalled Jennings: "People were looking over their shoulders. They weren't sure that it would happen. They worried whether there would be repercussions down the road. Also, they didn't understand anything. They didn't know the most basic things. What was equity ownership? What were shares? Who could buy those shares? What could the new shareholders do to them? How could this help them raise finances in the capital markets? Conceptually it was completely new. It was very peculiar to explain these simple concepts and, in a short time frame, to tell people that there was something in it for them."[10]

Slowly, Jordan and Jennings persuaded the Bolshevik Biscuit Company, one of the largest cracker and cookie makers in the former Soviet Union, to become the first company in Russia to be privatized via a voucher auction. Together with Chubais's team, they set up the auction center, trained 150 people, and advertised the auction. On December 9, 1992, the session of the Congress of People's Deputies started, with loud debates about Yeltsin's reforms. But the auction program was under way, and the Congress did not stop it.

On December 13, 1992, the government sold off 44 percent of Bolshevik's shares to the public in exchange for their vouchers. Jordan and Jennings, and the GKI team, had pulled off their mission. As they calculated the final results, Jordan later recalled, "I said to myself, 'Wait, how much did this company sell for?' And I took the market price of the vouchers and I took the shares outstanding and the price came out to something like $656,400. I looked over to Steven and said, 'You know, we just sold an identical company in Poland for $80 million.' And he looked back and said, 'You know, there's an opportunity here.' And we said, 'Jesus Christ, there's an incredible opportunity here. There's a massive opportunity here.'"

Jordan and Jennings eventually went on to exploit the opportunity that privatization offered to investors, both Russian and Western. But on that day they were disappointed that Chubais didn't even show up at the first privatization auction. Instead, he sent his deputy, Vasiliev. To Jordan, it was "the first sign of Chubais the politician. Up until then,

Chubais was viewed as a kamikaze. He was going to do things." But by not showing up, Chubais was protecting himself. "He was saying that if this thing bombs, I don't want my name attached to it," Jordan said.

Such caution, in this instance, wasn't necessary. Although the Congress did force Gaidar's resignation, it failed to stop privatization. Miraculously, privatization took hold. Local GKI offices auctioned more than one hundred companies in January and close to two hundred in February. Then the auctions took off. Across the country, every week, citizens and investors began exchanging vouchers for shares of dozens of enterprises. At a press conference in January 1993, Chubais declared: "If we are victorious in the first half of the year, it will be enough to make the process irreversible."[11]

As Chubais and his team labored to keep the auctions rolling, Russia's shrewdest entrepreneurs were eyeing the same opportunity that Jordan and Jennings recognized at that first privatization auction. One was Kakha Bendukidze. A thirty-six-year-old bachelor, he liked to work late in the plain, five-story brick building that his companies—Corporation NIPEK and Shareholding Society Bioprocess—shared with the Institute of Microeconomics. Nothing on the building's exterior revealed that the millionaire Georgian worked inside. Inside, a tall iron gate prevented visitors from ascending to the second floor of one wing. And two armed security guards controlled the entrance to the floor.

Bendukidze was unknown outside a small circle of businesspeople, but his empire was already impressive. NIPEK—the name was the Russian acronym for the People's Oil Industrial Investment Euro-Asian Corporation—had been one of the first Russian companies to issue shares to the public. Bioprocess had started as a cooperative in the late 1980s and built up a huge business trading oil and other natural resources. It also held significant real estate assets in Moscow.

Like many of his comrades in business, Bendukidze had become an entrepreneur more by chance than by planning. As a student in his hometown of Tbilisi, Georgia, he had been active in Komsomol. He became a Communist Party member in 1979 and held on to his card until 1989. A graduate of Tbilisi University with a Ph.D. from Moscow State University, he was the head of biogenetic research in his lab at the Institute of Biochemical and Physiological Organisms outside Moscow in 1988 when the cooperative movement began.

Times were growing increasingly difficult for scientists then. State allocations for research were dwindling, and researchers were among the lowest-paid workers in the country. So Bendukidze and two colleagues decided to set up a cooperative under the auspices of the Academy of Sciences to sell fine chemicals, biological components, and the Russian equivalent of the electrocardiograph machine to state enterprises. They called their cooperative Bioprocess.

Although Bendukidze had never contemplated running his own business, he enjoyed it, bringing to it his passion for experimentation. Bioprocess received orders from state enterprises and hired Academy of Science researchers to work after hours for extra money. Soon the cooperative was turning a profit.

"When we started Bioprocess, each of us had different motives. Some wanted to make more money. I understood that the institute was already on *khozrashyot* [self-financing]," Bendukidze explained to me. "In order to survive, it was necessary to earn money. I liked science and had no intention of dropping it. We thought we were going into business connected with science. We immediately started making good money—at least for those times. If my wage was 120 rubles a month, the company earned around 100,000 rubles a month, sometimes more, sometimes less. And all that time I was also working in the laboratory."[12]

It didn't take long for Bendukidze and his group to realize that lots of money could be made outside science. Bioprocess began importing clothes, food, and other goods from China, borrowing money to finance the trade deals. Interest rates were low, and inflation was rising. "It was easy to make money, because the state enterprises were given freedom to do what they wanted. The combination of the planned economy and elements of the market economy had a big effect. There was not much competition," Bendukidze explained. The company expanded its range of products to include shaving cream and a woman's face cream called Madonna. Although it failed to get in on the computer boom that brought riches to many other companies, it began acting as a middleman in oil export deals.

Gradually, business took over Bendukidze's life. He left the lab and spent all his time buying, selling, cutting deals, and thinking up new financial experiments. At the end of 1991, he dreamed up a way to raise capital from the Soviet public, which he planned to use toward investments in oil. He formed NIPEK, which began offering the public shares in December 1991. The aim was to soak up part of the vast "ruble overhang"—the millions in rubles that Russians kept in their bank accounts and under their beds.

Lines formed outside the Museum of the History of Moscow, where NIPEK had leased an office for selling the shares. Babushki, workers, militiamen—all came to take part in one of the first share offerings in Soviet history. They were hoping to shield themselves from inflation by owning a share in an oil company. No one seemed to mind that NIPEK offered few details about its assets and operations. (It didn't own any oil fields, for example.) NIPEK raised the ruble equivalent of $5 million but cut short the share offering in early 1992, when inflation soared in the wake of the price reforms. Bendukidze invested most of the money in Moscow real estate—another lucrative business that was just taking off. He also set up a bank, the Industrial and Trade Bank, which would help to finance his future activities.

Bendukidze had been patiently waiting for the sell-off of state assets to begin. He knew it would be a huge chance for anyone who had built up a cash hoard. His idea was to create a giant industrial holding company, with investments in chemicals, oil, shipping, machine building, and other industries. "We will continue to have state interference in the economy," he told me one afternoon in his office at the Institute of Microeconomics. A socialist realist painting decorated an entire wall behind his desk. "In this situation, the ones that will be most effective will turn out to be those that are close to the government, those that can get what they need—whether it is cheap credits or export privileges or special licenses or concessions. It's not important what. But it's understandable that the government cannot save 100,000 enterprises. These enterprises will form into groups. There will be maybe one hundred or two hundred very powerful groups, and they will have their own lobbyists. It will be the reason to unite."

"I plan to create a financial-industrial group," Bendukidze declared. An intelligent man with a good grasp of economics, he said he understood that the development of such conglomerates might discourage competition and thus in some ways prove to be bad for the Russian economy. But it seemed the best strategy for survival and growth, at least at that stage. "It could affect the whole process of the development of capitalism in Russia. Nevertheless, I am going to do it," he said firmly.

So, as the auctions took off in the winter of 1993, Bendukidze moved into action. Quietly, his bank began buying up vouchers all over the country—wherever it could get them cheapest. Colleagues from Bioprocess monitored the voucher price on the Russian Raw Materials and Commodities Exchange. They stayed in contact with voucher brokers, who sprang up in smaller cities like Yekaterinburg, Perm, and Volgograd. They assigned a person to buy vouchers from kiosks or from people on the street. "We spent some millions of dollars to buy vouchers, 7 to 8 million maybe. It's hard to count because the rates were always changing—dollars, vouchers, rubles," Bendukidze later told me. "It was very important to do everything quietly. I didn't want anyone to know. I considered that the fewer people who knew, the lower would be the price for vouchers."

In his office, Bendukidze spent hours every day poring over newspapers' descriptions of enterprises whose shares would soon be for sale. There wasn't enough time and information to be picky. Instead, the shrewd Georgian followed two strategies: to grab stakes in a few large and well-known enterprises, and to pursue what he called "blanket privatization," buying anything that he thought he could sell for a profit later on. "We didn't think about whether we needed the factory or didn't need it. We simply bought it. It wasn't important what it built. What was important was whether we thought we could sell it later on. If it was for sale, we should buy it. *Prodayotsa, nado kupit. Prodayotsa, nado kupit."*

So they did. Throughout 1993 they poured their newly purchased vouchers into factories: a shipbuilder in St. Petersburg, construction companies in the Far North, oil refineries, machine-tool factories— twenty enterprises in all. Handing over vouchers for shares, sometimes they gained as much as 25 percent of an enterprise, sometimes less. The biggest sensation, however, came when Bendukidze bought 18 percent of giant Uralmash—the showcase machine-tool factory in Yekaterinburg—in the spring of 1993 for just $700,000. That a Georgian millionaire could snatch a significant stake in a company as historic as Uralmash stunned not only the management but the government and much of the country. Uralmash turned the obscure Bendukidze into a public figure overnight.

What was Bendukidze thinking when he invested his vouchers? I suspected that he had politics in mind. As the jewel of the Soviet economy and the largest employer in Yeltsin's hometown, Uralmash could not be allowed to go bankrupt. The huge company might give Bendukidze's Bioprocess group better access to government credits, tax privileges, licenses, or other favors. But Bendukidze denied that Uralmash was the centerpiece of his strategy of building a financial-industrial group. "It isn't the key to our strategy," he later told me. "When we were buying companies we tried to figure which shares were expensive and which ones were cheap. The bigger the factory, the cheaper you could buy it for."[13]

Instead, if Uralmash could get on its feet, the acquisition actually made business sense for Bendukidze. His conglomerate would concentrate on three main areas: oil and chemicals, construction and real estate, and finance. As a major supplier of oil exploration and drilling equipment, Uralmash fit into the Bioprocess group. Its new director, Viktor Korovin, had already been shaking up the company, with an aim to turning it into a global player over the long haul.

Still, in Yekaterinburg, the questions were flying about Bendukidze's motives. Was he an asset-stripper, or would he provide real financing for the ailing company? How much would he interfere? Did he want to split the company up and sell off parts of it? Or did he plan to carry on its proud tradition? "We at Uralmash were afraid. We don't like to be shocked. We like to sit and think—is it good or bad and how should we do it so that it will be good?" one manager told me later. "Until the auction, we didn't know that there exists an organization called Bioprocess."[14]

It would take years for these questions to be answered. In the meantime, Bendukidze's purchase of Uralmash transformed Russia's privatization program. Suddenly, slower-moving entrepreneurs woke up and saw that they were missing the sale of the century. The price of vouchers began rising as entrepreneurs snapped them up and began investing in privatization auctions. Foreign investors began buying up vouchers and investing them, too, helped largely by CSFB's Jordan and Jennings.

By the end of 1993, Bendukidze had accumulated stakes in fifty enterprises with more than sixty-five thousand workers. Other entrepreneurs had also built up industrial holdings. These investments set the stage for critical battles between new entrepreneur-shareholders and former state enterprise managers, which would be played out over subsequent years. The outcome of these fights would help to determine the pace of Russia's industrial restructuring.

One such battle took shape in the historic town of Vladimir, one hundred miles from Moscow. There the main employer was the Vladimir Tractor Factory, a maker of tractors and diesel engines since 1945. Anatoly Grishin was the factory's general director. A tall, gruff, white-haired man, he had worked at the factory for more than forty years and had run it for eighteen years.

The factory was his life. He knew every inch of it. He knew many of its nineteen thousand workers by name. He was proud of the scores of apartments, the twenty-five day care centers, the sports complex, and the cultural palace that the factory had built for the entire city to enjoy. Grishin had struggled to ensure that his workers were well fed: the factory owned two farms outside the city, producing fruits and vegetables that were sold to the workers at subsidized prices. As the factory's general director, Grishin was one of the most powerful people in Vladimir. He presided over his enterprise like a stern but generous papa.

Now Yeltsin's reformers seemed determined to shake up that order, and Grishin was puzzled. How could he let outsiders take a stake in the factory? How could anyone know better than he how to run the sprawling operations, with its two factories for engines, its tractor assembly line, and its own heating plant and design bureau? Grishin had mastered the art of managing within the old boys' network that was the central planning system, where personal ties were the guarantee of success. He had built up close relationships with suppliers and customers, from the Lipetsk Tractor Factory to TraktorExport, the foreign trading firm. He had won the respect of officials at the Ministry of Agricultural Machinery in Moscow for boosting the factory's exports to Canada, the United States, and Europe and bringing in useful hard currency. Grishin hated all the new talk about profits and privatization. He despised, even feared, the rationality and harshness of the new market economy.

Yet the determined sixty-year-old boss could not block the changes sweeping over Vladimir and other industrial cities across the country. Privatization was happening, and there was no getting out of it. In September 1992, the workers voted to privatize the company in a way that would provide them with a 51 percent stake. Five percent would be allotted to the management; the rest would be auctioned to the public.

Meanwhile, thousands of miles away, a longtime rival of Grishin was already plotting to gain control of the factory when the state sold its shares. The first big takeover attempt and proxy battle in post-Soviet Russia would center around Grishin's pride and joy.

The audacious raider was Josef Bakaleynik, forty-two, who had worked side by side with Grishin as deputy director of the Vladimir plant for seven years in the 1980s. Bakaleynik was a native of Siberia, and his style and background contrasted sharply with those of his traditionalist Russian boss. Bakaleynik had never dirtied his hands on a factory assembly line. The son of professors at the Vladimir Technical University, he had graduated from Moscow State University with a Ph.D. in economics. There he had learned about market economics from Stanislav Shatalin, the same professor who had influenced reformer Yegor Gaidar. Bakaleynik had hoped for a career in academics, but he couldn't get a teaching job in Vladimir. He figured that was because he was Jewish and living in Vladimir, where such positions were few; local Communist Party bosses were more inclined to offer slots to ethnic Russians. As Bakaleynik didn't have the permit needed to live in Moscow, he joined the Vladimir Tractor Factory in 1982.

Bakaleynik was an ambitious young manager, and it didn't take long for him to clash with his boss. After learning the ropes for the first few years, he quietly came to the conclusion that he could run the factory better than Grishin did. Bakaleynik thought he could get more from the workers by giving them a sense that they were part of a team. The older manager, by contrast, had an authoritarian style. He easily lost his temper and didn't hesitate to yell and pound his fist on his desk. He concentrated all decision-making power in his hands and those of his close associate, the factory's chief engineer.

Gorbachev's perestroika reforms in the late 1980s gave Bakaleynik his first chance to experiment with new ways to manage. When Gorbachev imposed self-financing on enterprises in 1988, Bakaleynik introduced incentive pay systems and profit centers in a bid to boost efficiency. But Grishin didn't see the need for most of these experiments, which he believed distracted everyone from the key goal: exceeding the plan by producing more and more tractors, every hour, every day, every month, every year. "I was trying to get people interested in what they were doing, to find a mechanism to preserve the essential energy of the factory, so everyone was working together," Bakaleynik later explained to me. "It was a huge company, and it was clear that it was impossible to manage by just two people. But that was the culture."[15]

As time went on, Bakaleynik realized that he would never get the chance to rise to the general director's post. Soviet factory directors often stayed in their posts until retirement, and Grishin seemed in no hurry to leave. Bakaleynik began to think about returning to Moscow to study for another Ph.D. or to join the Ministry of Agricultural Machinery.

Then in 1989 came an unexpected opportunity. Bakaleynik heard about a scholarship program for Soviet managers at Harvard Business School. To win the scholarship, Bakaleynik, who was nearly fluent in English, beat one hundred candidates. Little did he know that while he sweated over business case studies for the next few years, the Soviet Union would fall apart, radical economic reforms would begin, and shares in the Vladimir Tractor Factory would be put up for sale to the public.

His desire to run the factory grew even stronger as he studied. "The way they teach you at Harvard, the punch line is that you assume you are the protagonist in the case, the chief executive," Bakaleynik recalled. "When you get indoctrinated that way, it really gets you. So somewhere in the middle of my first year at Harvard, it became an idée fixe. I became almost obsessed with it." For Bakaleynik, the sell-off of Russian industry therefore opened up the unexpected opportunity to return home, bid for the job that he had long wanted, and apply his new skills to the task of turning around the sluggish, inefficient plant.

But first he had to get his hands on a major stake in the company.

By chance, through a professor, Bakaleynik had met Len Blavatnik. Blavatnik was an immigrant from Ukraine, a Harvard MBA who had set up a company to invest in the former Soviet Union. "What do you want to do when you finish?" Blavatnik had asked Bakaleynik during one of their several meetings in Boston and New York. "Become the general director of the Vladimir Tractor Factory," he had replied. "Don't just become director; become an owner," Blavatnik advised him. Together, they developed a strategy.[16]

The plan was simple. They would buy privatization vouchers on the open market and invest them in the enterprise's shares, scheduled to be auctioned in March 1993. They hoped to win a large minority stake—enough to influence both Grishin and the workers. Then, at the first shareholders' meeting of the newly privatized company, Bakaleynik would bid to become general director of the company, ousting Grishin.

It seemed like a good plan. Who would want the Vladimir shares? Workers and local people perhaps, but surely few foreign investors would be eager to buy a stake in the enterprise. Through his company, Renova, Blavatnik accumulated vouchers at the cost of less than $1 million. Bakaleynik himself invested a small amount. He couldn't put in much, he told me, because he had lived in the United States on a student grant with his wife and child and had little money to invest.

But then the new partners made a tactical mistake. They disclosed their cards, suggesting that Grishin become chairman of the board and Bakaleynik, CEO. "It was one of our worst investments," Blavatnik later confided to me. He regretted that they had revealed their strategy to Grishin. "If we had done it quietly," Bakaleynik agreed, "we would have gotten much more."

The next step was to gain more voting rights through a proxy battle before the shareholders' meeting. Bakaleynik and Blavatnik hired a new local investment company, Blagovest, to help them gain the support of the factory's workers. Every morning at six o'clock, the team rolled up to the factory gate in a bus equipped with loudspeakers. As workers streamed into the plant, emerged for their lunch break, or left to head home, they heard the broadcast messages urging them to put their shares and voting rights in trust to Bakaleynik, in exchange for a

250 percent dividend worth 2,500 rubles per share; after the meeting and payment of the dividend, the shares and voting rights would return to the workers. Many workers considered this a good deal, for at the time the shares were trading at less than that on the black market.

Inside the factory gate, Grishin had his own ways of ensuring the workers' support. Determined not to lose control, he told his foremen to get the workers to hand over their voting rights. Voting at the meeting would be by worker representatives: surely all would vote in favor of Grishin for fear of losing their jobs.

The odds were against Bakaleynik. Within a week of the shareholders' meeting, he had control of just 15 percent of the shares. Grishin was counting on the support of shares held by the workers and Alfa Capital. But the boys from Harvard were still fighting. Bakaleynik learned that Grishin had received proxy rights for thousands of shares but had not had them notarized. That contravened government rules. Bakaleynik objected.

Panic broke out at the plant as Grishin hired nearly every notary public in Vladimir to work around the clock authorizing all his workers' proxy statements. But that wasn't all. To ensure that the voting would be all-inclusive and fair, Bakaleynik insisted that the meeting be held at a venue where all twenty thousand shareholders could be present. The only place large enough was the Torpedo football stadium, so the regional privatization committee ruled that the meeting would be held there on June 23, 1993, beginning at 10 A.M.

On the day of the meeting, dark clouds hung over Vladimir. Still, by nine o'clock the area outside the stadium bustled with workers waiting to enter for the meeting. Some drank Russian beer in dark bottles. Others clung to the white cards with which they would indicate their votes during the meeting. Inside the stadium, microphones and a table stood beneath the scoreboard, where Grishin and Bakaleynik would make their appeals. Just after ten o'clock, a voice boomed over the loudspeaker and echoed against the walls of the half-empty football stadium: "The first shareholders' meeting of the Shareholding Company

Vladimir Tractor Factory is declared open!" Grishin sat stiffly along-side managers and local officials at the dais that had been set up on the field beneath the scoreboard. His white hair was brushed back; he had donned a dark blue suit. He seemed uncomfortable in this new world of shareholding societies, shareholders' meetings, and challenges to his authority. Bakaleynik, meanwhile, sat in the stands with the sharehold-ers, a relaxed smile on his face. He enjoyed playing the role of under-dog. "This is my idea of a vacation," he joked to shareholders seated around him. And indeed he was waging his campaign while on vaca-tion from his new job at the IFC. He seemed an unlikely corporate raider.[17]

The meeting resembled a Communist Party gathering with a twist. Workers in overalls sat beside young biznesmen with briefcases, local politicians, and curious reporters. Microphones were placed in several positions around the stadium. Shareholders voted by holding up their large white signs. As rain began to fall and umbrellas opened up in the stands, Bakaleynik approached the microphone to present his views to the shareholders.

Standing there without an umbrella, rain streaming down his face, he began: "Uvazhaemye tovarishi . . . " "Respected comrades . . . " He paused to allow the traditional form of the Communist era to sink in. Although he had come home from Harvard and Washington, Baka-leynik wanted to show that he was still the *tovarish*—the comrade—of workers at the Vladimir plant. "Respected comrades, it's nice for me in these ten minutes to put forth the reason why I am here, to say how I see the future of the tractor factory."

The stadium was silent. Bakaleynik continued. "My desire to speak is determined by changes taking place in our country. They arise be-cause the country is going to the market system of economy. New de-mands are appearing for enterprises and companies. The changes will determine how we might have to work in the twenty-first century.

"You see, there are only seven years left and we will move into a new historical era. It seems to me that the future will demand a lot from the directors of big enterprises—much more than compared with just two or three years ago. For that reason, after I consulted with my comrades at the factory, they put forth my candidacy for the post of general director. These people did this taking into account today's situation in the factory, and seeing the cardinal changes that will take place in the next two or three or four years. There are big changes taking place in the country. The market is changing. Privatization is taking place in enterprises."

The stadium remained silent. Bakaleynik took a breath and went on.

"There will take place changes in the factory that are dictated by the changes in the country. We shareholders who are represented here are responsible for the prosperity of the factory. The factory needs additional funds. We cannot count on the savings of previous years. We should organize the work of the factory in this way: there should be a profit in the factory, and there should be free financial resources. And in this way we can maintain for ourselves our apartments, our kindergartens, our supplementary benefits, and so on. Then we can raise our economic status in such a way that we can compete successfully.

"Before we competed thanks to the low cost of gas, oil, aluminum. Now we will have to compete on equal terms with others. We need to find raw materials, components, and new technology so that our production should be competitive. We cannot compete because of our low technical qualifications. I would like to make these proposals in the plan of the factory: to look at the human factor, to solve the problems of finance so that people can understand and see what they will get if they work more effectively, steadily, rhythmically.

"These are my proposals and I would like to prove that what I am proposing will be successful. The demands on factories are changing, and demands on the management are changing. They are changing especially from what we had just two or three years ago under the system of central management of the economy. In the next few years on our market will appear leaders in the world market of tractors, and as the saying goes, 'May God give us energy and strength.' In a market economy, competition is cruel. It takes decisions independent of the will of the leadership of the plant, the government, the shareholders. It allows to remain afloat only those firms, companies, and societies that have the possibility to organize all resources and put them to work in concentrated form."

He completed his statement, the rain still coursing down his face. Now it was time for questions. From one of the microphones placed around the stadium, a worker bellowed: "I know Anatoly Vasilievich Grishin for more than twenty-five years. I am going to vote for him. But I have this question for you. You are persuading us that a market economy demands competition. You stand for new production. For as long as I have worked there and continue to work, the Vladimir Tractor Factory has always been in a process of reconstruction."

Bakaleynik: "You have touched on an important human factor. People who work in the factory and the shareholders should see the link between their own work and the income they receive—what production, how we are going to compete on quality, and on price. If we don't attract resources, our factory will go bankrupt."

Other workers asked questions about unemployment, possible cutbacks in social privileges for the workers, benefits for young workers. One worker stood up and declared: "I think a Harvard education will not help you. Today you need personal contacts, deep personal contacts." Bakaleynik did not reply. He thanked the shareholders and sat down.

It was Grishin's turn. He stood before the microphone as the rain continued to pour down. He shouted loudly, as if booming his message made it all the more correct. Although he felt sure he would win, he nonetheless wanted to stand up for his record. He was fighting for the life he was accustomed to and seemed almost bewildered that he was forced to defend himself.

"Respected shareholders," he began. "Today for the collective of the tractor factory is an atypical day. I draw attention particularly to the tractor constructors. They have a bigger packet of shares of the tractor factory. And they decide the future. I want to put forth how I have spent all my life in the tractor factory. It is for you, tovarishi, to judge my intentions and the quality of my work.

"I should tell everyone that today we stand on the threshold of absolutely new tractor business. As a shareholding company we have to rethink our position, our psychology, and our relationship to business. But before I go to my program, I would like to draw your attention to what we have managed to do. Let's go back several years."

"In the past fifteen years," Grishin recalled, "we have raised the capacity to produce tractors by three times. We built capacity to produce tractor engines. What did we do for the factory in the social plan? We built big institutions. We built several schools and technical colleges. All of this was built on the money and strength of the tractor constructors. We solved with you very complicated questions of the food program. We solved the problems of food for our pensioners. We have several pioneer camps. We have provided children's kindergartens at minimum cost, food at minimal cost. Now we have a big potential of labor resources. Practically, it is the whole apparat of the old management team. Our specialists are responsible, and Bakaleynik knows that. All our best cadres are working on bringing out new production."

"I would like to assure all shareholders, my tovarishi, and colleagues at work that here I have spent my entire life," Grishin exhorted. "If we cut back our workforce, our perfect workers, we will defend them socially. We cut back our workers because our hands have been tied; we have been given the market economy. But we know best what to do, how to do it, and for what price.

"Everything that was done in our factory was done with our hands. And if today we can choose the ideal director, the head of the board of directors, I will do stubborn, persistent work for our prosperity. I will work hard and doggedly for the good of our factory."

The shareholders applauded, and Grishin sat down.

Next came the discussion period.

"Tovarishi, ladies and gentlemen, friends," said one worker. "Bakaleynik is perfect. Grishin is even better. I don't want to say that I love Anatoly Grishin as a person; I don't trust him. But as a shareholder, I trust him because I know him for eighteen years. I will vote for Anatoly Vasilievich because he has been here for eighteen years. We don't know whether they will sell our factory. We live only thanks to the factory. I want to vote for the person who can keep the factory the way that we know it."

In the secret ballot that followed, Grishin won by 82 percent of the vote. Bakaleynik was disappointed but not surprised. "People in Russia tend to respect not law but authority, and the authority made itself clear. The local administration, the shareholders, depend on the management," Bakaleynik told reporters in the stands after the vote. "The system was very simple: if you don't give me your proxy, you are fired." Bakaleynik's 18 percent vote was enough to get him a seat on the board. Renova also won a seat.

Bakaleynik vowed to continue the fight. The meeting went long into the evening, but as he approached the microphone for the last time, he thanked shareholders for their attention and hinted that he would be back. "To be continued," he said, and walked away.

From the floors of factories in Vladimir or Vladivostok to the streets of Moscow, the battle for power and influence as well as riches intensified throughout 1993. Politically, it was a volatile year—nearly as apocalyptic as the summer and autumn of 1991. Week by week, the opposition grew more vociferous. The government and the opposition often clashed openly in the Russian parliament. At other times the fight took place behind the scenes, through the action and inaction of bureaucrats who knew that they had much to lose in the new Russia. The result was a process of always moving one step backward for every two, enormously difficult steps forward.

The year 1993 started out with a fight over monetary policy. Industrialists and collective farmers put mighty pressure on the new prime minister, Viktor Chernomyrdin, and Central Bank chairman Viktor

Geraschenko to open the taps and let credits flow to state enterprises and farms. In the first three months, Geraschenko issued hundreds of billions more in new credits, fueling already surging inflation. Prices began increasing nearly 30 percent a month, steering Russia toward hyperinflation and further squeezing Russians struggling to survive on fixed salaries and pensions.

Radical economists still advising the government warned about the dangers of easy money. Liberal economist Boris Fyodorov, who had taken over as finance minister in January, was vitriolic. "We have clashed with an unprecedented situation in world practice," the chubby, irreverent young minister declared at a press conference that spring. "We have clashed with a situation in which the Central Bank refuses to be a central bank but wants to be a state bank. Maybe because it has a leader that is from the old State Bank.

"There is not a country in the world where the government goes to the head of the Central Bank and says that he must fight for the currency. In all countries, the central bank watches over the government and criticizes it constantly for trying to spend more than is reasonable in its given economic situation. We have a different direction.

"Mr. Geraschenko makes a speech and says: 'Well, someone from the Supreme Soviet forces us to give credits. Someone from the government made a decision. The government is to blame—it couldn't maintain its tough monetary policy of last year.' But who heard anywhere that Mr. Geraschenko argued against those decisions of the Supreme Soviet? Who heard anything from Mr. Geraschenko about improving payments? Inflation is increasing. Payments are not improving. To stop inflation without the participation of the Central Bank is not possible."[18]

But Geraschenko paid no attention, blaming the government for the collapse in monetary discipline. "The budget was never real. The Ministry of Finance never proposed a budget that could be implemented. They needed to find a guilty party. It was Geraschenko. Fyodorov and his colleagues gave that impression," he later argued to me.[19]

Meanwhile, the Russian parliament was taking aim at Yeltsin. In early March 1993, it called another session of the Congress of People's Deputies to debate Yeltsin's plea for a national referendum on a new constitution in April. A real fight was on for control of the levers of power. According to the system devised and put in place by Gorbachev, the Congress was the final arbiter for all policy decisions in the land. But the Congress had been elected in 1990—before the collapse of the Soviet Union—and was filled with Communist-era factory directors, bureaucrats, and public figures who came to abhor the changes that Yeltsin had set in motion. In December 1992, when protesting Yeltsin's policies and successfully demanding Gaidar's resignation, the Congress had agreed to allow a spring referendum on changing Russia's constitution and system of governance. But now it was backtracking, because such a change would mean the end of power and perks for the Congress's 1,033 deputies.

Every day, the battle for power became more intertwined with the fight over Russia's economic policy. In the spring, Russians and westerners alike began voicing fears that the stalemate could not be resolved without violence.

At the congressional session in early March, the deputies severely criticized Yeltsin, awarded themselves the power to suspend the president's decrees, and refused to approve the planned spring referendum. Yeltsin's reforms had caused "chaos and the disintegration of Russia" and had "backfired against a majority of the people," the Congress declared.[20] Yeltsin stormed out of the Kremlin's ornate hall and, a few days later, counterattacked. In an address that was televised on a Saturday night, he told the country that he was assuming "special powers" until the referendum went ahead on April 25, 1993.

The parliament erupted. Once again, the Congress of People's Deputies gathered for an emergency session. This time, the main item on the agenda was a motion to impeach Yeltsin. Demonstrators clogged the center of Moscow to rally for and against the president and his reforms. Separated by barricades and militiamen, the crowds faced each

other on the cobblestones next to the Kremlin as deputies walked to
and from the Congress session. "Down with Yeltsin" and "No Capitalism in Russia," said signs on one side. On the other, demonstrators
waved placards declaring, "Boris, You Are Right!" Emerging from the
session, Yeltsin stood before the crowd and announced: "These people
are using all their strength to destroy Yeltsin, if not physically then by
removing him from office. I submit only to the will of the people." But
Yeltsin survived the political attack; the move to impeach him lost by
seventy-two votes.[21]

The April 25 referendum turned out to be a decisive victory for
Yeltsin. On the ballot were four questions: "(1) Do you have confidence
in Russian president Boris Yeltsin? (2) Do you approve of the socio-
economic policy carried out by the president of the Russian Federation
and the government of the Russian Federation since 1992? (3) Do you
consider it necessary to carry out early elections for the president of the
Russian Federation? (4) Do you consider it necessary to carry out early
elections for the deputies of the Russian Federation?"

The turnout was unexpectedly large. Sixty-four percent of the electorate headed to the polls to express their views—a sign that democracy was alive and well in Russia after all. Even more surprising were
the results: 58.5 percent of the voters checked "da," indicating their approval of Yeltsin's presidency. In spite of the collapse in living standards, a surprising 52.8 percent backed his program of economic reforms. (Both Western and Russian commentators had expected Yeltsin
to lose on this issue, once again misjudging the Russian people.) Only
32 percent of the voters backed early elections for president, whereas
41.4 percent called for early parliamentary elections. In a pre-referen-
dum campaign, Yeltsin's supporters had fanned across the country urging voters to cast their ballots "Da, da, nyet, da." And they had. It was
a striking victory for the beleaguered president.

The referendum victory should have spurred faster reform. But
Yeltsin failed to take advantage of the momentum gained by his win.
All through the summer, the Russian parliament attempted to stymie

economic reform. It passed an inflationary budget, with a deficit more than double that of the government's proposed budget. It voted to put Chubais's privatization committee out of business. Back and forth between government and parliamentary officials flew accusations about high-level corruption in the country. Then, on July 24, 1993, while Yeltsin was on vacation, Geraschenko announced that rubles printed before 1993 could no longer be used as valid currency. The decision sparked a public outcry as Russians hurried to try to exchange old notes for new ones.

Meanwhile, two separate commissions, one backed by Yeltsin and one backed by the parliament, worked on strikingly different draft constitutions. The country seemed deadlocked over how power should be separated in the new Russian state.

On September 16, 1993, Yeltsin invited Gaidar back into the government as deputy prime minister in charge of the economy. The message was clear: Yeltsin was determined to push ahead with reforms. Five days later, Yeltsin took the boldest and most controversial step of his career. Again appearing on television, he announced that he was suspending the parliament and calling new elections for December. The legislature, he said, "has ceased to be an organ of rule by the people. . . . Power in the Supreme Soviet of Russia has been seized by a group of persons who have turned it into the headquarters of irreconcilable opposition. . . . My duty as president is to state that the current corps of deputies has lost its right to be in control of crucial levers of state power." He added: "The security of Russia and her people is a higher value than formal compliance with the controversial laws produced by a legislature that has totally discredited itself. The time has come for the most serious decision."[22] Yeltsin signed Presidential Decree No. 1400 to put his decision into action.

The parliament's reaction was fierce and decisive. Gathering overnight, the deputies voted to oust Yeltsin and named Vice President Alexander Rutskoi acting president. A crowd gathered outside the White House. The stage was set for a siege.

Around the country and the world, people debated Yeltsin's commitment to democracy. In the United States, President Bill Clinton backed Yeltsin. In regions around Russia, legislatures began taking sides. Some, such as Novosibirsk and Sverdlovsk Oblast, where Yeltsin was born, called for joint presidential and parliamentary elections as a compromise to end the dispute. But Yeltsin would not be moved. For days, the parliamentarians remained in the White House as barricades formed outside. Arms had been stockpiled in the building, and deputies could be seen toting automatic weapons. On September 24, 1993, Moscow turned off the electricity and water to the building. Police armed with billy clubs, not assault rifles, surrounded the White House. From then on, deputies could leave, but no one was allowed to enter the parliament.

The tension rose every day, finally spilling into violence on October 3. Waving a *kalashnikov* assault rifle, Rutskoi urged an unruly crowd outside the White House to mount an armed insurrection against the government. Wild, armed Rutskoi supporters ran through the streets, shooting. They raced to the television tower north of the city, where a gun battle broke out for control of the nation's airwaves. Rutskoi had launched a civil war. Four central television channels were shut down as the violence raged, but Russian Television kept broadcasting. Gaidar called for all people who supported democracy to stand vigil outside Moscow's city hall. Although Yeltsin had declared a state of emergency and ordered troops to enter Moscow, the army had not responded.

Only hours later, at half past two in the morning, Yeltsin climbed into his Zil and raced to the Ministry of Defense, a white building a few blocks from the Russian parliament. There, together with Chernomyrdin, he met with Minister of Defense Pavel Grachev and other generals. They worked out a plan to attack the parliament that very day. Just after 10 A.M., on October 4, a tank fired a shot at the center of the parliament. The blast tore a large black hole in the center of the building, stopping the huge clock gracing the facade, and a fire started. Within hours, Rutskoi, parliament speaker Ruslan Khasbulatov, and

their supporters in parliament surrendered. The air of tension and dis-
quiet lasted several more days as snipers continued to fire on innocent
people from the rooftops in Moscow's center.[23]

The incident dealt a serious blow to Yeltsin's political reputation.
Russians were saddened and embittered that events had taken such a
turn. In the name of democracy, Yeltsin had taken actions that were
clearly undemocratic. He had allowed—even provoked—what the
Russians came to call "the second coup." Now apathy, exhaustion, depression, set in.

Some voiced doubt that Russia could ever build a solid democracy.
"When we say, 'Let's create a democracy,' you have to ask if there is a
historical basis for it," Kakha Bendukidze told me a few weeks after the
October events. "We want a democratic Russia and we want to fly. Neither one nor the other is natural. Russia has to go down a long road to
civilization. We cannot have Western-type democracy here. We don't
have the historical experience." He continued: "If you take off the incorrect glasses and ask, 'How do you create democracy?' War, death,
hunger, a failed attempt [at democracy], again war, death, hunger, another attempt, again war . . . Russia may want to develop democracy
quickly, but it can't."[24]

When parliamentary elections took place on December 12, 1993,
only slightly more than 50 percent of the voters headed to the polls. By
a tiny margin, they approved Yeltsin's new constitution, which established the state Duma and Council of the Federation and gave the president sweeping executive powers. Yeltsin was surprisingly quiet in the
weeks before the vote, holding himself aloof from politics and letting
Gaidar and other "democrats" fight for themselves.

To their dismay, they didn't win the majority. Instead, the Liberal
Democratic Party, headed by nationalist Vladimir Zhirinovsky, snared
the most votes. In the aftermath, the ruble started on a downward slide
that wouldn't stop until 1995.[25] A few weeks later, Gaidar resigned
from the government, followed by finance minister Boris Fyodorov.
With two key reformers gone, many Western commentators began pen-

ning essays with titles like "Who Lost Russia," declaring Russia's liberal experiment at an end. There would, of course, be many more zigs and zags yet to come.[26]

While the politicians skirmished over the right to determine the country's future economic and political course, many Russians were otherwise occupied. They were busy making money. The political chaos provided a surprisingly lucrative environment for entrepreneurs, financiers, and arbitrageurs who figured out how to take advantage of the distortions of the economy-in-transition. I called it playing the money game, and a remarkable number of Russians became adept at it. It was as if seventy years of suppressed talent for financial speculation had suddenly burst forth into the market.

Although it could be played in many different forms, the principles of the money game were simple. The key was to move fast, to bet as much money as possible, and to move on quickly to the next deal. With inflation rising and the ruble weakening, it was possible to borrow money for nothing. The trick was in using interest rates and the ruble-dollar exchange rates to your advantage. If you played your cards right, you could double your money or better.

A young man whom I'll call Yuri was an expert at playing the money game. Tall, handsome, with dark hair and eyes, he drove around Moscow in a silver Lexus. He made several million dollars in 1992 by exploiting the Russian penchant for smoking. Borrowing rubles for three months from a commercial bank, he exchanged the money for dollars and bought cigarettes from wholesalers in Turkey, India, China, and Poland. "The packages said Marlboros, but they really weren't Marlboros," he confided. Even though interest rates were rising, prices were rising faster, and the ruble was in a freefall from March 1992 on, as the government threw open the gates to the money supply. Yuri could sell the cigarettes at enough of a profit in rubles to pay off the loan and the interest—and start all over again. Soon Russians across the country were smoking his imported cigarettes. Yuri's story was repeated by thousands of kiosk owners and small-scale traders of everything from candy to beer.[27]

Banks and bankers profited, too. In the old days, banks never paid interest on deposits, so many people lived from pay packet to pay packet or kept their money at home. Since 1991, commercial banking had exploded in Russia. More than 2,500 banks had sprung up, and they attracted deposits by paying 60 percent, 80 percent, or 100 percent interest. But they charged much more for the three- and six-month loans. "There was a wild difference between the deposit rate and the interest we earned," recalled entrepreneur Ivan Kivelidi, who set up a bank to support small and medium-sized businesses in 1991. The banking business was especially lucrative in 1992 and 1993, before the Central Bank began demanding larger reserves to cover loans and currency risk.[28]

Of course, many illegal games were played. As commercial bankers dished out loans, a few percentage points of interest were often reserved for the private accounts of the bankers themselves. Some state factory directors, seeing that their days of privilege were waning, openly stole from their companies. Enterprises in the oil, aluminum, and timber businesses channeled part of their production for export and arranged for the proceeds to be paid into foreign bank accounts, some of it for the personal accounts of the directors. Shell companies were another common scam. A director could set up a private company to operate alongside the bigger state enterprise. The state enterprise would sell the raw materials or other goods to the private company at an artificially low Russian price. The private company would then export the commodity at world prices, pocketing the difference. Hundreds, perhaps thousands, of such companies were believed to have been set up in businesses ranging from oil and metals to coal and vodka.

Because the domestic price of oil was still a small percentage of the world price in 1992 and 1993, the potential profits were huge. Oil, aluminum, metals, timber, and even plutonium found their way to the West, thus enriching the managers of enterprises in those industries.

Meanwhile, as Geraschenko poured out cheap credits to military enterprises and state farms, the money rarely went to pay back salaries or bills. Instead, the enterprises deposited the money in Russian commercial banks at high interest rates or secretly banked it in Switzerland, Cyprus, or elsewhere in the West.

Indeed, capital was flying out of Russia at extraordinary speed. Estimates ranged from $5 billion to $50 billion by 1993. Entrepreneurs and managers were avoiding the government's stiff taxes on hard currency transactions. Many were also stashing money abroad for safekeeping. Businesspeople began heading in droves to Cyprus or Spain, buying villas with suitcases of cash. They also opened offshore bank accounts and companies.[29]

As the Russian elite lunged for wealth, Russian capitalism took on its own peculiar characteristics. Some entrepreneurs indeed followed the classic Western model: they were driven to earn profits, and as they accumulated profits, they reinvested them to create bigger businesses. But they were in a minority. Many others tried to create something from nothing, using arbitrage and distortions in the economy, or they tried to profit by grabbing a piece of state resources. Access to state funds was another route to fortune. In other words, just as Bendukidze had predicted, the way to power, influence, and wealth in Russia was still closely tied to the government. Chubais was certainly not succeeding in depoliticizing the economy.

Several leading commercial banks played the money game with the government's own money. They became known as "authorized banks"—banks authorized to hold government money (at the local, regional, or national level) on deposit or to channel money to finance government expenditures, such as those in the health budget. The banks paid little interest and sometimes no interest at all for holding the funds, yet they were allowed to invest it short-term and keep the returns. As one U.S. banker in Moscow explained to me, "It was as if the government pretended it didn't understand the time value of money."

Authorized banks were the invention of Vladimir Gusinsky. He was a quintessential moneyman. Although trained as a theater director, the tall, solidly built Gusinsky had a sharp instinct for doing business. In the early days of the cooperative movement, he set up a construction and real estate company. Eventually, his group became known as Most—Russian for "bridge."[30] In the early 1990s, the cooperative began bidding for, and winning, government contracts to renovate buildings in Moscow. Soon Moscow's suburbs became dotted with subdivisions of new "cottages," or single-family homes, many of them built by Gusinsky. "Why did I go into construction? Because in every transition economy, the thing that drags everything else along is construction, especially housing construction. It is natural in any developing economy. Everyone looks for his own happiness," he told me.[31]

Gusinsky understood that close ties to the government were important for success in Russia. In 1987, he had become friends with Yuri Luzhkov, then deputy head of the Moscow City Council. Luzhkov would go on to become Moscow's highly effective mayor—a real *khozyain,* or manager, as the Russians put it. The Russian media often hinted that Luzhkov and his city apparatus demanded bribes. They also implied that Gusinsky pulled a lot of strings in the city. Gusinsky denied it. "Any cooperator that was trying to get involved in business then knew that they could go to [Luzhkov] at any time. His door was always open. He never went home until he received all those who came to see him. Then he was accused of taking bribes from everyone. He didn't take any bribes. It's simply not the truth. If he took bribes, show it, prove it. Who can prove that he took bribes? No one. It is stupidity," Gusinsky told me.

Nevertheless, Gusinsky's Most Bank occupied a top floor in the former COMECON building, the skyscraper that the Moscow city government occupied after the August 1991 coup. And he managed to persuade Luzhkov to name Most Bank, along with Menatep, as authorized banks for the city of Moscow. As we chatted one day in his office overlooking the Moscow River, he explained: "There was one bank—a former state bank that serviced the budget, and it had enormous money.

The bank didn't pay any interest—ever. But for that, they gave the city very cheap credits. And for that, the bank lived well and the situation seemed to be acceptable to everyone."

"It was fine until financial problems started in the city," Gusinsky went on. "Suddenly, it became clear that the city didn't have enough money. It was [in 1991 or 1992], and I asked [Luzhkov], 'Why doesn't the bank pay you any interest?' I told him that the bank should pay interest. He said OK. Then I came to the second conclusion: all banks dealing with the budget should pay one and the same interest rate. It should be tied to the discount rate of the Central Bank. The rate [then] was 120 percent. The system was very strict. There was long bargaining with the Finance Ministry about how to do it."

"Then we said that there should be a group of banks that will work together," he recalled. "We started to create a market for money. That started a big scandal. Then our bank and Menatep decided to take the pressure together. We went through inspections, and we said that there would be two authorized banks—Most and Menatep. And all accounts would be done through a new system. And in the city appeared new possibilities. Money appeared. All big banks in Moscow later became authorized banks—Inkombank and Stolichny and Rossisky Kredit. The system was very open. But the state bureaucrats didn't like it. Why? Because without their involvement a system of banks had begun to pay exactly the same interest in very difficult conditions. The system then started to work everywhere—in Petersburg and in other cities."

Gusinsky painted a pretty picture: Moscow gained. I pressed him to admit that his own bank gained a lot, too. Even if it paid interest, which some said was debatable, it could use the state funds to earn its own profits. "We make money, of course. It is big, very big. But there is nothing wrong with that. It is like any bank. The city keeps money with me for a few days or for one day. We pay interest. But we manage this money. We pay the city, and we make some money ourselves. Maybe 2 percent, 3 percent, or 4 percent income, but since it is a lot of money, we make a lot of money."

Working as bankers for the city of Moscow, Most Bank, Menatep, and other banks grew much stronger in 1992 and 1993. Soon the national government was setting up networks of authorized banks to service its budget. Many of the same banks benefited by channeling the government's money through their accounts. Parallel to that, the government began creating a banking infrastructure: an interbank lending market, an improved settlement system, and a market for short-term bonds, or *gosudarstvennye kratkosrochnye obligatsii,* which soon became known as GKOs. Toward the end of 1993 and throughout 1994, the government financed its budget deficit by issuing bonds rather than printing money. In order to attract investors, it offered sky-high interest rates—sometimes more than 200 percent.

The GKO market became an engine generating new earnings for the banks. In fact, Russia's commercial banks did little traditional banking business. With interest rates so high on the government bond market, it wasn't worthwhile for them to lend money to enterprises or entrepreneurs at lower rates—and few hard-pressed enterprises were in a position to pay 200 percent for bank loans. So while financiers and natural-resource companies benefited from the money game (as did, of course, those directors who simply stole from their companies), many manufacturing companies and their employees continued to suffer. It was one of the ironies of the hyperinflation that Geraschenko presided over. He issued credits that were supposed to help enterprises. But the result was that they mainly helped factory directors, who diverted the money, or banks, who used inflation to earn even more.

Meanwhile, privatization offered a way to play the money game as well. Vouchers were the first securities, and all kinds of people began making money by arbitraging the price of vouchers on the street with that on the Russian Raw Materials and Commodities Exchange. For some fledgling financiers, this was their means of survival.

One chilly spring morning in 1993, I met two women near a metro station on the outskirts of Moscow. One held a cardboard sign: "I buy vouchers." They were mother and daughter. The mother, who wouldn't tell me her name, was fifty-seven years old. She had worked all her adult life as a welder in a factory and had retired at age fifty, putting aside one thousand rubles for her funeral. Now a kilo of butter cost more than that. She received a pension of seven thousand rubles a month—then the equivalent of about seven dollars. Her daughter, a nurse, was married to a doctor who also made about seven thousand rubles, she said; they had two children.

Now they were in the voucher arbitrage business to make extra cash. On this day, they were paying 4,200 rubles for vouchers (which, like all vouchers, had a face value of 10,000). They expected to sell them on the Raw Materials and Commodities Exchange for 4,900, a 700-ruble profit. They bought and sold about twenty-five vouchers a day. The mother worked every day, the daughter only on weekends. They earned about 5,000 a day, or 200,000 a month. That was about twenty dollars.

"The state pays you for one day of work a month. The other twenty-nine days you have to try to find some other way to earn money," the daughter, Lyuda, told me. "This is the shame of our state," the mother added. "I have brains. You have to have brains in order to survive, but I could be using these brains for some other good, useful purpose. I could be using them in some factory or institute." She said that she used the money she earned to buy dollars or "nice things made in the West," which she then resold.[32]

That's how people like Lyuda and her mother got by.

Of course, others used voucher privatization to build up serious businesses. Some eight hundred voucher investment funds sprang up in 1993 and 1994, each one promising to invest citizens' vouchers in privatizing factories and award them dividends. Some were scams. But others were legitimate and in time became significant financial institutions.

Alfa Group—the company that had helped Director Anatoly Grishin keep control of the Vladimir Tractor Factory—ran one of the most prominent funds. The company had started out as a window-washing cooperative operated by five students from the Moscow Institute of Metals and Alloys. In 1987, twenty-two-year-old Mikhail Frid-man and four of his friends at the institute began hiring students to wash windows for institutes and enterprises. "It was a big problem in Moscow, cleaning windows then. There was only one state company that did it. Institutes had lots of money, and they didn't know how to use it. We helped them," Fridman said in an interview nearly ten years later.[33] The profits came rolling in. "During our first month, our profit was 25,000 rubles. The average salary then was 160 rubles. My own profit was 10,000 rubles. It was huge, absolutely. I was practically a millionaire compared to Soviet standards. We had a lot of employees. Every day we had at least one hundred students cleaning windows," Fridman recalled.

The cooperative followed the typical path. It went into trading consumer goods, cigarettes, and perfumes and then moved on to computers, oil, and sugar. The company bought and sold real estate and set up a small commercial bank. But when privatization started, Fridman and his partners saw the opportunity to move into industry without risking much of their own money. They set up a voucher investment fund.

Hiring a U.S. company to run a big advertising campaign, they began collecting vouchers from Russian citizens in January 1993. By May they had accumulated some 650,000 vouchers, in exchange for Alfa shares. As local governments all over the country organized privatization auctions, Alfa began investing vouchers in cracker, candy, and macaroni producers, cement factories, a pharmaceutical company, and the nation's biggest producer of glass. The aim was to buy stakes that Alfa could later sell, at a huge profit, to Western investors or partners. As well as investing its voucher fund, Alfa also managed investments on behalf of clients.

Alfa was on its way to becoming a leading financial-industrial group. By the summer of 1994, when the voucher privatization program came to an end, the fund had invested 2.7 million vouchers, worth between $50 and $60 million, in fifty-two enterprises. During the next few years it was to work first on advising these companies on how to improve their results and then, after improvements came, on slowly selling off the assets. By setting its sights on creating a financial-industrial group—a holding company and conglomerate—Alfa was to follow the same path that Bendukidze had described to me. Indeed, a number of banks and industrial companies latched on to the same strategy in 1993 and 1994. These financial-industrial groups were to eventually become key actors in Russia's economy—and in its political life as well.

Not only Russians cashed in on the privatization bonanza. A handful of shrewd foreign investors and financiers did, too. Their numbers were tiny, but they played their own significant role.

Many of the foreign purchasers of vouchers and, later, the stock of newly privatized companies came to the fledgling market through Jordan and Jennings of Credit Suisse First Boston. As the duo that had helped Chubais's team set up the voucher auction mechanism, they had the keenest sense on how it worked—and how to bring foreigners in.

Their biggest problem at first was convincing CSFB to believe in the gold mine that they felt could be found in the mass sell-off of Russian state-owned assets. "We said, 'The heck with advising. The game to be played here is the investment game,'" Jordan said. "Because we had developed the system, we knew it better than anyone. So it gave us an enormous edge over a lot of people on what was happening in the country."[34] CSFB, however, didn't want to take the risk. They urged Jordan and Jennings to continue advising clients and not to invest any money. In frustration, the partners threatened to quit in mid-1993. But by then a new management team had just been appointed, and they invited Jordan and Jennings to make a presentation to the board. That's when the young financiers got the green light to begin investing CSFB and client money into brand-new Russian securities.

So, like the Russians, CSFB began buying up vouchers and taking part in auctions on behalf of clients. In the beginning they were private clients—shrewd individuals or families who had already made millions or billions investing in emerging markets in Latin America and Asia. Later they included investment funds geared for high-risk markets.

In making this transition, Jordan and Jennings had to come up with a mechanism for buying vouchers on behalf of foreign investors and exchanging the vouchers for shares at privatization auctions, because the market on the Russian Raw Material and Commodities Exchange wasn't big enough to accommodate their purchases. "We were trading millions of dollars. The Russian Raw Materials and Commodity Exchange was trading a few hundred thousand rubles," Jordan recalled. "We needed to accumulate size. We started with half a million a day. At our peak we were buying sometimes ten or twenty million a day. [But] there was no infrastructure, so we created a whole system."

Jordan's explanation of their system showed just how primitive Russia's early capitalism was. CSFB had hired three Russian brokers who took short-term debt lines from a Russian bank and then used the loans to buy vouchers in the market. But there was no mechanism for storing and keeping track of so many vouchers. "We couldn't take physical delivery of the things," Jordan recalled. "We found a system that allowed us to put the vouchers in a vault. The company that ran the vault would tell us how many vouchers had been deposited, and only after those vouchers were deposited would we actually pay for them." ("I went down there one day," he added, "and the girls that were working there were taking scissors and slicing condoms, and when they would count one hundred vouchers, they would wrap the vouchers with the condoms." Why condoms? "There were no rubber bands." The next day, CSFB ordered a shipment.)

Jordan continued: "When an actual auction came up, we'd have to take the vouchers, put them in an armored car, and walk in with these vouchers to this auction. This was terribly dangerous. Later, the system became more sophisticated because everybody started using this depository. So we paid the company to do a deal with the auction center. The company would present a sheet and say, 'These guys have so many vouchers in the vault.' We would get a piece of paper from the depository, and the auction center would give us credit for the vouchers. And the auction center would call the depository and tell them to destroy so many vouchers. This was how we worked through what was called the First Central Depository, in the basement of the Moscow mayor's building."

This was yet another example of the rough-and-ready improvisation that characterized capitalism's rebirth in Russia. CSFB charged their clients a fixed fee for every voucher thus bought, which became in itself a rich source of income. "We were the only international market maker, and we were the only international house participating in the auctions," Jennings acknowledged. They invested in any company that they considered attractive, whether its niche was natural resources, utilities, communications, or industrial products like pulp and paper. They also began buying shares of companies directly from employees, who in many cases had collectively won the biggest stake in the company. "CSFB was the largest nominating shareholder in every good company—all the oils, Norilsk Nickel, Unified Energy System," Jennings recalled. The company bought stakes sometimes as large as 15 percent on behalf of its clients.

Meanwhile, secondary trading was taking off. The market was tiny and illiquid, but CSFB dominated it, controlling as much as 80 percent of the shares in early 1994. Jordan and Jennings began trading shares on behalf of their clients. Other brokerages were gearing up as well, including Troika Dialog, part of the Dialog Bank group, and Brunswick International, founded by a group of Swedish advisers to Chubais on privatization. At a conference of the European Bank for Reconstruction and Development in St. Petersburg in the spring of 1994, Jordan and Jennings made a presentation to emerging-market investors. "We told them Russia is going to make it, and the market really started to take off. Every hedge fund, emerging-market investor could understand it," Jennings said. All that spring and summer, the tiny market soared as foreign investors blindly plunged in. From July to September alone, the market capitalization of the two hundred largest firms traded on the market more than doubled to $36 billion.[35]

Money frenzy had gripped Russia. As foreigners poured into Russia's stock market, Russians also seemed to develop suddenly a whole new attitude toward money. Ordinary Russians began speaking in a new financial slang. A one-thousand-ruble note, worth less than one dollar in 1994, was called a *shtuka,* a thing. The value of Russian currency had collapsed so dramatically that some Russians now referred to a one-thousand-ruble note as simply a ruble. A million rubles was a *limon* (lemon). And a billion rubles was an *arbuz* (watermelon). Russians referred to dollars as *baks* (bucks) or *griny* (from the English word "green"). And in stores, on street corners, and in railway stations appeared exchange points where Russians and foreigners could easily exchange rubles and dollars. (Changing money was far easier in Russia than in most European capitals or in the United States. Except during a crisis, such as a sharp currency devaluation or a sudden currency shortage, anyone could change money at almost any time of the day or night.)

In February 1994, the government issued a decree requiring all retail transactions to be made in rubles. Two years earlier, both Russians and foreigners had simply ignored a similar decree. This time, to my surprise, it stuck. One reason was that the ruble, despite its previous uselessness and despite inflation, had gained real purchasing power in the past two years. At stores in Moscow now, the price tag on a pair of jeans might be twenty-four dollars, but to buy them a Russian would hand over, say, forty-five thousand rubles. It was a sign that the Russian ruble was playing its real role as a currency, as a means of exchange.

Still, rising inflation had played its part in deceiving Russians. Some were persuaded that they could begin to make money almost literally from nothing. Dozens of new "investment funds" took cash deposits from citizens, promising unbelievable—but supposedly "guaranteed"—returns of 100 percent, 200 percent, or even more. Most ordinary Russians did not understand what a pyramid scheme was. The most notorious but certainly not the only such fund was known as MMM, named after its founders, the three Mavrodi brothers.

MMM was a phenomenon of advertising and played strongly on Russians' gullibility and desire to make a fast ruble. Night after night, television advertisements depicted the story of a simple Russian named Lyonya Golubkov. Dressed usually in a cap, Golubkov was a Russian worker who invested in MMM, the fund set up by Sergei Mavrodi and his brothers. Week by week, Lyonya's life improved as a result of dividends from MMM. He bought a house, a car, a new wardrobe for himself and his wife. He headed off to the United States to watch the World Cup soccer championship. To top off his run of success, he met "Maria," the star of Russia's most popular soap opera, an import from Mexico called *Simply Maria*. Television viewers saw Golubkov dancing with Maria, a dreamy expression on his face. What more could a Russian man want? The advertisements always ended with the slogan "MMM—nyet problem."

All over Russia, people headed for one of MMM's many local offices to buy its "shares"—certificates that, in the end, didn't represent ownership in anything. Some MMM investors were clever speculators who understood the nature of a pyramid scheme and managed to withdraw their funds—including huge profits—on time. (One Russian financial source informed me that his friend had banked hundreds of thousands of dollars of MMM profits in Cyprus, taking the money out stage by stage in suitcases.) Other purchasers were gullible investors who believed they could get at least a little richer quick.

MMM—nyet problem? In July 1994, the Russian government called a halt. State tax authorities served notice that MMM was liable for billions in back taxes. On the Russian Raw Materials and Commodities Exchange, where a secondary market in MMM shares had sprung up, the price fell from 118,000 to 50,000 rubles in a single day.[36] Without warning, MMM closed its offices and stopped selling shares and paying out redemptions. On the outskirts of Moscow, thousands of share-holders gathered outside MMM's rectangular, redbrick headquarters on Varshavskoye Shosse. Standing for hours on end, sometimes camping out overnight, they waited anxiously for news of their investments.

I spent an afternoon wandering through the crowd outside the MMM building. Over the years I had witnessed anti-Communist protests and pro-Communist protests. Now shareholder protests had come to Moscow. An air of disbelief hung over the crowd, especially among older people and families who had believed Mavrodi's advertisements. Many were looking on Mavrodi as a kind of folk hero, an underdog now under attack from the government. "The government wants to stop him because they are afraid. He was growing too powerful, too popular," a retired schoolteacher told me sternly. Indeed, a few days later, leaflets began to circulate around Moscow: "Mavrodi for President of Russia!" Over time, though, MMM investors realized that they had been taken. Some had poured what remained of their savings into the scheme. Most would never get their money back.

Sergei Mavrodi barred himself in his Moscow apartment and refused to open the door. When he didn't emerge after several days, KGB special forces scaled his apartment building and broke through the window. They arrested the financier and led him away. He was later released while awaiting trial and managed to save himself by running for, and winning, a vacant parliamentary seat in the autumn of 1994. A few years later he was to try to revive his company, but most Russians were already wiser.

The MMM episode underscored once again the primitiveness of Russia's early transition to capitalism. And yet it also proved that ordinary Russians were increasingly willing to part with their money—to take a risk and invest. They had changed their attitudes toward speculators and profiteers. They had become speculators themselves. Unfortunately, the majority had lost their gamble. Later, a Russian newspaper estimated that as many as "three hundred firm swindlers" had taken as much as 20 trillion rubles from 20 million Russians.[37] The numbers were too round to be accurate, but there was no doubt that millions of Russians lost something.

Everything seemed to come unraveled at once that autumn. After the stock market reached its peak in August 1994, share prices tumbled. One reason was a technical glitch at CSFB. "We had an instrument we were using to bring in non-hedge-fund money. We realized it had a flaw and so we had to pull the instrument. That dried up the flow of funds into the market," Jordan explained. But at the same time, the supply of shares increased as entrepreneurial Russian brokers bought more and more shares from employees of companies in the regions, increasing the supply of stock for possible foreign investors in Moscow. "All of a sudden you had this flood of paper in Moscow that showed up from everywhere. Investors were buying 2, 3, 4 percent of these companies, and the employees held 51 percent. So in October, November, and December, more and more paper hit the market and prices went down because the demand wasn't there," the young financier added.

Others simply figured that CSFB's clients—and the bank itself—were taking profits. Perhaps, having run the market up themselves, they decided to get out when it was riding high. Whatever the explanation, the newly created *Moscow Times* stock index collapsed in 1994. It wouldn't recover until 1996.

Not only was the market plunging. Pressure was also growing on the ruble in the fall of 1994. The government had once again released credits to agriculture, nudging inflation up from 5 percent in August to 7 percent in September and 15 percent in October. In September, when the ruble was trading at about 2,400 to the dollar, Central Bank chief Geraschenko announced that the currency was too strong. That gave the market the jitters. Then the bank chief and his colleagues told the world that the bank had been intervening to support the ruble but that they would have to stop because reserves were down.[38] On Tuesday, October 11, 1994, a day that became known as Black Tuesday, the exchange rate collapsed 27 percent.

As the news spread through Moscow, kiosk owners jacked up the prices on their wares by several times that Tuesday. The Central Bank did not intervene to support the currency. On October 12, the exchange rate recovered, but the damage was done. The government narrowly survived a parliamentary vote of confidence a few days later. Yeltsin fired both Geraschenko and acting finance minister Sergei Dubinin for failing to contain the debacle.

Even though the currency did recover, the ruble collapse seriously undermined public confidence. Few merchants cut their prices after raising them. Shortly after Black Tuesday, I chatted with sociologist Natalia Tikhonova, who worked at the Center for Political and Economic History of Russia in Moscow. The ruble shock hit hard, she explained, because it came at a time when people were beginning to feel more confident in their ability to carve out an existence in Russia's new economy. "Many small businesses suffered. Many came close to bankruptcy. I don't know one family that did not somehow suffer. In the past there were big leaps. But this time it was worse because people were just beginning to feel that the situation was getting to be more stable. People will not put so much of their money in banks, in financial companies. They will [again] put money in goods," she predicted.[39]

Yet Tikhonova felt that the society as a whole had progressed in the two years since Yeltsin had shocked them by liberalizing prices. "When we understood that we were rejecting the kind of society where we lived before, our vision of how to live further was very idealized. We knew it would be better to live in a different kind of society, but we did not understand how it would be. After the price reforms, we faced a new situation. Of course it was a shock for the whole society."

"But, according to our polls, the most difficult year was 1992," Tikhonova added. "Already by 1993, people were beginning to understand where things were going. Now, in 1994, they already understand how you can live in this society and how you can solve your own problems."

The ruble shock took its toll on the banking system, too. One bank,

Chara Bank, closed its doors. Depositors were unable to withdraw their funds. In fact, Chara Bank itself operated almost as if it were a pyramid scheme, banking regulators later said. It did not invest its deposits well and kept insufficient reserves to back deposits. This was common among commercial banks, who lived on profits from currency trading and, later, GKOs. Every once in a while, Russia's volatility caught a bank unawares.

The autumn of 1994 proved a peculiar time for Russia's commercial banks. On one hand, organized criminals began closing in on banks. More than one hundred bankers were murdered in what were apparently contract killings. Following the example of Gusinsky's Most Bank, which had set up a virtual private army, banks stepped up their security, investing hundreds of thousands of dollars in bulletproof glass, sophisticated protected entrances, and security guards.

Yet the mafia was not alone in eyeing Russia's banks and bankers. Also doing so, it seemed, was someone in the Kremlin: Alexander Korzhakov, Yeltsin's bodyguard and confidant and the head of the Kremlin's own security detail. On December 2, 1994, a group of elite soldiers surrounded the mayor's building, where Most Group was located, and seized several Most security guards. The elite soldiers did not wear markings, but it was later determined that they came from the Kremlin guard. They forced the Most guards to lie in the snow and roughed them up. From his office high above, in the skyscraper, Gusinsky could see the conflict unfolding. He phoned the mayor and the Kremlin to find out what was going on. Finally, after several hours, the Kremlin detail withdrew. Gusinsky was badly shaken. Several of his guards were hospitalized.

Only in Russia, it seemed, could the president's guards attack one of the country's leading bankers. The Russian press went wild. It was a warning to Gusinsky and perhaps Luzhkov, the papers speculated. Luzhkov had grown immensely popular and was already rumored to be a potential challenger for Yeltsin as president. The theory went like this:

by attacking Luzhkov's banker friend, whom Korzhakov openly despised in any case, Korzhakov was warning Luzhkov not to mount any kind of a challenge to Yeltsin. And he was warning all bankers that they should not assume that their riches meant that they were powerful.

Other banks were attacked that autumn. A similar incident took place in the elaborate mansion owned by Rossisky Kredit just a few blocks from the Foreign Ministry. The mansion had been the property of the Morozovs, the family of industrialists, before the revolution. The bank had beautifully restored its many paneled and chandeliered rooms, each one decorated to represent a different part of the world. The mansion served as the bank's headquarters and the center of its private banking business. But one fall afternoon, security guards rushed into the building, ordered customers to leave, and closed the bank down for several hours. Some of the guards searched through documents and files, not telling the dumbfounded bankers and clerks what they were doing or why. Other guards ran upstairs to the offices of the president and vice presidents of the bank and tried to get in. But the bankers stood behind a bulletproof glass wall and wouldn't emerge.

No one ever knew who had ordered either attack, but the bankers and Russian press generally assumed that it was Korzhakov. Leading bankers openly worried that Korzhakov or others in the Kremlin were trying to steer Russia back to a darker time. "The collapse of the Soviet Union created big losses for our society and for Russia. We have already paid. We paid in 1991 and we paid in 1993," said Vladimir Vinogradov, president of Inkombank, one of the largest retail banks. He was referring to the coup of 1991 and the 1993 battle over the parliament. "We want to create a civil society. We don't want to go back to dictatorship. We want to ask the president, as guarantor of our constitution and our laws, to defend our banks against direct attacks."[40]

These would not be the first signs of tension between representatives of the new elite—representatives of capitalism—and Korzhakov. It was to all come to a head during Boris Yeltsin's reelection campaign.

The frenzy of financial speculation did not spread to all parts of the economy. Many industrial enterprises suffered deeply as inflation raged. Prices for raw materials soared, while demand for many industrial goods plunged. Makers of machine tools, textiles, weapons, and cars were all just barely surviving. By the fall of 1993, the industrial debt crisis had reached abominable proportions. Enterprises owed each other trillions of rubles—a total of 28 trillion in October, for example.[41] Most were bankrupt by Western standards, but the government had not yet drawn up bankruptcy procedures. And it feared the political consequences of mass unemployment.

But the government could not keep bailing out industry with cheap credits; they defeated the effort to stabilize the country's finances and strengthen the ruble. As the government tightened its finances, factories ran out of money. They started engaging in huge barter operations, some of which involved ten or more transactions each, in order to purchase raw materials or cover electricity bills. The cash or "live money"— *zhiviye dengi*—went to workers when there was enough to pay wages. When there wasn't, managers delayed payment or put workers on short-term vacation or issued promissory notes. The virtual industrial economy, as I called it, was still operating alongside the cash economy. The factories somehow hung on, even though they could not afford to keep operating. Still, official unemployment remained low—less than 2 percent of the workforce.

The Vladimir Tractor Factory was one company feeling the pinch. Indeed, its story reflected many of the difficulties of industrial restructuring in Russia, even when directors wanted to fix their companies rather than bleed them dry.

After winning the election for general director at its first shareholders' meeting in June 1992, Anatoly Grishin had continued with business as usual. But his tried-and-true methods of running the factory, built up over eighteen years as director and close to forty years at the factory, began to let him down. Orders from state farms, which themselves had no cash, were plunging drastically. Customers who had purchased tractors weren't paying their bills. Export orders also slipped. Because his suppliers were increasingly demanding payment in advance, Grishin couldn't scrounge up the money to keep components rolling in. The assembly line stopped from time to time while the plant awaited delivery. By September 1993, Grishin was short of money for paying workers' wages. The direst predictions of his rival and former deputy, Josef Bakaleynik, were coming true.

Desperate, Grishin took a short-term loan from a commercial bank at a punishing 210 percent interest rate. (After two years of offering easy credits, the Central Bank began charging commercial banks positive real interest rates in the fall of 1993, and the banks passed them on to customers.) Grishin sent a shipment of engines to his long-time customer, the Lipetsk Tractor Factory. But Lipetsk didn't pay. Shout as Grishin might at his old contacts at Lipetsk or at the ministry, they did nothing. Unable to pay salaries, Grishin stopped the assembly line and put his workers on vacation. The plant closed down through most of October, November, and December.

It was a bitter blow to a man who considered the factory his home and the workers his family. In January 1993, Grishin offered his resignation to the board, which accepted it. He retired into seclusion at his dacha outside the city. He spent his time beekeeping, declining all requests for interviews.

The plant's board turned to Bakaleynik. As a board member, the intense economist had kept in touch with the factory in the months after the shareholders' meeting, even as he worked in Asia for the IFC. The financial collapse had taken place faster than he predicted it would. Now Bakaleynik wavered about taking the job that he had sought earlier. He was no longer sure he could turn the troubled plant around. But he agreed to try. At an extraordinary shareholders' meeting, this one held on the grounds of the plant, Bakaleynik was voted in as general director with a 98 percent majority. There were no other candidates for the job.

In May 1994 Bakaleynik launched his bid to save the Vladimir Tractor Factory, and during the next few years I visited the plant on several occasions. Sitting in his general director's office (still furnished with the requisite Soviet-era conference table, bookcase, bank of telephones, . . . just about everything but Lenin's portrait), we discussed the ups and downs of applying American management techniques to a struggling Russian manufacturing enterprise.

My first visit was in August 1994. Bakaleynik had been on the job three months but hadn't yet put his name on his office door, where Grishin's had been. He looked tense and exhausted. He had just returned from Moscow, where he had met with bankers to discuss the company's financial plight. "We are going through a difficult period, obviously," he admitted.[42]

When Bakaleynik took over, his first surprise was that the company's accountants had no idea how much cash the plant had on hand. The books were a mess, and the company was nearly $4 million in debt. The plant had stood idle for nearly four months. It didn't have key components in stock, while mountains of unnecessary parts and equipment cluttered warehouses. The plant lacked working capital to get production moving.

Drawing on his reputation (as well as his chutzpah), Bakaleynik talked a Moscow commercial bank into excusing the factory from paying sky-high interest on an outstanding loan of 6 billion rubles, and then he negotiated a $10 million line of credit at lower interest. That was enough to start the assembly line rolling. To make a little extra money for the factory, he banked part of the money at higher interest rates in Malta, where it would not be taxable. "Right now, it's easier to make money on finance than on tractors," Bakaleynik told me.

Yet he talked confidently about his plans. He was shaking up the management team, although so carefully as not to alarm people. "I don't want to create a climate of uncertainty," he said. He had appointed a vice president for marketing and sales. And he was working on setting up a leasing company to boost sales among cash-strapped private farmers and collective farms. "We try to sell tractors for cash, and it's very difficult. That doesn't happen anywhere else in the world," Bakaleynik said.

Finally, Bakaleynik planned to start spinning off parts of the company—the housing maintenance department and the two collective farms. He also wanted to sell two buildings that had once housed day care centers. And he was turning a former defense plant, which made tank treads, into a separate company responsible for its own sales and profits; the plant now made gas engines. "It didn't have its own responsibility, didn't have its own balance sheet, and didn't care about financing. But now there's a certain change in attitudes," the young CEO said.

From behind his desk, Bakaleynik pulled out a copy of *The Great Game of Business,* by Jack Stack. He was growing more enthused. The key, he explained, was changing workers' and managers' attitudes. Employees had to be involved in decision-making. They had to believe that their pay was directly connected to their involvement in the company. "We want people to be more responsible, more in charge of their destiny. We are trying to break the habit of people looking to the top management for all the answers."

It all sounded very nice. But, I wondered, was he being naive?

Bakaleynik had given up a three-figure salary at the IFC to come home to Vladimir and work for much less money. (He claimed his official salary was about 1 million rubles, or under five hundred dollars a month.) With his wife and son, he was living in a small apartment opposite the factory gate. Sure, there was something prestigious and challenging about running the biggest factory in the town where one had grown up. But why choose all the hassle? "The bottom line is that I want to be able to sell the company for a good price," Bakaleynik told me. "What's important is that this company should go for a price that is appropriate for the size of the establishment—certainly with the caveat that it is in Russia."

As part of his contract, Bakaleynik had received options that could increase his ownership stake to 10 percent, depending on his performance. (His partner, Len Blavatnik, gradually boosted his company's stake in the plant to a controlling 40 percent after the initial voucher auction.) If Bakaleynik took the company public for $50 million, he could earn up to $5 million. "If I can turn this company around," he confided, "I hope that I will walk away with a small fortune."

That was an enticing opportunity. But Bakaleynik would have to succeed with a turnaround far more difficult than any he had encountered in his case studies at Harvard Business School. Still, if anyone could have fixed a fifty-one-year-old manufacturer with equipment dating back to the U.S. lend-lease program, it ought to have been Bakaleynik. He could draw on his background as a socialist-era deputy general director as well as the lessons he had learned at Harvard about business in a market economy.

He explained: "To be a good director before, you had to have good connections in the ministry, Gosplan [the state planning committee], government. Directors were responsible for volumes, . . . [for] numbers every day and even every hour. You had to be intense and very much involved in the everyday kind of thing." But now it was different: "You have to be able to think in terms of the global market—competition. So you need a good education. You need to be able to get the best out of people. It's very important to get the best results, and that takes the combined efforts of all the people involved. And they only give their best if they have the incentive to do it."

Bakaleynik's enthusiasm and determination were one plus for the workers of the Vladimir Tractor Factory. In that sense, they were far better off than were their counterparts in scores of other factories in Russia. In 1993 and 1994, the majority of Russian factories were still run by Red Directors; whereas a few of these socialist-era managers adapted to the new climate, most could not or would not. They continued to operate much as they always had, begging the government to bail them out or to abandon its policy. Secretly, many longed for a change in power that would end all the disruptive experimentation with market economics, privatization, and capitalism.

Other directors simply drained their companies of resources. While they put their workers on vacations, they banked millions in the West or, like the managers of the metals giant Norilsk Nickel, called board meetings in Barbados. From their point of view, their behavior was perfectly rational, because the government didn't step in to stop them. Only a minority of companies made serious moves to refocus their strategies, develop new product lines, cut costs, and boost sales in the early years of reform.[43]

The Vladimir city government understood this dilemma well. At city hall, Sergei I. Postnov told me of his frustrations as director of international affairs. He was supposed to attract foreign investment to the city, but enterprises were resisting. "Directors of factories live well personally," Postnov explained. "They have high wages, and when the factory goes private, the government can no longer interfere. There isn't any income; they don't pay taxes. The directors simply say Yeltsin is bad, the regional government is bad, the city government is bad. There's always someone else to blame." Foreign investors often made it harder for directors to maintain their positions. "If an investor comes, it will soon become clear that the entire top team needs to be changed. And why should a director be interested in that? For that reason many directors are not interested."[44]

Yet, while they weren't sure what to expect from Bakaleynik, Vladimir's city fathers welcomed him back. "The tractor factory used to be the most successful factory in town. It had money from exports. It paid good wages, gave its workers refrigerators and vacuum cleaners, but didn't put its money into production and new technology. When they realized their tractor was already old, it was too late. They had eaten all the money," Postnov said. Now he hoped that would change.

What did the workers think about Bakaleynik returning as boss? On that visit in August 1994, I strolled around the plant with Gennady Petrov, vice president of the plant's trade union. A short man with a wrinkled face, he looked much older than his forty-four years. He had worked at the plant since he was seventeen.

Walking toward the building where the main assembly line was lo-

cated, Petrov reminisced about the good old days. "We had the planning system. There was something planned for you for the future. It was
insurance for life. Now we don't know what to expect the next day," he
said.

"In one sense I didn't like the planning system because it was the plan
at any cost. If you didn't fulfill it, you were bad. And people lied to each
other. There was no accounting. People did whatever they could to get
the premium earlier. We worked on the days off." Petrov led me
through a courtyard where a statue of A. A. Zhdanov, a Stalin-era minister, had stood. Before perestroika, the factory had been called the
A. A. Zhdanov Vladimir Tractor Works. But then workers voted to
change the name, and Zhdanov was removed, he said.

We walked past the line of red tractors near the factory gate—examples of the company's product line. "To tell you the truth," Petrov
continued, "our factory was built for one capacity, but we tried to hide
that." So they could overfulfill the plan? He nodded. "Maybe there
should have been changes. But now the system has changed at its roots.
I think that without planning, there's no way to live. People need to plan
for what they are aiming."

The sound of clanging metal greeted us as he opened the door to the
building holding the main assembly line. It was dark inside, and the
metal floor was greasy. On one side of the plant, a conveyor moved
slowly as workers assembled tractors. On the other side, they assembled engines. Parts dangled from hooks above our heads. We walked
past workers banging and manually screwing parts on the tractors. Farther along, the line had stopped. "Some parts didn't arrive today,"
Petrov explained. "We used to work every day and assemble incomplete units with one or another detail missing. Then we decided, why
should we assemble incomplete tractors? So we will wait for the parts."

We walked up to an older worker who was hoisting an engine onto a
hook. "I've worked here forty-four years," declared Alexander Martisyanov, age fifty-nine, shouting to be heard above the noise. "The conditions have worsened in relation to everything. We produce one-half

of what we used to produce. Socially, we are poorly protected. The official minimum living wage is seventy thousand, and we get forty to fifty thousand a month [less than twenty dollars]."

Wages were a big problem, Petrov acknowledged. Not only were they low, but the factory delayed paying them because cash was short. "Everything depends on the consciousness of the workers. We had this kind of consciousness: you came to work, you got money. Whether you worked or not, it didn't matter. Now the situation is different. It's a shareholders' society, you have to provide for yourself. You come to work, you realize production, you get money. That's the system. But there was a moment when the wages weren't paid. There was tension. We didn't have a strike, but we had a stoppage. You have to live on something," he said.

Those who could find work at higher pay had already left the plant. The workforce had already shrunk from nineteen thousand to fourteen thousand. Those who couldn't leave stayed on and did odd jobs on the side to make extra money. "I have worked here twenty-five years. I already can't imagine where else to go. For me it is my second home. The people who stayed are those who couldn't find themselves in the new system. But the young people mainly left," Petrov said.

We left the main assembly line and walked for about ten minutes down a narrow road. Like many enterprises built in the Soviet era, the Vladimir Tractor Factory was huge, with several buildings and warehouses sprawled over many acres. Railroad tracks abutted the plant. In its heyday, the late 1980s, the Vladimir Tractor Factory had churned out 36,000 tractors and 178,000 engines every year. Now it was lucky to squeak out 16,000 tractors and 45,000 engines. As we walked, we passed piles of rusty parts, carelessly discarded outside. Then we entered a fairly new plant built at the end of the 1980s by order of the Ministry of Defense. It was meant to produce tank treads, but when the Cold War ended, the Soviet Union didn't need tank treads anymore. Now workers assembled small gas engines there.

This was the factory that Bakaleynik was spinning off. The workers and managers now would be responsible for their results. They weren't sure what they were going to do besides make gas engines. Some wanted to open a restaurant or motel, because the building abutted the main Moscow–Nizhny Novgorod road. Others wanted to find a new product to manufacture.

Yuri Shalin, fifty-seven, an engineer-mechanic, voiced hope for the company as a whole. "We think there is a future for our tractor, that there will be demand for it, that we will improve the technical and financial position of the factory," he told me. As a "master," Shalin was ranked at the top of his field, yet his monthly wage was only 130,000— about sixty-five dollars. "Painful periods are always painful. My wage is horrible. But if we stabilize, maybe we will get higher wages." He stood beneath an old red poster from the days of central planning; it read, "The quality of his work is the worker's conscience."

Changing a mindset takes more than a few months or years. And it's especially hard to do when you are buffeted by external problems largely beyond your control. Industrial production fell more than 20 percent in Russia in 1994, and companies owed each other close to 200 trillion rubles by the end of the year.[45] Yet when I returned to Vladimir in November, Bakaleynik was pleased with his turnaround effort so far. And he was even more confident that he could apply American management practices to the Russian experience: "Now I can say that everything is applicable almost to the T. We only need to know about the Russian environment."

"You come to a company like this, the first thing you try to do is stop the cash bleeding" Bakaleynik elaborated. "You refinance to get the company going again. So if there was a success in the first five months, it was to consolidate the order portfolio and restructure the loans. In this situation, when no one really knows what they want, it's possible to get something done. I know what I want to do and it allows me to push people to go farther than they might want to." Now, he added, was the time to begin working on "strategic issues" such as the company's product line.

I was a little surprised by Bakaleynik's cheeriness. I told him that I couldn't believe that the idiosyncrasies of Russian business and life weren't complicating his every move.

"Like what?" he countered.

Like the fact that companies don't pay each other, I ventured.

Bakaleynik insisted that his problems were not much different from those of an American CEO. "It is very difficult to get paying customers. But that's not different from the United States. In the States, for every paying customer you have competition. In Russia, there are very few paying customers, but the competitors are very few. The end result is the same. You have to fight for customers—especially in our industry, capital goods. In the States, nobody buys for cash, but we are trying to sell for cash. And that's not the way it works. We have to catch up with them. That's why we want to set up a finance company."

Bakaleynik did acknowledge that the cost of capital had soared out of sight in Russia. "That is one special thing about Russia. It is impossible to sustain these kinds of interest rates in manufacturing. I'm speaking in real terms—they are very high. Still, it's not something that never happened before."

Since my previous visit just a few months before, Bakaleynik had lost two thousand more workers. Now he was down to twelve thousand and was considering more layoffs. The company had set up an unemployment office to help former workers find jobs. I spent some time hanging around the office, which was located in an old two-story building with concrete floors, in the center of town. The flow of visitors, both men and women, was steady. Each job seeker sat down at a desk, where an employment counselor typed details into a computer and then checked a database for job possibilities.

It was surprisingly well organized. The counselors gave each unemployed worker a job referral on a piece of paper. To get their unemployment payments—which amounted to 75 percent of their wage for the first three months after they were laid off, and then gradually declined—the workers had to go and check out the job openings. Except for skilled industrial jobs, which were few and far between, most of the jobs were low-paying. Women had it the worst, because there were mainly cleaning and other manual jobs available. "For women, it's difficult," admitted Tatyana Makarova, thirty-eight, who had done clerical work at the factory before she was laid off. It was hardest in families where father, mother, and children all worked in the factory. Their plight was to become much worse before the situation at the factory improved.

No matter what Bakaleynik said, the complexities of Russian business and life heavily influenced the Vladimir Tractor Factory and his ability to save it. He longed to attract investment from a strategic partner, and even entered into negotiations with a major U.S. company. But the group hesitated because of Russia's political and economic stability.

Meanwhile, the backwardness of Russia's banking system—together with government policy—kept the cost of borrowing high. Bakaleynik sought government money for his leasing company, but the powerful lobby of state and collective farm directors beat him to it, receiving the funds in order to prop up their nearly bankrupt farms. And Russia's quirky tax system strained the tractor factory's resources as well. With inflation still high and the ruble plunging, the company had to pay the government more in taxes for every dollar earned abroad.

Even though Bakaleynik supported economic reform and Russia's transition to capitalism, he criticized the government's policy toward industry. "All factories have to go through the process we are going through. They will, but the question is, How long will it take, and is the government going to support them or not?" he said. "There's no grand plan or strategy. There's no clear sense of what role the government has to play in economic development."

Caught up in the fight for power and property along with the push to control inflation, the government seemed to lack the will and energy for devoting serious attention to industrial policy as well. It was a problem not just in Vladimir but all over the country. Even industrial enterprises with good management—like Vladimir or Uralmash, the giant heavy equipment manufacturer in Yekaterinburg that had been purchased by entrepreneur Kakha Bendukidze—barely hung on.

"The tax policy of the government is impossible," Bendukidze told me one afternoon, as I visited his office in Moscow. He, too, was voicing his frustration over the government's industrial policy. "To make a profit on a contract at Uralmash takes one and a half years. And in that one and a half years you have to spend an enormous amount of money. You can rationalize. You can do everything. But it is senseless to demand from the general director to do this or that, or put in this line or that line if it only means more losses."[46]

Each of Uralmash's nineteen thousand workers, he continued, brought roughly a five-hundred-dollar annual loss to the company, even if he or she worked well. That was partly because of taxes, partly because Uralmash's order book had totally collapsed. If Uralmash slashed its workforce, it would have fewer losses. But how far should he cut? That was the dilemma. In 1988, Uralmash had produced half a million tons of heavy equipment, Bendukidze said. "Now, in 1994," he added, "it produces ten times less because its main customers, which are in the same position it is in, don't order. Yet Uralmash is trying to support a gigantic institute, one of the best engineering institutes in the world. Uralmash's products are competitive on the world market. We have good production because several generations of engineers work at the factory. They were raised to do it. So we are trying to hold onto the engineering potential. You can find workers, but you can't find that potential. Workers you need to prepare for a year, but engineers you need to prepare for ten years."

Uralmash had one advantage, however, he conceded. "It is very big. The factory is continuing to work. You understand that it is eating its basic capital, but that capital you can use for a long time. Uralmash will not die soon because it is very big. And we hope we will improve the situation with time."

Like Bakaleynik, Bendukidze felt the government should conduct a more thoughtful industrial policy. The problem was how to do it. "Our economy is so ineffective. We cannot reject 90 percent of the economy. If you do reject it and say that all of the economy is bad, you cannot close it. It is politically impossible. So the government will have to regulate the process and decide how many enterprises must be closed, and so on."

Instead, what developed was an ad hoc approach of handing out tax breaks and special privileges to the loudest or the best connected. Rather than industrial companies, energy giants like Gazprom and Lukoil were the most visible recipients of such benefits. Gazprom, the huge former state gas monopoly that had been run by Prime Minister Viktor Chernomyrdin before he joined the government, was excused from paying taxes for years (until, in fact, 1995). The company saved billions of dollars, which it could pour into financial investments or into building its towering new headquarters in Moscow.

Lukoil, while it was quickly developing into one of Russia's most progressive companies, also benefited from the close links that its president, Vagit Alikperov, had developed over the years with Prime Minister Chernomyrdin. In the Gorbachev era, they had worked together in the Soviet Ministry of Fuel and Energy. A shrewd and ambitious manager, Alikperov secured for Lukoil the status of "special exporter," which meant that it could export oil for itself and on behalf of other oil companies.

Because Russia moved very slowly in deregulating its oil prices, Lukoil benefited handsomely from the difference between domestic and world oil prices. In 1994, the domestic oil price was still less than half of the world oil price. This enhanced the profitability of exports. Only in 1995 would the government begin to deregulate oil prices so that they could climb to world levels.

Yeltsin and the government handed out tax breaks and customs benefits to many other groups as well. They ranged from the Russian Orthodox church (which earned revenues importing cigarettes and booze) to so-called charity groups that later proved to be infiltrated by the mafia. While draining the government budget of billions in revenues, these benefits encouraged corruption and conveyed to the Russian people the impression that business involved anything but fair competition and market values. Soon the government would be catering more and more to leading commercial banks as well.

After Yeltsin fired Geraschenko and Dubinin in the wake of Black Tuesday in October 1994, he appointed Anatoly Chubais as first deputy minister in charge of the economy, promoting him from his position as GKI chief. Tatiana Paramonova, a longtime staffer in the Central Bank, became acting Central Bank governor. Together, they launched Russia on a long, slow push toward financial stabilization.

Paramonova was an unlikely monetarist and an even unlikelier Central Bank governor. For starters, she was a woman, and women rarely held such prominent posts in Russia, whatever Communist rhetoric had once proclaimed. On top of that, she was a plain-speaking professional—not the kind of person to try to charm the bankers and politicians around her. For nineteen years, she had worked closely with Geraschenko at the State Bank of the Soviet Union, until it was dissolved in the wake of the Soviet Union's collapse. When Geraschenko was appointed Russia's Central Bank chief in July 1992, he brought her back as deputy chairman in charge of settlements and coordination with the Ministry of Finance. In turn, after Geraschenko's ouster, Paramonova asked Geraschenko to stay on as a consultant to the Central Bank. Some Russian analysts claimed that she remained under Geraschenko's thumb all the time she governed the bank. I wasn't so sure.

In fact, Paramonova proved a surprisingly tough Central Bank chairman. "Mrs. Paramonova can say no to anybody—even Yeltsin," Geraschenko told me a few years later.[47] Dubbed the Iron Lady by the Russian press, she wasn't afraid to rile the parliament, the industrial lobbies, or the commercial banks. As a woman, she had moved slowly and doggedly up the career ladder at the bank, excluded from the man's world of after-hours vodka binges and sauna sessions. Perhaps for that reason she was able to resist the pressure of her critics. On the other hand, the male establishment, from parliamentarians to bankers, resented her for failing to consult them about her decisions. Mikhail Berger, then *Izvestia*'s highly respected economics editor, wrote that many in the banking community and government considered her "institutionally egotistical" and "difficult to work with."[48] Her career as Russia's chief banker was to prove short-lived.

The country's finances were in a precarious condition at the end of 1994 and the beginning of 1995. Hard-currency reserves were down to just a few days' worth, drained by the Central Bank's intervention to prop up the flagging ruble. The Chechen war, launched in December in what the generals had mistakenly told Yeltsin would be a lightning strike, put further pressure on the budget.

In response, Paramonova scrambled to shore up the Central Bank's reserves. In February 1995, she announced new rules requiring banks to increase their reserves to cover both ruble and hard-currency deposits. The new rules would force them to lodge reserves of 20 percent of their deposits of up to thirty days with the Central Bank and reserves of 10 percent for their hard-currency accounts. Bankers reacted angrily. Paramonova offered to give the banks until June 1995 to meet the rules, but she would not back down and reverse them.

Indeed, when I interviewed Paramonova later, she recalled this moment in January 1995 as one of the most difficult in her stint as acting Central Bank governor: "Our hard-currency reserves were almost gone, and we were close to hyperinflation. The only way to lower inflation was to take that measure of raising the reserves. We took several measures in the space of about ten days. We changed our hard-currency position, raised the interest rate, increased reserve requirements. That was the most painful for the commercial banks. They didn't understand what was being demanded of them at first."

"It was the only correct step," she continued. "And it brought the right result. I took that step very consciously. Even though I later paid for it [when the parliament voted against her], I knew that if we didn't take that step we could in just a few days fall into a very serious position because our hard-currency reserves would have run out. And we would have exploded into enormous hyperinflation. So I took the step, and we did stop inflation."[49]

To my surprise, Paramonova told me that she had decided to shake up the banking requirements without consulting anyone else. "Under the law of the Central Bank, it was our right to do it without consultations or agreement. And we did it. I knew if we tried to have an agreement [with the government and the banks], I wouldn't have been allowed to take such a step. They would try to talk me out of it. But we didn't have any time at that point."

Paramonova was castigated in the press after her series of moves. Once again, a physical shortage of cash rubles developed on the market as banks scrambled to find rubles to meet their reserve requirements. "Nobody understood it. Even Chubais was against it at first," she said. But the pace of price rises began to slow down. Inflation was in retreat. It was a small but significant turning point in Russia's post-Communist economic history.

Meanwhile, the government sought a way to finance its 72 trillion–ruble budget deficit by means other than printing money. The solution was twofold: to borrow from the International Monetary Fund and to issue Treasury bills. The government had launched its market for short-term government obligations, or GKOs, in May 1993. Every Wednesday, the government issued three- and six-month bonds at an auction on the Moscow Interbank Currency Exchange. Brokers traded the bonds in a secondary market on other days. The government began issuing larger tranches at higher interest rates—more than 100 percent, on an annualized basis—to attract investors. The market boomed.[50] In April 1995, the IMF approved a $6.8 billion loan, dependent on the government lowering its budget deficit and inflation.

By May 1995, the ruble had stopped its plunge and begun strengthening against the dollar. The Central Bank had boosted its hard-currency reserves to nearly $10 billion. The stage was set for the next big decision: pegging the ruble to the dollar. On July 5, 1995, Paramonova and Chubais teamed up to announce that the ruble's exchange rate would not be allowed to fluctuate beyond the range of 4,300 to 4,900 rubles to the dollar. The "ruble corridor," as it was called, was planned to be in effect until October 1, 1995, although the government later extended it indefinitely. The introduction of the ruble corridor was a highly important moment in the history of Russia's reform efforts. It seemed that the government was finally closing in on its elusive goal: financial stabilization.

But the banks again fell into panic. The ruble corridor took away a chief source of their profits—currency speculation. They had grown accustomed to operating in an inflationary environment where they could arbitrage the falling ruble and rising inflation. The Central Bank had stuck to its promise to force the banks to meet reserve requirements by the end of June 1995. With money tight, rumors of an imminent banking crisis swirled all summer. The press printed reports that banks had already stopped offering interbank loans to one major bank, Nationalny Kredit. Nationalny Kredit was the bank owned by Oleg Boiko, one of the early business wunderkinds who had set up a chain of retail stores and the first Russian debit cards.

The ruble corridor also hurt Russian exporters of everything from oil and gas to tractors. Their powerful lobby had strong backing among hard-line deputies in parliament. Paramonova's candidacy for Central Bank governor was up for a parliamentary vote for a second time on July 29, 1995. She had been serving as acting governor already for nine months and had been rejected once before.

Her record was clear. She had curbed inflation and strengthened the ruble, but she had made too many enemies. In a secret ballot, the Duma rejected her nomination. Both Geraschenko and hard-liner Vladimir Zhirinovsky later claimed that deputies were offered money to vote against the Iron Lady. Some commercial banks, Geraschenko told me, had promised to finance the campaigns of deputies who helped out.[51]

Paramonova rarely gave interviews to the press. When she did, she was unapologetic. In June of 1995, she told the newspaper *Segodnya:* "I am a careful person, although people accuse me of being tough. I know the price of what I am saying. . . . I myself worked in a commercial bank, and I know that before I open a corresponding account with some bank, I should clarify what is the bank and study its balance independent of whether my friends work there or not.

"The banking system . . . developed in very liberal conditions. We couldn't immediately work according to world standards. I remember how our first commercial banks were formed. It was a difficult job. Everyone was afraid that it wasn't for long and that soon they would all be closed. Then the situation changed. There came the time to introduce norms that regulate the operation of banks according to international standards. . . . We obligated the banks to create necessary reserves and put a limit on their open valuta position. We took licenses away from 140 banks."[52]

Later, she explained her philosophy as a central banker to me. "I was a professional. I had visited central banks all over the world, and they had given me advice. I understood that a central bank should be a supervisory body. And it should be completely neutral as far as other banks are concerned. It should be completely dispassionate.

"I told all my colleagues that we should not keep any ties with any particular commercial banks. And so all our relations with the banks were only official. That was my main task—to be neutral and objective. This gave me freedom. Even the commercial banks understood that I wouldn't allow any exceptions for anyone."

Unlike many others in the rest of the government, Paramonova wasn't willing to play the insider game. It was one of the main reasons her career didn't last. Meanwhile, though, because of a legal loophole, Yeltsin wasn't required to remove Paramonova immediately after the Duma's rejection of her candidacy, and she continued to work. On August 24, 1995, a bank called A/O Chasprom defaulted on its overnight interbank loan. Suddenly banks stopped supplying credit to each other, and interest rates soared to 1,000 percent. Menatep, Inkombank, Na-tionalny Kredit, and several other large banks, as well as scores of smaller banks, faced a dangerous liquidity crisis. "This is the Black Thursday of the interbank market," declared Peter Derby, president of Dialog Bank.[53]

The Central Bank stepped in, effectively bailing out the banking system. It bought more than 1 trillion in government bonds from the banks and set up special credit lines for the bigger, more solid banks. Para-monova's moves averted a major disaster, although some banks, in-cluding Nationalny Kredit, eventually went under as a result of the crisis. Yeltsin invited the country's banking leaders to the Kremlin and gave them a tongue-lashing for "lacking the skills to work under new conditions." "Frankly," Yeltsin told them, "we have some doubts now about your capabilities."[54]

Once again, Russia was experiencing the autumn jitters. The bank-ing system had seized up, and crucial parliamentary elections, sched-uled for December 17, 1995, were just weeks away. "The Pinochet sce-nario looks more and more like the only future for Russia," wrote *Izvestia*'s Berger in the wake of the banking crisis, referring to the Chilean military coup whereby the army's commander in chief, Au-gusto Pinochet Ugarte, became head of state. If the banking system couldn't meet the needs of its clients, he reasoned, "panic would ensue as depositors rushed to demand their money back, which would com-pletely paralyze the monetary system. As a result, businesses would be unable to pay wages and other debts or their taxes. The state, without taxes, would be unable to pay for the army, social benefits, etc." Con-cluded Berger ominously: "In the best possible case, some sort of Pinochet would step forward to bring order."[55]

Yeltsin finally dismissed Paramonova on November 8, 1995. A week later, he nominated former finance minister Sergei Dubinin, who had been sacked after Black Tuesday, to take her place. Although Dubinin didn't much change Paramonova's policies, he was more acceptable to the commercial bankers. He was a man, and he was willing to consult with them on his policies. As the acerbic Boris Fyodorov, another former finance minister, later told me: "Mrs. Paramonova was better than Mr. Geraschenko. She was good with numbers and with getting inflation down. But Dubinin was an economist. He had a better understanding of the policies he was implementing."[56]

That fall, Yeltsin wanted to avoid a damaging banking collapse. The strength of the banking system was important to the government for more than just monetary reasons. Since Chubais had been named first deputy chairman, the second phase of privatization had moved excruciatingly slowly. Rather than transfer ownership through voucher auctions, the government aimed to raise funds by selling off additional stakes in some already privatized enterprises and shares in some of Russia's natural-resource and industrial gems—in some defense plants and shipping companies, in metals exporters like Norilsk Nickel, and in oil giants like Lukoil, Sidanko, and Yukos. The goal was to raise 8.7 trillion rubles, or $1.9 billion, by the end of 1995, but by September 1 the government had raised only 162 billion rubles through privatization.

The government was locked in debate over a controversial proposal to speed up privatization. In March 1995, Vladimir Potanin, chairman of UnExim Bank, one of the strongest commercial banks, had approached Chubais with a scheme of his own devising. Under the plan, a consortium of banks, including UnExim Bank, Inkombank, Menatep, Stolichny Bank, and Imperial Bank, would lend the government close to $2 billion in exchange for shares of the country's leading companies. The banks would hold the shares in trust for the government and work on restructuring the companies until the government paid back the loans. If the government failed to pay back the loans, the banks would have the right to keep the shares or sell them. The program, called "loans for shares," was attacked by opponents of privatization, by those who were afraid of giving the banks greater control over the economy, and by those fearful of selling off Russia's jewels for a song. (Some of the last-mentioned group, of course, wanted to be the buyers in such a scenario.)

Potanin, the architect of this complicated scheme, had enjoyed a meteoric rise as a commercial banker. He had started comparatively late in the game—1993—but by 1995 his United Export Import Bank, or UnExim Bank, was vying for the position of Russia's most powerful commercial bank. Undoubtedly one of the country's smartest, best-connected bankers, Potanin was a smooth-talking graduate of the prestigious Moscow State Institute of International Relations, where scores of Soviet diplomats had been groomed, and had worked at Soyuzpromexport, a unit of the Soviet Ministry of Foreign Trade, where he got to know the heads of many of the largest exporting and importing agencies in the Soviet Union.

By the time the Soviet Union collapsed in 1991, he and his partner, Mikhail Prokhorov, had created a foreign trade association called Interros. It was a consulting and trading company made up of smaller, newer trade organizations set up during perestroika. Its starting capital was 200,000 rubles. But Potanin soon discovered that what was really needed was a financial institution, so a year later Interros teamed up with other shareholders to form the International Company for Finance and Investments. Besides Interros, the shareholders included the former COMECON bank known as IBEC, or the International Bank for Economic Cooperation; Russia's state-controlled savings bank, Sberbank; and the Bank for Foreign Trade. Explained Potanin, in an interview much later in his beautifully paneled office: "I understood that something new should be brought to this business to attract bigger organizations. The most important thing was financial services, management of money."[57]

Potanin got a lucky break early on. The Council for Mutual Economic Assistance, or COMECON, the trade bloc established in 1949 to link the Soviet Union and its Eastern European satellites, had decided to disband itself in 1991, and IBEC, its bank, was in chaos. That played right into the clever Russian's hands. "We received from IBEC about $300 million—not all deposit, but as part of our balance. We received within half a year this amount of money, together with IBEC's clients." As it turned out, Potanin explained, the Russian Central Bank issued a letter prohibiting IBEC from working with Russian clients, because the bank was in danger of bankruptcy. "Because they had a lot of Russian clients, we got all of them."

Potanin called it "a good start." That certainly was an understatement. A year earlier, he had been pleased with starting capital of ten thousand dollars for Interros. Now he had $300 million in his own, new bank. That meant he could start serving clients almost immediately— lending money, offering letters of credit, arranging settlements—and growing.

Thanks to his head start, Potanin was able to attract newer, bigger clients from the twenty to thirty large, proud foreign trade organizations that previously hadn't given him the time of day. Then he had another idea. "While we were working with the bigger organizations, by the end of 1992, we understood that it would be interesting for them not only to be clients of our bank but to be owners of a bank. So we proposed to them to create a new bank, UnExim Bank, especially for exporters and importers as well as for suppliers and receivers of import licenses." In April 1993, some fifteen big foreign trade organizations and several companies from the Interros group joined together to create UnExim Bank. Potanin became its president.

I wanted to know how much Potanin himself controlled of UnExim Bank, but he wouldn't say. He said openly that his Interros company owned a stake. And he said that no shareholder owned more than 20 percent. But he wouldn't be more specific than that. He explained his reasoning: "The problem is, in Russia, it is not a good thing to say that you are an owner of something. The country and public opinion are not prepared for ownership. You know we have 35 percent of Communists in our country and really people do not understand this. And that's why I do not hide it, but it's not a good thing to talk about it."

The pace of Potanin's life and his business accelerated after April 1993, when UnExim Bank targeted a market crying out to be better served. The bank started working with the country's largest importers and exporters—Surgutneftegaz, Norilsk Nickel, oil companies, ma-

chinery manufacturers. One by one, the bank's leading clients also became its shareholders. "By 1994, we already had twenty to twenty-five
shareholders of good quality," Potanin recalled.

Like other banks, UnExim made money trading currency. It invested
in GKOs. It also began lending to regional and local governments in the
provinces, extending loans guaranteed by the Ministry of Finance. This
was lucrative, low-risk lending. "The Ministry of Finance gave [loan]
guarantees for trillions of rubles. The loans paid a little bit more than
the government (via GKOs), but it was still 100 percent secured. It was
a rather big business."

But for UnExim Bank the biggest business of all was handling the
government's customs accounts. Potanin explained his idea: "When we
started this, all taxes and customs payments were made after goods
cleared [the border]. Then there was an experiment on improving customs, and we proposed a system of advanced payments. In order to
make for an easier customs clearance procedure, we proposed to have
a certain amount of money on deposit. That would guarantee that companies would pay all taxes for the customs service."

This proved to be a great business. Importers had a strong incentive
to pay in advance, because they were charged astronomically high interest if their payments were delayed while their goods were on the border. UnExim gained, because it was able to use the money that was deposited in its accounts, earning interest on overnight deposits or by
investing in currency. "Our gain from this was a lot," Potanin acknowledged. But he argued that UnExim also contributed significantly.
It helped the government collect far more in customs duties and to do
so more quickly. "It really worked for Customs, for MinFin [the Ministry of Finance], for everybody. We gained, but it was not given to us
from the sky. We worked on this, we proposed the scheme. We gave
something good to the government. That was the job we did."

The government was to eventually take this revenue away from Un-
Exim Bank, but not before the bank had grown into a formidable financial-industrial powerhouse. And the bank was to do so not only on

the strength of its banking business but also thanks to Potanin's timely but extraordinarily controversial (as well as blatantly opportunistic) privatization proposal.

Potanin's plan did not please the heads of the enterprises to be auctioned. Many headed to their patrons in the government to plea to be excluded from the program. Other banks and entrepreneurs protested that the consortium of banks would be gaining unfair advantage in the scramble for Russia's wealth. Warned Bendukidze, who was still busy trying to set up his own financial-industrial empire: "This proposal shows that strong banks and weak enterprises together want to set up an oligarchy in the Russian economy. This is a very dangerous proposal. Instead of separating the banks from the government trough, it draws them in closer."[58]

The government took no action on the proposal until late in the summer of 1995. By then, Chubais was getting worried that a Communist victory in the parliamentary elections scheduled for December 1995 would scotch the second phase of privatization altogether. It was time for another Chubais compromise, one reminiscent of his summer 1992 agreement allowing industrial managers to gain 51 percent control of their companies. If the only way to get Russia's leading energy and transport companies into private hands before the December 17, 1995, elections was through the loans-for-shares program, he decided, so be it.

In spite of the banking crisis, Yeltsin signed Decree No. 889 on August 31, 1995, authorizing the loans-for-shares auctions. The plan contrasted somewhat with the one proposed by the banking consortium. Now, because of the banking crisis and the lack of time before year-end, the government expected the auctions to raise around 2 trillion rubles, less than $500 million, rather than $2 billion. If the government did not repay the loans by September 1996, banks winning the auctions would be allowed to sell the shares and pocket 30 percent of the proceeds. The government would get the rest. The auctions were open not just to banks but to other investors. But foreigners were excluded from buying shares because the companies on the block were considered strategic companies. Shares would go to the banks that offered the most over a minimum amount set by the government. UnExim and Menatep would conduct the auctions.

It was a system virtually designed for insider deals. But in spite of mounting opposition, Chubais backed it. "This plan is very elegant," he told reporters. "It is so well written I would almost call it a work of art."[59] Although in the end no one was to be able to prove any outright cheating, the results of the auction were to raise eyebrows around the world and spur complaints by rival banks in Russia.

On November 17, 1995, UnExim Bank won 38 percent of Norilsk Nickel, the world's largest nickel producer and a huge exporter of other metals, for $170.1 million; the government had set the minimum bid at $170 million. Rossisky Kredit threatened to sue GKI for rejecting its higher bid (GKI cited Rossisky Kredit's lack of financial guarantees). On the same day, UnExim Bank also bought 25.5 percent of NorthWest Shipping for $6.05 million, just $50,000 more than the minimum bid. A few days later, Alfa Bank, Inkombank, and Rossisky Kredit all publicly criticized the loans-for-shares program for favoring insiders.

On December 7, UnExim Bank won control of 51 percent of Sidanko Oil Holding for a bid of $130 million, $5 million more than the minimum bid. UnExim's sister organization, International Financial Company, gained 14.8 percent of the Novolipetsk steel company, a major producer that was to later become the center of a big fight over shareholders' rights.

On December 8, two different companies backed by Menatep bid in two auctions held for Yukos Oil Holding, the country's second largest oil company. On the block was 45 percent of Yukos shares for a starting price of $150 million under the loans-for-shares program, plus 33 percent in a straight cash sale. One of the two Menatep-based companies, Laguna Company, won both auctions. Menatep conducted the auction. Only a month before, Menatep's first deputy chairman had told the *Moscow Times:* "We will get Yukos. There should be no two opinions about this." Yukos did not oppose Menatep's bid.[60]

THE BATTLE FOR RUSSIA'S WEALTH 141

Talking to me later, Potanin made no apologies for the loans-for-shares auctions. In his original proposal, he pointed out, he had suggested that foreigners also take part in the auctions. That might have raised prices and ensured more openness. But, he added: "There was a very difficult struggle with the Red Directors and the ex-Soviet nomenklatura. You can believe me that it was unbelievably difficult to start this. That's why it was a certain compromise between the reformers in the government who wanted to continue this and proceed with a big plan and with the Red Directors and Soviet nomenklatura which didn't want to allow foreigners to come.

"As soon as it was announced that only Russian bidders are allowed to bid, of course, it was already some kind of insider deal. I agree that it was cheap, it was not international market price. No question. How could it be international price when the foreigners are not allowed? It was some kind of internal Russian price."

By Western standards, of course, it looked terrible that the banks running the auctions had won the best assets on sale. What did Potanin think of this?

"There were scandals after all auctions. Those who lost were very angry and there was a lot of noise in press," he replied. "There was no agreement among us. The problem was that there were only a very few players who were ready to bid this money. Everybody forgets they were not good enterprises. The reason why they were sold was that the Red Directors could not prove that their enterprises were working well. If everything was OK in these plants, we could never even talk about purchasing them. Our political declaration was that they were bad and we will make them work."

"It happened because of different compromises during the privatization process," he continued. "Voucher privatization was made in interests of management and not in interest of investors. Almost all directors that were not completely stupid got all the assets under their control. It was some kind of compromise. Either we satisfied the Red Directors, or we did not make privatization. And because of this, the management of companies was very poor. They were stealing, they were incompetent."

"During the auctions, it was not possible to declare this, because it was politically unacceptable," Potanin explained. "But the real reason of the auctions was to bring normal management to sizable companies and to break the Red Directors' lobby. It was the most important thing. I mean, we could say that maybe the relatively cheap price for this loan was payment for breaking of the Red Directors' lobby."

Breaking the lobby of the Red Directors was truly a significant step, and it was clearly crucial for Russia's industrial restructuring. But still, I pressed, wasn't it a bad precedent: the banks winning auctions that they themselves ran—and winning with such low bids?

Potanin looked uncomfortable. "Well, if there is no other bidder . . ."

I finished the sentence for him: " . . . why pay more?" He nodded and shrugged, smiling slightly and looking resigned.

"I don't know. It was a piece of our history," he continued, a little exasperated. "We had a few players. To a certain extent it was insider trading. We created the conditions of auctions in a way that those who wanted really to compete should really pay money. Those who just wrote on paper that they were ready to pay $1 billion had to prove that they were able to do this. If they did not prove it, their proposal was rejected. That was the reason for scandals. Some of the banks who really could not buy just made bids in order to spoil business for us."

Also, time was short, he pointed out. "We had very few bidders at that time. Yeltsin signed the decree, and by the end of the year we had only two months to sell everything. Again, because of the Red Directors." And because the parliamentary elections were imminent.

"So it was really bad," Potanin at last conceded. "But we created the precedent when the enterprise was sold to the investor and not to the manager. OK, cheap, with scandals, but to the investor. And, second, we broke the practice of management of the Red Directors. For our country, it was very important. The major problem of our economy has been the inappropriate management of our enterprises. What we tried to do was to completely change the system of management."

Yes, UnExim had gained. But Potanin had a point.

By the end of the auctions in November and December 1995, Un-Exim Bank and Menatep in particular had increased their industrial shareholdings dramatically. If they would be allowed to keep their assets, they would use these purchases as the core of new, powerful financial-industrial conglomerates. Chubais had not accomplished all that he had hoped, but he had managed to push the privatization process one step further.

On December 17, 1995, the voters headed to the polls to elect a new Duma. Yeltsin, recovering from a heart attack suffered on October 26, appeared on television a few days before the election and exhorted Russians to vote for the future and not the past. "The most dangerous thing is that there are parties that want to turn the country back to the past. I am convinced that this would be a tragic mistake," he intoned. "Remember your parents. They knew what hunger was, and real fear, and mass repressions. They had a very difficult life, and it is only because they sheltered us that we recall the old days with such fondness. Let us work together to preserve this hard-won, fragile stability and accord in our common home—Russia—on the eve of parliamentary elections."[61]

The voters didn't listen. Gennady Zyuganov's Communist Party of the Russian Federation walked away with nearly 35 percent of the vote. Prime Minister Viktor Chernomyrdin's party, Our Home Is Russia, came in second, with 12.2 percent. Vladimir Zhirinovsky's Liberal Democrats won 11.3 percent, and Grigory Yavlinsky's, 10 percent. It was another political blow for Yeltsin and the reformers.[62]

As the bankers and politicians struggled for power and property, they largely ignored the other, darker side of life in Russia. Russia's leaders were mostly blind to the plight of poorer, more unfortunate people, especially those who had completely lost their way in the economic upheaval beginning in 1992. But this darker side was in fact not hard to find. It was visible in the gutters, where drunks collapsed. At railway stations, where invalids begged. And on Moscow riverbanks, where young boys washed cars, smoked, and hung out, when they should have been in school.

One November afternoon in 1994, I stopped along the banks of the Yauza River, where a cluster of boys were washing cars. Metal buckets of water were lined up, as the boys awaited clients. Rough-looking and shivering, they huddled near a small fire that they had made in a trash can. They looked to be about thirteen or fourteen years old. I was with my friend Elena Antonenko, who has a special talent for making people feel at ease, even when they are speaking to a Western reporter. I wanted to see if the boys would talk to us as they cleaned the grime from my white Russian jeep.

A blond boy, his hands shoved into a faux-leather bomber jacket, seemed to be the leader. He had cloudy blue eyes rimmed by dark shadows. His black jeans were wet from the water being splashed onto cars. He eyed us suspiciously but agreed to answer a few questions as his partners scrubbed away.

His name was Maxim, and he was almost fourteen years old. He didn't go to school. His fifteen-year-old brother was in jail for purse-snatching, and his older brother, who was nineteen, had already been in prison once but now spent most of his time at home, drinking vodka. Maxim's mother was bedridden, an invalid hardly able to walk. They lived in a communal apartment, sharing the kitchen and bathroom with another family. They had once lived in their own three-room apartment, he said, but it had been taken away from them.

"I work here two years already," Maxim said matter-of-factly, taking a drag on a cigarette. "I am used to it." The boys had staked out this spot near a bridge on the Yauza. They didn't have to pay money to the raket, they claimed. "We had a talk with the guys. They decided not to ask for money from us," Maxim said. The boys earned about 150,000 rubles—roughly fifty dollars in November 1994—a day. Most of his share Maxim brought home to his mother, some he kept for himself. "For cigarettes, jeans," he said.

His mother had lost their apartment in what sounded like a scam.

"They took our apartment from us. My older brother hit another guy's car, a Mercedes. We ended up giving up the apartment because of that car. My mother sold the apartment for thirty-seven thousand bucks. We gave them two lemons [2 million rubles, or about two thousand dollars in 1993, when the incident took place] for the car. They said, 'Give us the rest of the money and we will get you another apartment.'" But they disappeared.[63]

It sounded almost too miserable to be true. Was this young man angling for a big donation from an impressionable foreigner? Maxim took Elena and me to visit his mother in their apartment not far away. A frail-looking woman, her gray hair falling into her eyes, lay in a bed in one dark room. On another bed, a young girl, Maxim's sixteen-year-old sister, lay sleeping. In the kitchen, a couple were laughing and drinking vodka.

Maxim's mother gave her version of what had happened. A broker had come to her and offered to help her sell her apartment. With the money, she planned to buy a small house outside of town. She signed a paper saying that she agreed to sell the apartment for 37 million rubles. "But they only gave me 1 million rubles," she said. The broker then disappeared. She fell ill and could not search for him. "I went to the woman who lives in my apartment and asked, 'Why did you give the money to someone else and not to me?' And she said, 'I thought the man was your brother or your relation.' She said to me, 'Give me my money back, and I will give you your apartment.' Now I am left with nothing."

Maxim's mother seemed truly sick. She said she was forty years old, but she looked about sixty. She had huge circles under her eyes. She could barely walk, relying on her daughter for help. Her older son didn't work. "He wakes up and says, 'Vodka, vodka, vodka. Give me vodka,'" she said. Then he would drink himself into a stupor again.

"I am sorry for Maxim. He works from day until night. He buys the food. We are all living off what he is earning," she said.

I saw Maxim and his family as victims of Russia's new capitalism. No matter which version of the apartment story was true—or even if both

versions were fictions—the fact remained that a young boy was washing cars in the freezing cold and seemed to be supporting his mother,
brothers, and sister. Perhaps Maxim's mother was an alcoholic and
someone had taken advantage of her. Or perhaps she truly had no idea
how to function in a rapidly changing economic environment where the
laws were unclear, ignored, or unenforced and where some people
would do anything for money.

Many others like Maxim and his mother struggled in Moscow and
other Russian cities in the early years of Russia's reforms. While great
numbers of ordinary people managed to adapt to Russia's transition
better than many doomsayers had predicted, millions still suffered in
one way or another from the economic revolution. Some suffered because the government failed to fulfill its obligations to the people. These
were the doctors, teachers, civil servants, and other state workers whose
pay packets were months late because the government could not or
would not come up with the money. These were the hospital patients
who didn't receive adequate care because of shortages of funds.
(Health care had been poor during much of the Soviet period, but it
was even worse in the first years of economic reform.)

These were also the people, from babushki to bankers, victimized by
crime. Robberies, extortion, even contract killings had exploded in
number. The Western press tended to exaggerate the terror of the "wild
East," but it was true that the militia and the government were slow in
addressing a very real problem. Part of the problem had to do with corruption in the militia and the bureaucracy, but another part had to do
with Russians' ambivalent attitude toward the law. In the Soviet era, the
Communist Party had used the law against the people. As a result, people did not view the law as a means for protecting their rights. They were
particularly ambivalent about paying taxes. Personal income taxes
were tiny in the Soviet era—just 13 percent—and many people didn't
bother to pay. Why give the government one's hard-earned money? The
verkhushka—the people at the top—would only spend it on themselves, the logic went. Corporate taxes didn't exist at all. Until Gor-

bachev began changing the system, enterprises' funds were completely controlled by central planners.

Alexander Minakov once gave me some insight into Russians' attitude toward the law. "There are a few reasons why people don't respect the law," began the prominent Moscow lawyer. "The first reason is that, yes, there was very severe law under Stalinist rule. There was criminal law only. There wasn't law that would regulate normal relations between people, civil relations and market relations. But at the same time, people were accustomed to the idea that law was selective. If you look at the criminal code in the Stalinist era, every one of your steps may have been considered an infringement of the law. That's why people had the idea that every step was punishable. Therefore, there was no space to live and act in a legal way, and everything we did was an infringement of the law."[64]

Minakov elaborated: "What was the law under the Communist system? The law was that if you said something wrong about the Communist government and the Communist Party, you were a criminal. And so there was political suppression of the people and control over their mind. If you look at society as a pyramid, on the top of this pyramid was political pressure. The law was part of this political pressure. And the majority of people supported it. They considered it was fair and necessary to fight enemies inside and outside. Otherwise, they thought, the enemies would spoil and undermine everything."

"Now it is possible to find people looking for law and order," Minakov continued. But too many people equated law and order with authoritarianism. They called for a strong hand, a strong leader. "It's a reflection of Communist brainwashing," he said. Market relations were still new to Russians, and many people didn't understand what regulating the market economy meant. "To them, democracy means freedom with no frontiers," Minakov explained, echoing the view that Natalia Tikhonova had expressed to me. Some Russians didn't understand that you could live in a democratic society that also ran by the rule of law.

Of course, corruption was a problem. Many older Russians remembered the Communist era as one in which officials didn't steal. In truth, they simply didn't see what went on. But there was no doubt, Minakov added, that corruption had exploded in the post-Soviet era. Years before, Gorbachev had put Brezhnev's son-in-law in jail for stealing from the state. But "his bribe was just one-tenth of a bribe of a very small clerk in a city council," Minakov said. In the Yeltsin era, it was common for prominent supporters of democracy to refer to bribes as "'well, not a bribe, but a kind of payment,'" he noted.

With those attitudes at the top, no wonder the population as a whole didn't believe in the law. Moreover, Russia's laws were contradictory. Business law was just developing in the 1990s, and the authorities poorly enforced the laws that did exist. The judicial system was weak, and many judges understood little about the market economy. "It's a question of time. It's necessary first of all to educate people to give them a proper sense of values—not only market values but values such as goodwill, honest work," Minakov added.

Indeed, what worried Minakov most was the degradation of the Russian soul. "All big revolutions involve some disorder," he conceded. But in Russia many people had stopped treating each other decently or behaving according to socially acceptable norms, he told me. They drank too much. They vandalized property. They carried on in public. Minakov cited these simple examples to point out how the losers in the new game were often overcome by their feelings of malaise.

For many Russians, life under capitalism was far more difficult than life under socialism, especially in 1992, 1993, and 1994, when the country struggled to adjust to the transition. Money was so scarce that there was no longer such a thing as doing a favor for a friend. Everything was for sale. Doctors and dentists who used to treat their friends for free began charging money. Some Russians charged fees for introducing people to each other.

For others, the abundance of the new life was soul-destroying. Newly rich husbands left families that they had started in the old days, before they were biznesmen. Now the fast life of nightclubs and casinos attracted them. They dressed in Versace jackets and drove Mercedes 600s. "Do I look like a *solidol?*" a biznesman would ask. "Solidol" was slang for "a solid-looking person." The appearance was far more important than what was underneath.

"The Russian person is standing on the first step of change," my friend Elena explained. "He understands that capitalism is much more complicated than socialism. You have to have a strong character and a smart head to make capital and to make honest capital. The Soviet person lost those brains during Soviet history. Honest brains were murdered, extinguished, or exiled. And the brains that remained were those that were patient and kept quiet and gave the impression that they didn't notice anything.

"For the person brought up in socialism, today it is very difficult for him to reject hypocrisy, to reject the show for outside effect. It's very hard for him to get away from the idea that he wants an outward beautiful shine and it's not as important what he is made of inside."

The stress of the transition took its toll on the health of the nation as well. While visiting Vladimir, I heard that the general director of a local factory had committed suicide. He had been a civic leader, an important man in town, but he had made a serious business mistake, and his company was on the edge of bankruptcy. Suicide was increasing among older people, too. Among Russians over ninety years of age, the suicide rate tripled in the first half of the 1990s. Men who could not support their families began to have "accidents"—many of which were thought to be suicides. At the same time, conditions in cash-starved hospitals were so poor that 10 to 20 percent of newborn babies were dying.[65]

The dark side of Russian life, the weakness of some people and the weakness of the state, all provided fertile ground for organized crime. Criminals exploited Russians' ambivalence toward the law as well as the corruption and incompetence of the law enforcement authorities. Maxim and his mother weren't the only ones to lose their apartment. In

Moscow's roaring real estate market, apartments were bought, remodeled, and sold at an astonishing pace in the 1990s, and unwitting Russians were deceived all the time. In fact, the Moscow militia had a file of almost three thousand people, many of them elderly, who had gone missing after signing papers to privatize their apartments. Russians were being murdered for their property.

Since the collapse of the Soviet Union, the Russian mafia—a vast network of loosely connected groups, from small-time bandits to serious criminals—had caught many businesses by the throat. The spiritual leaders of the mafia were so-called *vor v zakone*, "thieves in law." These were criminals who had spent time in prison and built up for themselves *avtoritet*—authority. They lived by their own internal code of ethics (which, for example, forbade them from marrying), yet they could be brutal, as the gang wars around Moscow demonstrated.

"Viktor," a raketeer whom I met in 1994, had explained the brutality of the mafia business: "A person comes home. We put a plastic bag on his head. We hold it there for a long time. We beat the person, or hold the plastic bag—and there, the person signs all the documents. That's all there is to it. There are a lot of murders connected to real estate—alcoholics, old people."[66] I was sickened to hear such an account, yet Viktor was matter-of-fact about it. No wonder Minakov worried about the degradation of the Russian soul.

As the mafia grew more powerful and the legal authorities more impotent, contract murders also became common events. Hundreds of bankers and businesspeople were gunned down or bombed. (In fact, many suspected murder rather than suicide in the case of the Vladimir factory director, although there was no proof.) The killings occurred when businesspeople owed money to the raket and didn't pay up. Other killings happened when executives refused to fulfill the demands of the mafia, such as handing over a percentage of the ownership in their business. Still others were the result of business disputes. Instead of going to the courts—which were slow-moving, corrupt, and not yet adapted to a market economy—businesses "sorted things out." It was called a *razborka,* a "settling of affairs" through a shootout, bombing, or contract killing. Sometimes the victims were public figures. Banker Ivan Kivelidi, a leader of Russia's Business Roundtable—a lobby group set up by Bendukidze and other business figures—was poisoned in 1995 in an apparent contract hit. He had strongly criticized the government for failing to protect its citizens and defend property rights against the mob.

"The state is not fulfilling its function," Kivelidi had argued in an interview with me several months before he was killed. "The state should not pressure you, but defend you." He continued: "The ridiculous tax system links business to the criminal world." (To avoid paying taxes, Russian companies did far more business in cash than did their counterparts in Western economies.) "The money goes into your pocket rather than taxes and that attracts criminals. Either you lose everything or you start to work with the criminal world. This is the big problem for small- and medium-sized business especially," he said.[67]

In my years in Russia, the only self-confessed raketeer who ever granted me an interview was the aforementioned Viktor. He struck me as a relatively small-time bandit when I first met him, although I was in no position to judge. I met him through a go-between, an acquaintance of an acquaintance who (at the least) had contacts in the raket. Viktor came to my apartment one night, and we chatted over tea and cookies. It was an odd scene. He sat in a straight-backed chair and chain-smoked nervously, agreeing to talk only if I didn't use his real name and if I destroyed the audiotape of the interview immediately after transcribing it. I felt edgy, too. As he recounted his story, I wanted to ask him how many people he had killed. But I couldn't summon up the nerve. Perhaps he had killed no one, but he talked big.

"I was born in Moscow," he began. "Both of my parents were robbers. My father was in prison for twelve years. My mother was in prison when I was a kid. For four years, we had that kind of situation. When I was in tenth grade, I started to steal. When I was twenty, I was put in prison for three and a half years. I was in the Urals. I came back to

Moscow, but I couldn't get a permit to live here. So I went to Yakutia to work."

A rough beginning in life. Viktor may well have ended up a criminal whether or not the Soviet Union had leapt from socialism to capitalism. But the upheaval had also provided opportunities for people like him.

"In 1985, I came back to Moscow," he continued. "I couldn't find a job. Some friends gave me a call, and I again started to steal with them. Then I got very sick. I had tuberculosis, and I had a serious operation on my right lung. What next? There was no work for me, nowhere. I started to spend time working out, and I went back to stealing. When the wave of commerce and everything came, I got back in touch with old friends. They were former athletes. What else is there to say?"

For some reason that I never understood, it was quite common for athletes—*sportzmen,* as they called themselves—to join the raket. Perhaps it was because the job required speed and physical strength. Perhaps it was because they had nothing else to do, especially when the government cut back funds for the training of athletes. Viktor had hung out with sportzmen, and that's how he got into his gang, one of a handful of groups that had divided the territory of Moscow between them.

He continued his story: "At the beginning, the bread came with difficulty. There were fights all the time, shootouts all the time. Then we started to try to work so that people met us halfway—so that they asked for our help themselves. At some point, they had to give us money."

But when they didn't, the gangsters got rough. Viktor gave an example: "There was one man in recent days, the director of a firm. He didn't want to give us money. But we had invested $200,000 into his factory. We took him, tied him up, brought him to the forest. We told him what was the intelligent decision to make. And that was it. As soon as he gave us the money, we fired him and put our own man in his place. That's the kind of work we do, in principle."

I asked him about his daily routine. "I get up in the morning. There's nothing to do. But then a certain person calls. He says, 'Viktor, you have to go and collect ten thousand greens.'" Ten thousand dollars, in other words. "We naturally go there. The guy is a big guy. He sends us away with three letters." Cursing. "Naturally we put a *stvol* [an automatic weapon] to his belly. We take him to his apartment, handcuff him, and start to beat him hard. There you have it. He starts to acknowledge his debt and that, yes, he should pay. That's it. In two days, he goes to the bank and withdraws all the cash. And that's it. Everything is done correctly." Viktor added: "More and more, we are trying to work without using force. It's not profitable to use force. The cops now have a law that they can shoot to kill. We also passed a law that we should also shoot."

Not seeming to notice the self-contradictions that were creeping into his account, Viktor concluded: "I am thirty-three years old now. I have two children. My life is such that I can do anything I want now, but one perfect day maybe that won't be. Everything is more or less quiet, but we use guns. We kill. We kill. We kill. It's not simple."

I asked about the price for a contract killing. Like prices for most anything else, it varied depending on the market and the complexity of the job. But on average, he said, it cost five thousand dollars to kill a person and two thousand dollars to get some information from him.

Meeting Viktor was at once sobering and eerie—a window opening to another aspect of the dark side of Russian life. That darkness was more than just the absence of order and the state's inability to fulfill its obligation to its people. It was more than Russians' ambivalent attitude toward the law, which had been used against them during the Soviet period. It was more than their familiarity with paying bribes or giving "presents" or contributing to corruption. It was more than the mafia, in all its brutality. It was a complex web of all these things.

In some greater or lesser sense, each of these people were losers in the battle for Russia's wealth: Maxim and his mother, the general director in Vladimir, the old ladies committing suicide or being murdered for their property, the workers who lost their jobs or weren't paid on time, the newly rich husbands who left their wives and families behind, and Viktor and his cohorts, the raketeers and probable murderers, who found it easier to make a living through crime than through honest work.

It was sad. And yet, even if the government had done a much better job than it had, the dark side of the reforms could not have been completely avoided.

In October 1993, opposition to Yeltsin and his reforms came to a head when Yeltsin dissolved the parliament. After a standoff, opposition politicians called for an armed attack on Moscow's television tower and mayor's office. Yeltsin ordered the army to storm the White House and arrest the renegades. Dozens were injured or killed. Above, special police carry a wounded person away from the White House. Below, a Russian priest waves a white flag during the siege. *Photographs by Sergei Voronin.*

After the privatization of the Vladimir Tractor Factory (below), one of Russia's largest producers of tractors and diesel engines, Josef Bakaleynik (above), the enterprise's former deputy director, launched a bid to become its general director. He failed on the first attempt in 1993 but was invited to head the plant a year later after it fell into financial difficulties. Bakaleynik, a Harvard MBA, tried to use Western management techniques to turn around the plant. *Photographs by G. Popov, Itar-Tass (above), and A. Morkobkin, Itar-Tass (below).*

As inflation raged in 1993 and 1994, an "investment fund" known as MMM launched a massive advertising campaign to attract investors from all over Russia. In reality a pyramid scheme, MMM collapsed in July 1994 when the tax police tried to force its founder, Sergei Mavrodi, to pay back taxes. Shareholders who lost money protested against the closure. The signs say, "Save MMM, Save Russia!" and "Shareholders of Russia—Unite!" One woman holds a picture of Mavrodi. *Photograph by I. Chokhonelidze, Itar-Tass.*

To make extra money for their families or themselves, children went into business washing cars along the Yauza River in Moscow, both winter and summer. Some children dropped out of school altogether. *Photograph by V. Sozinova, Itar-Tass.*

Mikhail Khodorkovsky, a former leader of Komsomol, founded Menatep Bank in 1988, before he was thirty years old. Menatep went on to become one of Russia's leading financial-industrial groups, specializing in oil as well as finance. *Photograph by P. Denisov, Itar-Tass.*

Vladimir Potanin was another shrewd businessman. His UnExim Bank, founded in 1993, quickly became one of Russia's largest. Potanin became known in 1995 as the initiator of the controversial loans-for-shares privatization scheme, which allowed banks like his to acquire control of some of Russia's largest oil and natural-resource companies for low prices. Potanin's UnExim Bank and its industrial holdings were considered by many to be Russia's most powerful financial-industrial group by 1997. *Photograph by V. Velikjanin, Itar-Tass.*

By 1995 and 1996, the Russian economy was beginning to be dominated by large, powerful corporations. Vagit Alikperov had the foresight and the political connections necessary to found Lukoil, Russia's first vertically integrated oil company, even before the collapse of the Soviet Union. By the mid-1990s it was one of Russia's most successful and progressive companies, with a retail network that was expanding across Russia and into other republics. *Photographs by G. Popov, Itar-Tass (top), and N. Malishev, Itar-Tass (bottom).*

In early 1996, it looked as if Boris Yeltsin was in serious danger of losing his presidency to Communist leader Gennady Zyuganov in the June 1996 elections. But with backing from business and the media, Yeltsin launched an energetic campaign that led to his reelection in July 1996. *Photograph by I. Chokhonelidze, Itar-Tass.*

In 1997, Russia remained a country of dramatic contrasts. One-fifth of the population still lived below the poverty line, and some elderly people resorted to begging. At the other end of the economic spectrum, wealthy "new Russians" thought nothing of tipping with fifty- or one-hundred-dollar bills in their frequent forays to the new restaurants and bars that sprang up to serve them. *Photographs by Alexei Rogov (above) and Sergei Voronin (below).*

Elderly and poor people often begged in pedestrian underpasses. The woman's sign says: "I have two orphans to take care of, grandchildren, ages twelve and thirteen. My son's wife died. My son is an invalid." *Photograph by Alexei Rogov.*

5
Capitalism Versus Communism

I'm the wife of an enemy of the people. What do I
think of [Gennady] Zyuganov? I'd like to bury
him alive. Stalin, Brezhnev—I curse them all. I
stand for Yeltsin. *Serafima Ivanovna, pensioner*

Politics and economics have always been tightly intertwined in Russia,
but that was never more true than in 1996. The country was transfixed
by the prospect of presidential elections in June. The victory of Communists and nationalists in the December 1995 elections, plus Yeltsin's
poor popularity rating early in 1996—8 percent versus 20 percent for his
Communist rival, Gennady Zyuganov—played on the nerves of government officials, businesspeople, and Western observers alike.[1]

Would the elections go ahead, or would Yeltsin find a reason to delay them (thus extending his presidency)? If the elections went ahead,
would Yeltsin find a way to stuff ballot boxes to ensure his own victory?
Was it possible that Russia could return to Communist rule, only five
years after the failed August coup and the demise of the Communist
Party of the Soviet Union? Did Russians really want to turn back the
clock? Would Zyuganov renationalize property if he became president? Would there be civil war?

Yeltsin was under extreme pressure. On January 29, 1996, Sergei Kovalev, Yeltsin's adviser and a campaigner for human rights, resigned. As he did, he wrote a harsh and bitter letter to Yeltsin, castigating the president for his failures. Although the letter wasn't intended to warn Yeltsin against canceling the elections, it made clear how history would judge the president if he did so. In the letter, which was published in Russian newspapers and, in translation, in the *Washington Post*, Kovalev wrote: "In electing you, Russia saw not only a politician ready to demolish the former state structure, but a person who was sincerely trying to change himself, his views, his prejudices and his habits of rule. You convinced many—myself included—that humane and democratic values could become the foundation of your life, your work and your policies. We weren't blind. We saw the typical traits of a Communist Party secretary preserved in your behavior. But all Russia, like a man striving to overcome a serious defect, was struggling with itself." Then Kovalev continued:

Beginning in late 1993 if not even earlier, you have consistently taken decisions which—instead of strengthening the rule of law in a democratic society—have revived the blunt and inhuman might of a state machine that stands above justice, the law and the individual. . . . You have virtually halted judicial reform, which was designed to make the administration of justice truly independent from the other branches of government. . . . You loudly proclaimed the launching of a war on organized crime. . . . The criminals continue to roam freely while law abiding citizens have to tolerate the abuse of the uniformed forces without gaining the security they were promised. . . . You speak of a policy of openness, of transparency and of public accountability, yet at the same time you sign secret decrees concerning the most important matters of state. . . .

You began your democratic career as a forceful and energetic crusader against official deceit and party disposition, but you are ending it as the obedient executor of the will of the power seekers in your entourage. You took an oath to build a government of the people and for the people but instead you have built a bureaucratic pyramid over the people and against the people. Moreover, having rejected democratic values and principles, you haven't stopped using the word "democracy" so that naive people may well believe that "democrats" remain in power in the Kremlin. Your policies have compromised the very word, and if democracy is fated to someday exist in Russia (and I believe it will), it will exist not because of you but in spite of you.[2]

Prominent figures like Kovalev were not the only ones turning their backs on Yeltsin's style of democracy. Already capital was betting not on democracy's future in Russia but on Communism's revival. All through the first part of 1996, money flew out of Russia and into bank accounts in Switzerland and Cyprus.[3] Businesspeople began making contingency plans in case of a Communist victory. Democratic politicians were also worried. Boris Nemtsov, the reformist governor of Nizhny Novgorod, came to New York in the spring of 1996. As well as speaking at an academic conference, he was looking for a publisher. "My wife is sure the Communists will throw me in jail," Nemtsov told me over drinks at the Algonquin Hotel. "But she thinks it might go easier for me if I have a book published in the West."[4]

He was glum about the possible election outcome, especially if victory went to the Communist Party of the Russian Federation. "I am not sure that everything will stop if the Communists come. But it won't be democracy. Think of China—no democracy, huge amounts of money. Or South Korea—no democracy, huge amounts of money." In any event, Nemtsov was already developing strategies on how to preserve some of Nizhny Novgorod's reforms if the Communists did win. "One of the suggestions if the Communists come is to sign a peaceful agreement with them. Make Nizhny Novgorod like a free zone—free-market development with investment security—maybe like zones in Communist China. But a lot of people are skeptical about this idea. They are afraid that the main task of the Communists will be to destroy me immediately. Not to establish free zones, but to destroy me."

"Of course," he added, "there may be such an opportunity, but I will struggle against it."

We talked about whether Yeltsin or his team might fix the election in his favor. Nemtsov doubted it. In fact, he thought the tampering would come, if it did, from the opposite side. "The Communists might try to fix the elections. This is my estimation. They did it in my region [when there were local elections for governor]. I won, but in some districts the results showed that I lost by ten times. Maybe I lost, but I don't think I could have lost by ten times. It is difficult for me to check. But I am afraid that the Communists will do that."

On the other hand, he acknowledged, given Yeltsin's pitiful popularity rating, it was possible that the Communists would win fair and square. "I think that Russia is an absolutely democratic country. Russia is not in the Middle Ages," he said. The biggest problem, he felt, was that ordinary people had not seen enough results from economic reforms. Because of Russia's high inflation and the scarcity of funds to invest in privatized enterprises, "there were very few examples of successful industrial restructuring." He admitted, "It has been difficult to show progress—the successful results of reforms itself. This is one of the reasons people will vote against us."

Sensing their strength, the Communists launched a full-scale attack on the privatization program in early 1996. The Duma set up a commission to investigate privatization and "establish the responsibility of officials for its negative results"—a commission that one deputy compared, ironically, to Senator Joseph McCarthy's Communist-routing committee in 1950s America.[5] Russia's chief prosecutor announced that he would investigate the legality of the sell-offs through the loans-for-shares program. As the anti-Yeltsin attack mounted, the president dismissed Chubais from his post as first deputy prime minister in charge of the economy. He took the heat for the public's discontent.

But Chubais quickly found a new forum where he could express his deepening fear about the upcoming presidential elections. In late January and early February every year, a select group of business and political leaders gather at Davos, Switzerland, for a week of lectures and informal meetings known as the World Economic Forum. It was a chance for hobnobbing as well as serious image-building. In recent years, Russian reformers and entrepreneurs had joined the list of high-profile guests at the Swiss ski resort.

This time, for the 1996 World Economic Forum, Zyuganov headed to Davos to ease Western fears of his intentions—and Chubais followed to warn westerners to beware of sweet Communist words. Indeed, Zyuganov assured his audience that he and his party would not roll back the clock. Pointing to Eastern Europe, where former Communists had already been elected in several countries, he pledged to support social democratic ideas. But Chubais immediately cast aspersions on the Communist leader's words. Zyuganov's talk about his party's social democratic ideas was "the same old traditional, classical Communist lie," Chubais said at a press conference at the resort. The Communists' policies of renationalization "will inevitably lead to big bloodshed in Russia," he warned.[6]

Wandering the halls of the resort hotel and mingling at Davos receptions, Chubais found a group of like-minded Russian bankers, among them Vladimir Gusinsky and entrepreneur Boris Berezovsky. A controversial businessman, Berezovsky was a former mathematician who had made his fortune as one of the Soviet Union's first car dealers and then moved into banking and other businesses. A few years before he had narrowly survived what appeared to be an attempted contract murder: his Mercedes had been bombed, and his chauffeur had died in the blast. Somewhat like Potanin, Berezovsky had leapt into the limelight rather late in the game, in 1994 and 1995. But he was keen on preserving what he and other new Russian *kapitalisti* had gained.

Later, in an interview, Berezovsky recalled the Davos meeting: "Davos helped us to understand the dangers of Zyuganov and the Communists—that they were really powerful. What made an impression on us was that the West—different important figures in politics and in business—accepted Zyuganov as a new leader of Russia. And we realized that the only way was to help each other, that no one would help us from abroad. That helped us to consolidate our forces."[7]

Taking the lead, Berezovsky met privately with Chubais at Davos. "I proposed to him to create a real intellectual group for the elections, and he accepted my proposal to head an analytical group—and to be part of the election team," Berezovsky told me. "At the time, Chubais was thinking about his future. He wasn't in government, and he was analyzing different proposals that he got from different companies and different people. And when I told him about this idea, he immediately reacted, because he knew he was a very good analyst and he immediately estimated the sense of this proposal. In reality he became the number one organizer of the election campaign."

Thus Russia's leading businesspeople hired Chubais to ensure that their wealth would not be destroyed. And they paid him quite well for his analytical work. Many numbers were later floated; I had heard $4 million. Berezovsky wouldn't confirm the exact figure, but he acknowledged that I was not far off the mark: "It was several million—not more. It was payment for the analysis of the situation because we wanted to know better and after that understand what we had to do."

On February 16, 1996, Yeltsin traveled to Yekaterinburg, his hometown, to announce that he would run for reelection. He bantered with the crowd of supporters, but then became deadly serious. "Can I really in this situation take no part in the presidential elections? I have asked myself this question time and time again," he said. "But while there is still the threat of conflict between Reds and Whites," he explained, referring to the fight between the Communists and anti-Communists or Bolsheviks and anti-Bolsheviks dating back to the 1917 revolution, "my human and civic duty, my duty as a politician who stood at the front of reform, is to bring about the consolidation of the healthy forces of society. My withdrawal from participation in the elections would be an irresponsible step and an unjustifiable error. I am sure I can lead the country out of despair, fear, uncertainty." He then predicted gravely,

"On June 16, we are faced with a choice, not simply for the president but for our future, the fate of Russia."[8]

But the election was not merely a fight between Yeltsin and Zyuganov. Economist Grigory Yavlinsky, eye surgeon Svyatoslov Fyodorov, former Soviet president Mikhail Gorbachev, nationalist Vladimir Zhirinovsky, and the populist former general Alexander Lebed all threw their hats in the ring. A few days after Yeltsin's announcement, a television poll gave Zyuganov the lead, with 18 percent of the popular support; trailing him were Yavlinsky (11 percent), Zhirinovsky and Lebed (9 percent each), and Yeltsin (8 percent). If the election did go forward, there was a danger that several candidates would split the pro-reform vote, paving the way for a victory by either Zyuganov or Zhirinovsky.[9]

The race got under way. Yeltsin began barnstorming the countryside, promising to ensure that the $2.8 billion in back wages owed to workers would be paid in March 1996, three months before election day. Sometimes he handed out cash right on the campaign trail. One woman received three hundred dollars after complaining that her pension was too low.[10] Recognizing the danger of a Zyuganov or Zhirinovsky win, Yeltsin's democratic critics began to come over to his camp. The acerbic former finance minister Boris Fyodorov, who had started a liberal political movement called Forward, Russia! was the first prominent "democrat" to announce his support. Gaidar, who had broken with Yeltsin over the Chechen war, soon followed. Moscow mayor Yuri Luzhkov, the effective manager who had been rumored as a serious rival to Yeltsin, gave the president unqualified backing, blanketing Moscow with posters of the two politicians shaking hands beneath the slogan "Muscovites Have Made Their Choice."

But the business community still seemed confused. They knew they wanted to preserve the empires, whether small or large, that they had built up over the past several years. But how best to do that? Should they throw all their muscle behind Yeltsin? Should they hedge their bets by helping to finance the Communists as well as pro-reform candidates? Not a few businesspeople had earlier suggested that the elections be delayed; Russians weren't ready for true democracy, they argued.

"The West wants democracy here. The West wants elections," said Leonid Skoptsov, an executive with Bendukidze's Bioprocess group and vice chairman of the Uralmash board of directors. "But if the West demands that, in the best case a dictator will come to power here." Skoptsov wanted Yeltsin to cancel the elections for the sake of stability: "We want him to stay in power not because we like him, but because we don't need any more changes."[11]

The temperature of the election fight was rising. In March 1996, the Communist-led Duma voted to nullify the 1991 agreement whereby Russia, Ukraine, and Belarus had dissolved the Soviet Union. The deputies demanded that Yeltsin reestablish the Soviet empire. The government saw this move as a direct attack on Russia's independent statehood.

Businesspeople were increasingly frightened. Led by Berezovsky, thirteen leading bankers and industrialists, including Gusinsky, Potanin, Khodorkovsky, and Fridman—a veritable Who's Who of Russia's wealthy—issued a document calling for Yeltsin and the Communists to craft a political compromise rather than risk new violence in society. The document, which became known as "The Appeal of the Thirteen," was a clumsy effort at fence-sitting, and Yeltsin's backers as well as other political observers criticized it immediately. But it signaled the terror that had crept into the highest ranks of Russia's capitalists.

"Society is split. This split is widening day by day. And the void, dividing us into Red and White, into 'ours' and others, goes through the heart of Russia," the document began. "In this crucial hour, we, businessmen of Russia, offer the intellectuals, military, representatives of executive and legislative authorities, law-enforcement bodies and mass media (all those who concentrate real power in their hands and who are responsible for Russia's destiny) to unite their efforts in search of a political compromise, which will prevent sharp conflicts threatening Russia's basic interests and its statehood."

The lengthy appeal, which chided both Yeltsin and the Communists for mistakes even as it called for concessions, ended with a warning: "Those who infringe upon Russia's statehood by staking on ideological revenge and social confrontation, must be aware that Russian businessmen possess the necessary resources and the will to influence unprincipled and uncompromising politicians. Russia must enter the 21st century as a flourishing and great power. We owe it to our ancestors and descendants."[12]

Not long after, Andranik Migrayan, a political analyst, castigated the "Appeal" in a scathing column in *Nezavisimaya Gazeta*. Commenting that Russian business was unable to cut itself from "the umbilical cord of the state budget," he called the "Appeal" a "serious mistake": "It is hard for me to say what is the greatest [ingredient] in this appeal—stupidity, naivete or craftiness. . . . This action on behalf of the entrepreneurs has no chance of being implemented. . . . This action raises the legitimacy of the communist leader, makes him the basic figure in the political field and hands over political initiative to him." Migrayan added, referring to the "Appeal" as a whole, "Zyuganov received from local businessmen a gift beyond his dreams."[13]

Later, Berezovsky explained the "Appeal" to me: "The target was to demonstrate that in Russia a new power had appeared—an important power, capital. And capital in difficulties is able to be united, in spite of a lot of problems. The second was to say that this power had a clear understanding of the future of Russia. And this power will fight for this future. What does it mean to fight? We didn't have any doubts that we will fight within the framework of democracy and democratic institutions. I think that really we reached the target that we planned. We were very strong in our formulation, when we said we have enough power and enough will to realize our rights if political groups will not be successful through the peaceful way of elections." He sighed. "That's all."[14]

It was hard to know what he really had had in mind. Buying up the army or the Interior Ministry troops? Refusing to go along with the orders of a new president, if it were Zyuganov? In any case, nothing came of "The Appeal of the Thirteen." The businesspeople quickly realized the futility of trying to carve out a compromise between Yeltsin and Zyuganov. Berezovsky wouldn't comment on it, but another source told me that a delegation from the thirteen had met with Zyuganov and come away appalled at his economic policies.

Chubais threw all his administrative skills into organizing an extraordinary campaign for Yeltsin's reelection. A crucial role would be played by business. First, Chubais needed money and media support, and Berezovsky and Gusinsky stepped forward. Berezovsky was a major investor in ORT, the main former state-owned television channel. Gusinsky had founded NTV, an independent television station that had harshly criticized Yeltsin's handling of the bitter war in Chechnya, launched in December 1994. Now it began airing pro-Yeltsin programs. Gusinsky's newspaper, *Segodnya,* also began to strongly back Yeltsin.

In fact, the majority of Russia's journalists suddenly abandoned pretensions of objectivity and came out wholeheartedly in favor of Yeltsin. The scrappy *Moskovsky Komsomolets,* one of whose reporters, Dmitri Kholodov, had been assassinated in a bombing after he wrote articles about corruption in the Defense Ministry, ran a tireless front-page campaign urging voters to back Yeltsin. *Izvestia* published news articles and columns questioning the Communists' policies. "The Communists Want to Return Gosplan, Gosnab, and Empty Shelves!" exclaimed the headline for a story on plans to recreate elements of central planning. "Can Zyuganov Be Trusted?" asked another headline; the accompanying article did not hold back as it analyzed Zyuganov's "lies, deception, disinformation, and twisting of facts."[15]

Igor Malashenko, president of NTV, also didn't fret about appearances of conflicts of interest; he simply joined the campaign as the president's media adviser. Later, he explained why he decided that it was more important to back Yeltsin, even though he knew the president was in dubious health, than to worry about conflicts of interest: "The choice was between a sick Yeltsin and a healthy Zyuganov and I preferred a sick Yeltsin. It was very serious. I believe in a free press. Basically it was a difficult choice and I would prefer not to face this choice. . . . I was trying to preserve what the Russian media had achieved. I knew I would pay the price personally and so would the journalistic community [if Zyuganov won]. Many journalists were critical of Gennady Zyuganov. They knew he would have controlled the media." Malashenko added: "There is a big difference between Russia and the U.S. In the U.S., it is not about a choice between two political and economic systems. I hope that the next election in Russia will not [present] that kind of choice."[16]

When Malashenko joined the campaign in March 1996, a fierce internal debate still raged over whether to delay the election. The debate pitted old rivals and enemies against each other. Chubais felt very strongly that the election must go ahead. On the other hand, Alexander Korzhakov, Yeltsin's bodyguard, friend, and now adviser, feared that the president would lose; he was pushing hard for a delay. Korzhakov, of course, was no friend of Chubais's new allies in business (his Kremlin guard had attacked Gusinsky's security forces and possibly raided Rossisky Kredit), but his influence seemed to be waning.[17]

Yeltsin had a choice: to go down in history as the man who had brought democracy to Russia, or to be remembered as the president who lacked the courage to face the electorate at the crucial moment. Gorbachev had always been afraid to test himself at the ballot box, but Yeltsin had counted on the Russian people time and again. Would Yeltsin repeat Gorbachev's mistakes and hold back out of fear? Or would he press ahead?

Malashenko worked hard to ensure that the election go ahead. "When I joined Boris Yeltsin there was a danger the election would be canceled because people like Korzhakov thought he would lose," he later explained. "So when I met Yeltsin in early March I told him we had a lot of sociological information about his problems. We told him every day he should produce some news-making stories; he should dominate the news for the next several months. I had watched the election of Ronald Reagan. Politics is theater, and he knew it all too well. Both Yeltsin and Reagan are charismatic leaders and don't care too much about particulars."

The team moved into high gear. First on the agenda was fashioning a sympathetic advertising campaign, so Chubais and Malashenko hired a successful Russian agency, Video International, which had represented Russian rock groups and film stars. Chubais also began working closely with Yeltsin's daughter, Tatyana, who, at twenty-eight years of age, was already a shrewd political analyst in her own right. She had joined the campaign and relayed messages to the president when Chubais could not get in to see him.

Big businesses—many of them thankful that Chubais had made them wealthy through privatization—footed the bill. How much did "the thirteen" and other companies pay? Estimates and boasts ranged widely. The numbers that I heard ran as high as $140 million—an astonishing sum and far more than what was allowed by Russia's election laws. When I met Berezovsky, long after the election, I asked him how much business had paid. He replied: "You see, as far as our group is concerned, I may tell you that we supported the campaign through mass media, but we did not participate in terms of money. But for sure general business participated, not only those involved in mass media." A consultant who worked on the campaign told me frankly, "Of course it was illegally financed."

In contrast to Yeltsin, Zyuganov received next to nothing from business donors. Entrepreneurs were afraid that he would take back their privatized property or break up their companies. Even the Russian Union of Industrialists and Entrepreneurs, which had so doggedly resisted Chubais's privatization in its early stages, came out on behalf of Yeltsin. Now that 70 percent of the economy was in private hands, they saw no point in going back.

Moreover, while Zyuganov made big promises about improving the living standards of ordinary Russians, there was no evidence that his plan to recontrol prices and boost state spending would create a stronger economy. In a second public letter, dated May 1996, Berezovsky, Gusinsky, Potanin, and other business leaders declared that Zyuganov's program was "aimed at returning the country to the condition in the best case of the mid-1980s and principally repeats the politics that destroyed the Soviet Union in a period of four years. The plans will lead to the collapse of all the main segments of the financial base of today's major capital by worsening financial conditions and seriously limiting foreign economic ties."[18]

Yeltsin's forces hammered away at both political and economic issues. In ads and newspaper articles, they reminded Russians that the country had seen civil war, repression, and hunger under fascism. They plastered Moscow and other cities with posters depicting the long lines and bare shelves of the late Communist era, contrasting them with the full shelves and smiling families of the new Russia. "Think. Vote," the posters urged.

But Zyuganov had some economic ammunition of his own. He could point to the malaise of industrial cities, especially towns whose livelihood depended on defense factories that now had no orders. He pointed to the billions in back wages owed to Russian workers and pensioners, the shortage of money to pay them, and mounting unemployment. A minority of entrepreneurs and industrialists had become vastly wealthy while the ordinary people had suffered, he declared over and over. It was time to give power back to the people.

A few days before the first round of balloting on June 16, 1996, the atmosphere grew tense in Moscow. A bomb exploded on a subway, killing and maiming passengers. Would some other strange event delay the elections at the last minute? The Communists continued to predict that Yeltsin would falsify the results to ensure himself a victory. Yeltsin's popularity had leapt up in the polls, but he still wasn't sure of victory. The stock market, though, was certainly voting for Yeltsin. It had surged more than 70 percent since March.[19]

Even so, nobody knew what to expect, right up until election day. There was even a joke about ballot-box stuffing making the rounds. As the joke went, Yeltsin was on the campaign trail when a citizen shouted out, "What happens if we elect you in June, Boris Nikolayevich?" "You'll get a new president," he replied. "And what happens if we elect Zyuganov?" "You'll keep the old president."[20]

On election day, the sun shone brightly. I went to a voting place in an industrial neighborhood on Moscow's outskirts, where I was living. A Russian flag flew outside a local primary school, headquarters for Election District 1075. Two militiamen hung lazily around the entrance, looking as if they didn't expect any trouble. In the lobby just inside, cheerful Russian music screeched from a worn-out record player. Women stood behind a table selling chocolates, cakes, and juice, while an enterprising couple hawked a new edition of Russian encyclopedias for children. The atmosphere was almost festive.

Voters streamed in and out, stopping to chat with neighbors or heading straight upstairs to the second floor to mark their ballots in simple voting booths. Then they shoved the papers into a large box. Here, the votes were collected. Later, poll workers would count the ballots by hand.

I tried to talk with voters as they entered or left the school. Some were happy to say a few words. Others glared and hurried away.

An eighteen-year-old girl stopped for a moment. This was her first election. "I'm going to vote for Yeltsin because I have an unusual profession. I am a musician and I am not sure that life would be OK under the Communists," she told me. She didn't remember much about life under Communism before. "I was too young. My parents protected me from lines and shortages. But from what they say, it was terrible."

Yuri, a thirty-two-year-old who worked in a print shop, told me that he had supported Zyuganov. Walking away from the polls with his wife and two young daughters, Yuri seemed cynical and discouraged. He said: "I voted for the Bolsheviks, of course. I don't think life will be better, but we didn't have such a collapse of the economy before. Our children didn't wash cars. There was guaranteed education. I don't want my daughters to work on the street. The country has become unpredictable. If before we had a guaranteed wage, now it's a different situation."

An elderly woman sat on a bench, waiting for her husband. A pensioner, she was dressed neatly in a flowered dress and sweater. "I'll tell you right away whom I will not support—not the KPRF [the Communist Party of the Russian Federation]," she said emphatically. "They should never come to power again. All my youth, I suffered from the Communists. They told me what to wear, what to eat, what to sing. We should never have that again. Yeltsin has made mistakes. But you have to think of the future, of the lives of our children and grandchildren. All the pensioners in my building are for Yeltsin."

Later, I drove to the center of the city. There was almost no traffic. The atmosphere was calm. Russian flags lined the main streets. Every few blocks, the images of Yeltsin and Mayor Yuri Luzhkov, shaking hands, beamed down from billboards along the roadsides. In other ads, Yeltsin stood by himself. "Yeltsin, only Yeltsin," some of the signs read. Others were more sentimental: "I believe. I love. I hope. Boris Yeltsin." A red, white, and blue banner warned Muscovites, "Vote or Lose!" Another banner, near the Leningrad train station, declared, "For Civil Order and Social Consensus." I saw few posters for Yeltsin's opponents. They seemed to have been removed overnight.

Near the Arbat, the pedestrian thoroughfare that Luzhkov had cleaned up (and where street traders had formerly sold everything from matrioska dolls to Communist banners), McDonald's was doing a brisk business. But diners were more interested in Big Macs than ballots. A young man, perhaps in his early twenties, told me that he supported General Alexander Lebed because "he will bring order." Back on the street, a portrait artist called out: "Let me do your portrait on the last day of democracy in Russia!"

The race was close, but the portrait painter turned out to be wrong. That night, I watched the results come in on NTV, Gusinsky's station, with Russian friends. I was nervous, but I also felt a sense of amazement, almost pride. Russia had gone through with its election. There seemed to be no major irregularities at the polls. Western and Russian observers who had doubted that Russians, or Yeltsin himself, would take the election seriously were wrong once again. Yeltsin came in first, with 35 percent of the votes. Zyuganov came in second, with 32 percent. Surprisingly, Alexander Lebed garnered 15 percent.[21]

The next morning, at nine o'clock, Yeltsin appeared on television and thanked voters for supporting him. Then he immediately appointed Lebed as his national security adviser. The tough-talking general, in turn, asked his voters to support Yeltsin in the second round of the election, which was scheduled for July 3, 1996. Only later would it become known that the businesspeople backing Yeltsin had also poured money into Lebed's campaign. Chubais and his strategists had cleverly foreseen that Lebed might take votes from Zyuganov and Zhirinovsky. Their financial gamble had paid off.

The majority of Muscovites had voted for Yeltsin. (They had also re-elected Luzhkov as mayor, with an astonishing 90 percent of the vote.) But Moscow was not Russia, and I wanted to test the mood of workers, managers, and other ordinary Russians away from the capital. I used the time between the two rounds to visit the provinces. I headed first to Vladimir to check up on Josef Bakaleynik and his workers at the Vladimir Tractor Factory.

Bakaleynik smiled warmly as he opened the door to his office at the factory. (His name was now on the door.) But the tale he had to tell was grim. The plant was operating at only 10 to 20 percent of capacity. The labor force had slimmed down to nine thousand people, but nearly everyone was on extended vacation. Workers had not been paid in three months.

Bakaleynik blamed the government. "We are substantially short on working capital. There are no sources to turn to. The government is short of money. Banks are not lending. We are waiting for the Ministry of Finance to make good on an agreement to finance our export program. It's the only way we can pull out. Otherwise we may have to have a major restructuring. I wouldn't say bankruptcy but certainly shaving assets and reducing the workforce even further and reducing the scale of operations. That would be the case if we were in a developed market economy," he said.[22]

The key problem, he argued, was interest rates. "It's not that we don't want to restructure. We make mistakes. We have to compromise here and there. But I believe the fundamental problem is the macro-economy. Interest rates. No business can survive with 100 percent real interest rates. Just imagine if you had 30 percent real interest rates in the U.S.—half of American business would go under in six months. But in Russia it seems you can live in limbo for a long time. The government is chasing everybody else from the market, and they think they have every right to do this. Only the government has the right to borrow at any rate they choose. That's convenient."

Like many other exporters, Bakaleynik had been hurt by the stable ruble and the government's fight against inflation. "I came in to this job with the idea that the government would be sensible along the lines of other countries—Poland, Brazil, Japan. But nobody has been as severe as Russia. Until last year, I was able to do something, and then Chubais introduced the ruble corridor. I told him it was a bad idea, but he didn't listen. That's the second time I talked to him. I talked to him three years ago when privatization started. He was thinking about how to deal with the queue of foreign investors lining up to buy Russian industry. I told him he was thinking about the wrong problem, that there was no queue." He laughed.

"Chernomyrdin and Chubais say they have to continue the way they have been or else lots of banks will go under," Bakaleynik added. "As a taxpayer, I don't want them propping up the banks. Is it three or four huge banks doing most of the lobbying? The banks aren't investing in industry, even if they hold assets." He paused. "Every time I think about it," he laughed again, this time ironically, "it bites me. We're just giving the banks more and more money."

Bakaleynik's lessons from Harvard had not helped him much so far, it turned out. I had suspected as much, but still I was sorry to hear it. "They are applicable, but on the other hand they don't work." He sighed. "In the U.S., we would refinance in a situation like this, but it's impossible here because of the elections and the government borrowing. The financial market doesn't work the way you want it to work."

He continued: "Fundamentally, we still have many of the same problems as we would in the U.S.—marketing, pricing, personnel, financing, losses that happen in every economy. But everything is put in a different twist because of the absurdity of an economy with 100 percent interest rates. The other thing is that we are still liable for taxes—property taxes and taxes based on sales. We are losing 5 to 6 billion rubles a month."

Even so, Bakaleynik supported Yeltsin and expected him to win. "If Yeltsin wins, lots of things will fall into line. It means the end of substantial political uncertainty. I hope the government will take a more reasonable stance. It's very difficult when the government is trying to fight inflation at the cost of losing industry."

I understood Bakaleynik's words better when I strolled down the assembly line, where I had seen his employees pounding tractors and hoisting engines on previous visits. The green machine tools were quiet; black carcasses of half-built tractors hung on hooks along the line. The factory was totally still. Tacked to the wall was a sign, "Announcement from the General Director"—that is, Bakaleynik. "Due to the factory's insufficient funds, the chief accountant will disburse one month's wages when the worker begins his annual vacation," it said. In other words, workers would receive just one month's pay, not the total amount that the factory owed them. Next to the announcement, another sign informed workers that they could obtain twelve trolleybus tickets each at the expense of the factory.

Where were all the people? Most likely they were at home or at their dachas, growing vegetables or raising chickens. Perhaps they were off working some other job or trading items to raise cash. Suddenly I heard some clanging and looked up to see three men standing atop a ladder, fixing a broken window. Then, in the center of the building, I came upon three men hanging about, talking. They were the *okrana*—the security guards. There was no one else in sight.

"Before this factory used to work two shifts. We haven't worked since the eighth of June, and we aren't supposed to work until the fifteenth of July," said one of the three men, who had long hair and was wearing a plaid shirt. He gave his name as Alexander Shary, his age as thirty-eight. "This is Russia. There are robbers everywhere. If I see a person here, it means either he came to work or he came to steal. People will steal the machine tools, an engine if they get the chance."

When I asked him about the situation at the factory now, he replied: "The wages aren't paid. Sometimes it happens that both the husband and the wife work at the plant. That's very difficult. I am working three jobs right now—here, at another factory, and I work for myself. I am a photographer. From all three jobs I earn about 800,000 rubles a month." That was about $160.

Still, Alexander continued, "things have gotten better. Under the Communists, I couldn't tell you that Zyuganov was no good or that Yeltsin was no good. Or that Lebed was no good. If I did that before, they would have . . . " He puts his fingers in front of his face to show that they would have put him behind bars. "Now, if you have a bad life, go to work and it will be better. The chance to speak your mind is everything. Those who want to work, will work. Those who don't want to work, won't. I am going to vote for Yeltsin, and my wife is going to vote for Yeltsin. So things are better."

His comrades, however, strongly disagreed. Anatoly, fifty-four, who smelled of vodka, said that he was for Zyuganov. "There won't be civil war. It won't be bad. It won't be that the Communists will take power and turn everything around. I hope it will be better. If I go to the hospital now, I have to bring thousands of rubles of medicine with me. Before we had free medical care. I give thirty thousand rubles a month to pay for the kindergarten for my granddaughter. Last week, I wanted to get my car fixed. I had to pay ten thousand rubles just to pull in. The mechanic said something was knocking. I gave him sixty thousand rubles, and it still knocks. In the end, I didn't even have enough to buy bread. Well, how to live further?" Anatoly was also voting for Zyuganov because he thought that other candidates wouldn't be able to confront the country's crime problem. "Lebed says you have to fight crime. Well, let's see how he fights. You have to shoot in the temple first and later in the air, not the other way around. Under the Communists, there will be stability and order. What do we have under Yeltsin? It's mafia."

The third man, a kind-looking white-haired fellow, sat on a bench the whole time we spoke. His name was Nikolai Kazyanov. He was sixty years old and said he used to work in the Interior Ministry, Russia's internal security forces. "I'm also voting for Zyuganov—of course. I want the factory to start to work. I want us to get paid. I want us to receive our pensions on time. I want the state to be the manager of the factory again, because as a private company nothing is working. Maybe Bakaleynik is a good specialist, but he's not a good leader. Maybe he isn't completely to blame, but a lot depends on him. Some other firms are working, and he gets a big wage himself. There's a big gap between the workers and the management," he said.

It was clear that the workers had little patience for Bakaleynik. All they saw was that everything had gone downhill since the factory had been privatized. In the courtyard near the administrative headquarters of the plant, I ran into one more worker. His name was Sergei, and he had come in to check when the workers would be paid. He boiled with anger. "My wife and daughter and I all work at the factory. We have not received our wages for four months. Four months! So what do you think we can live on?"

I mentioned that some of the other workers had gone out and found temporary jobs. "What do you mean go out and work? And where can we work?" Sergei countered. "I took my daughter to the employment center. Our former deputy director works there. I asked him to get her a job. He said, 'Sergei, there are jobs, but they are for miserly wages—150,000 a month, 200,000 a month.'" That is, about thirty or forty dollars a month. "Who is going to go and work for such a wage? Before there was stability. I knew that I would get my advance—130 rubles. I had enough to provide for the family *vot tak*—so much," he said, holding his hand, palm downward, at eye level, as if to show a plentiful pile of goods. "You know what I have in my refrigerator at home? Nothing. Yesterday we had eggs and a little bit of pork. Today, I have nothing in my refrigerator."

He declared: "I am voting for Zyuganov. *Kak zhe?*" "How else?" He had worked at the plant since 1964, and he was now forty-nine years old. "Before I could take care of my family. Now look at us."

That afternoon, Bakaleynik called a meeting for the plant's top managers and the trade union representatives. He had learned that the Ministry of Finance had authorized a subsidy of 12 billion rubles for the factory. He wanted to use it, not to pay the workers, but to buy raw materials to start up production. Smiling and calm, he told the group that he wanted permission for more layoffs or to take a loan from the workers and pay them in promissory notes, rather than wages, for two months. "The financial situation is not simple. It is getting worse," Bakaleynik told them. "With every month, our chances of getting out of the hole are worsening." If they agreed, the workers would be paid back in one year, with 2 percent monthly interest. He appealed to the union representatives to explain the situation to the workers. "If we have strikes, the situation will get even worse," he insisted.

One of the union representatives stood up. "This is anarchy. Today we work. Tomorrow we don't. We need to have order," he said. "For some families to get their wages in promissory notes—their eyes will pop out in surprise. You will have to pay wages for March and April at least so that they will have received some money."

"Everything will depend on the moral climate," Bakaleynik answered. "Please get the workers to understand."

The meeting was over. As I left the plant, I noticed graffiti on the yellow apartment blocks near the factory. These were apartments that Bakaleynik's predecessor, Anatoly Grishin, had built for the workers and managers. "Zyuganov—da! Natsionalizm—da!" Given such harsh working and living conditions, the local support for the Communist was natural.

I managed to get to two other cities before the second round of the election. One was Novgorod, an ancient city located between Moscow and St. Petersburg. The center of the city was dominated by a kremlin surrounded by white walls. Inside, was a magnificent church. In contrast to Vladimir, the city seemed enveloped in an atmosphere of calm. The stores were stocked with goods—not as plentifully as in Moscow, but shoppers certainly weren't suffering from lack of choice.

Novgorod was a quiet success story. Like the rest of Russia, it had suffered from the collapse in industrial production, but it had managed to attract more direct investment in manufacturing than had any other region. Its local government had been the first to offer tax breaks for new investment, absolving investors of all local taxes and offering guarantees for credits extended to small- and medium-sized businesses. Local officials also publicized the city's peacefulness and stability, contrasting it sharply with the demonstrations and mafia wars in Moscow and St. Petersburg and with the frequent civil wars in the Caucasus. And the local government tried to cut red tape for investors rather than entangling them in bureaucracy.

As a result, such multinational companies as Britain's Cadbury Schweppes and South Korea's Goldstar were pouring big money into factories in Novgorod—between $150 and $200 million each—and providing hundreds of jobs. "We are working seriously to pull the oblast out of crisis," said Vladislav Alexeev, head of the region's economic committee, in an interview in his crowded, paper-strewn office. "We don't take tax from any new investors. And small business is also a big priority."[23]

Meanwhile, local radio and electronics factories had all but closed down, laying off hundreds of women. Alexeev said that 40 percent of the unemployed in Novgorod were women and that 40 percent of new businesses were started by women. The government was trying to help by setting up business centers to support small start-ups. I visited one in what appeared to be a former institute. On one floor, shops sold women's and men's clothing, some of it imported from the United States and Europe (usually brought by hand in someone's suitcase). On another floor, a small café was open, though it was doing very little business.

It wasn't clear that the small-business experiment would work. But it was a start. Natalia Mikhailova, an official at the local chamber of commerce, told me: "One problem is that our population doesn't have much money to spend. So it will take time. The government tries to help, but it doesn't have a big budget. We know it will be hard, but I hope we will gradually get results. Nothing in this world happens as quickly as you would like."

Novgorod was a Yeltsin town. His election posters hung in the center of the city. I saw little of his rivals' literature. Almost everyone I chatted with, both officials and people on the street, said that they would vote to reelect the president.

I headed next to a city in Russia's industrial heartland. In Magnitogorsk, a steel town in the Urals, the economic situation was more dire. The smokestacks of the Magnitogorsk Metallurgical Kombinat dominated the landscape on one end of this grimy town. The city's economy revolved around the *kombinat,* as the locals called it. Indeed, the city had been built around the factory under Stalin's direction in 1929. It was modeled after what had then been the world's most technologically advanced steel mill, located in Gary, Indiana.

The kombinat employed half the workers in Magnitogorsk. But it hadn't kept up with the times, and it couldn't produce steel cheaply enough for it to compete on the world market. The stable ruble had hit its export earnings hard. Moreover, demand had fallen in Russia, so the kombinat—and Magnitogorsk—were facing hard times. As the biggest employer, the kombinat was also the biggest taxpayer in town, and the local government was therefore having a harder time financing its schools, polyclinics, and theaters. There just was not enough *zhiviye dengi*—"live money," or real cash—to go around, locals told me. The town survived on promissory notes and lines of credit that the kombinat extended to its workers in place of wages. Everyone, from the director of the local theater to heads of families, engaged in long chains of complicated barter deals to get by.

"Who needs that kombinat?" Alexey Gorenkov, a local entrepreneur, asked me scornfully. "They don't understand that I could buy metal on the world market for $250 a ton and they are selling it for $450. There's no way they can compete."[24] Gorenkov, an energetic thirty-year-old, had built up a business manufacturing and selling furniture locally in the early 1990s. Then, when the kombinat ran into financial trouble, plunging the entire city into depression, he essentially went bankrupt. Now he was back in business, running supermarkets. On his desk was a Russian translation of Dale Carnegie's *How to Win Friends and Influence People.* Gorenkov held seminars every day for his own employees, he said, using Carnegie's book as the text.

How did Magnitogorsk cope with its cash shortage? At the local branch of Promstroi Bank, manager Alexander Graborski had come up with a novel idea that was easing the strain at least a bit. Credit cards. He arranged for the kombinat to issue credit cards to its qualified workers. Instead of actual cash wages, workers received a credit line from the kombinat every month. They could then go to local stores, which agreed to accept the card, and buy goods. Some stores also accepted promissory notes issued by the kombinat, which guaranteed eventual payment. (The kombinat itself would usually have to barter its production to secure cash.) Thus Magnitogorsk got by with its own monetary system, even when there weren't enough rubles to go around. It was a prime example of Russia's virtual industrial economy in action.

Despite the economic difficulties, Magnitogorsk had come out strongly in favor of Yeltsin in the first round of the elections. I learned this from an official at the local Communist Party headquarters. Zoya Ivanovna Pronina, first secretary of the local party, seemed resigned to the fact that she was fighting a losing battle. In the first round, she told me, Yeltsin had won 50 percent of the local vote; Lebed, 17 percent; and Zyuganov, just 13 percent. Dressed in a black suit and white blouse, she sat stiffly at her desk in her tiny office. There was no secretary. Nothing seemed to be going on. What a difference from the busy, pompous offices of first party secretaries in the old days, I thought. "I don't think that what we have had is reform. What we have now is wild capitalism. But the results of the vote seem to show that people support it," she said with a sigh.[25]

Later that day, I approached an elderly woman who was sitting on a park bench in the sun, and I asked about her views of the candidates, the election, and life in Magnitogorsk. Serafima Ivanovna was reading a newspaper, her head covered by a babushka. She seemed quite willing to chat, so I sat down next to her and we began to talk. "I can't complain. I live alone. I receive 300,000. That's enough to live on," she ventured. "I have always lived modestly. Those who can work, work. Those who are lazy, complain. People complain about prices but they come home with bags full of food."

"I am living," she continued. "My pension was delayed for almost a month because there wasn't any money in the town. I can adapt. And then they brought it to us. I'm not starving. I can't complain. I get enough. I buy milk, bread, sour cream—I don't deny myself."

"I worked in the steel kombinat thirty years," she informed me. "And before that I was head of a kindergarten and a *dom otdikha*—resort. I have three children—and not one of them is an alcoholic. There's not a hooligan among them!" She smiled, clearly proud.

Ya zhena vraga naroda. "I am the wife of an enemy of the people," she then said quietly. "My husband was arrested. He was a mining boss. First they arrested one boss, and then my husband. It was in 1938 that he was arrested. And I all the time looked for him, filled out forms. They always said my affair was being looked at. I wrote until 1958. And I never heard anything—just 'we are sorting it out, we are sorting it out.' He was being transferred to another place, to another town. In 1958, I received a document to fill out for a funeral in Magnitki, the old part of town. It turns out they took him on the eighth of April 1938 and on the twenty-ninth of April shot him here. And they told me 125 people were shot in the canal here. I was left with three children by myself. And I raised them all by myself. In 1958, they told me the truth, and before that I looked for twenty years."

She must have been a strong young woman. She still looked strong and healthy. "I was kicked out of my apartment as the wife of an enemy of the people," Serafim Ivanovna said. "I stayed near the house with two children, and I was pregnant with my third. I didn't think anything. I didn't feel anything. A friend in the building helped me."

She talked a little about her childhood. Her family had been kulaks, rich peasants, and the Communists had broken up their household. The term was *razkulachivanie,* from the word "kulak." "We were six people all together—four children. My father was rich. He was a hard worker. They arrested him and put him in prison. It was in 1929. After that, he said, 'Give me some kind of mud hut so that I can die. If you need my house, take it.' They gave him a mud hut, and he became a watchman for the town.

"When I was already around thirty years old, I went to work for the factory. I had a daughter. She died when she was sixty. My sons are on pension, sixty and sixty-three. But they still do some work in the kombinat. I have a grandson. He is a foreman in the kombinat. And I have four great-grandsons. And I am the wife of an enemy of the people."

She obviously was proud of all that she had accomplished in spite of her hardships. And, I thought, she had a right to be. Of course, she wasn't voting for the Communists. "I stand for Yeltsin," she said, firmly. "Some people around here say they want to strangle him and I say, 'What did Yeltsin do bad to you?' They say, 'Before you could buy everything for a ruble.' And I say, 'What could you get to eat for a ruble?'"

"I can't say I am living well. But for me to wait for something wonderful, why should I wait? I have enough money. My grandsons don't complain. They are bosses. They have their own cars. Those who don't work make a mistake."

I complimented her on her looks. She smiled, pleased. "I always make up my lips and brows," she said.

Serafima Ivanovna was ninety years old.

That night, before I returned to my hotel to pack my belongings, I stopped by a kiosk to buy beer and peanuts. Sitting inside was the owner, a woman wearing a big floppy hat, a white dress, and large bangly bracelets. She was intrigued to hear that I was from the United States, and she walked me back to my hotel.

I asked her about her business. "All the bad things about life in the West are coming here—crime, greed, materialism," she replied as we walked down the hill. The smokestacks of the steel kombinat rose in the distance behind us. "I am working in business so that I can give my son a good future. I want him to get a good education."

"I have been running this business—three kiosks—for three years," she added. "It's very difficult, but I am trying to raise my son by the ten commandments—not to lie, not to steal. I'm taking all the sins on myself so that he can live better. I want him to be a lawyer."

As we reached my hotel, I shook her hand and said goodbye. But she returned an hour later and presented me with a gift—an egg made of malachite, a stone mined in the Urals, topped with a Russian Orthodox cross. Another oddly touching, chance meeting in Russia.

Yeltsin disappeared from sight between the first and second rounds of the elections. Only later would the world learn that he had suffered another heart attack—a nightmare scenario for his campaign staff. The handful of people who knew the truth simply kept the lie going: Yeltsin had a bad cold, he was extremely tired. Meanwhile, the fight between Chubais and Korzhakov came to a head on June 19, when Korzhakov's

Kremlin guard arrested two top campaign workers—Video International's chief, Sergei Lisovsky, and Arkady Yevstafiev, a longtime aide to Chubais. The pair had allegedly spirited a box containing half a million dollars in campaign money from government offices in the White House.

After a tense night and morning of negotiations, Chubais convinced Yeltsin to fire Korzhakov.[26] In one of his few public appearances between the rounds, Yeltsin appeared on television and announced his decision. Exuberant, Chubais called a press conference and proclaimed victory. Russian observers said that he was far too gleeful and thus had probably killed his chances of winning a post in the next Yeltsin administration. But the confrontation over Lisovsky and Yevstafiev had been Korzhakov's last effort to sabotage the ballot. Now it would go ahead.

Two days before the runoff, Chernomyrdin traveled to Lyons, France, to take part in the annual economic summit held by the alliance of industrially advanced countries known as the Group of Seven. At a press conference, which was widely covered in the Russian press, he confidently declared: "The President of Russia is in brilliant form. There is no doubt that for the next four years he can perfectly fulfill the obligations of head of state if he wins the election."[27]

Two nights before the election—the last night that advertising was allowed—television stations broadcast frequent election ads. They were moving and in some cases frightening. (Although I watched for several hours, I saw none for Zyuganov.) "In 1917, no one thought that there would be civil war," intoned the voice-over in one commercial, as images rolled past of war and of people struggling to scavenge tiny bits of food from the ground. Then, in old-style lettering reminiscent of that used by the Russian Orthodox church, appeared the message, in Russian, "Save, preserve Russia. Don't vote for the Red color."

Other advertisements simply reminded voters to get to the polls. In one, viewers saw a cartoon-style picture that a little girl had drawn of her family. *Eto Ya.* "This is me," she says, before talking about her future. Then, in white letters on a black background, came the words: "There are 39 million children in Russia. They don't have the right to vote. Can you think of any stronger reason why you should go to the polls?" Then the scene switched to a digital clock indicating the time left to election day: twenty-six hours, six minutes, and three seconds.

On July 3, 1996, voters returned to the polls to choose between Yeltsin and Zyuganov. This time the turnout was lower, but Yeltsin pulled off his victory with 54 percent of the vote. He did not make a victory speech, although Chernomyrdin appeared on television the next day. Zyuganov conceded defeat and pledged that he would head "a loyal opposition." There would be no efforts to contest the election or to seize power illegally.

Russia was moving ahead along its road from socialism to democratic capitalism. But it still faced dangerous bumps and curves.

The Wary Westerners

The Russian market today is the most awesome
opportunity of our time. *Leonard Tsomik, young
Russian-American financier*

Russians weren't the only ones discovering pockets of wealth in the
changed Russian landscape. Westerners were, too, but for them the
new territory seemed especially confusing and dangerous. For Western
businesspeople, the Russian market promised a wild ride: high expectations often met with dashed hopes, unbelievable hassles sometimes
masked extraordinary rewards. It was not a market for the fainthearted.
Robert Strauss—businessman, Democratic Party bigwig, and U.S. am-
bassador to Russia from 1991 to 1993—put it bluntly: "The Russians
are constantly complaining about the lack of investment, the lack of
American capital coming to Russia. I tell them, 'Our people aren't risk-
adverse, but the ratio between risk and reward has to be proper. And
it's not right here.'" Strauss declared: "Capital to be invested is like a
beautiful woman. It has a lot of suitors. If the Russians don't create a favorable climate for the American business dollar, there are a lot of other
places in the world that will reach for it and welcome it."[1]

It had always taken a pioneering spirit to plunge into Russia, especially for Americans. Foreign companies had been active in manufacturing, insurance, and banking before the Russian Revolution, but they had been scared away when the Bolsheviks came to power in 1917. In the 1920s, when Lenin tried to achieve economic and political order with his New Economic Policy, he had enticed some investors back to Soviet Russia by handing out concessions to foreign companies in timber and other resources. But Stalin had ended all that. Although Western-Soviet trade continued, especially in grain, it frequently fell hostage to politics, both before and after the Cold War. Beginning in 1929, foreign direct investment in the Soviet Union was banned. Certainly in 1987, when Mikhail Gorbachev carefully reopened the door to direct investment by authorizing joint ventures, the United States and the Soviet Union were still highly suspicious of each other.

The early U.S.-Soviet ventures were set up by businesspeople with more than the usual store of patience, persistence, and vision. George Cohon, the American-born chief executive of McDonald's Restaurants of Canada, first began negotiating to open a Moscow restaurant in 1976, after a chance meeting with Soviet officials at the Montreal Olympics. He finally opened the nine-hundred-seat restaurant, then McDonald's largest, in January 1990. Joseph Ritchie, a successful commodities trader from Chicago, decided to open his Dialog joint venture after meeting his future Soviet partner at the Exhibition of Economic Achievements in Moscow in 1988. "I've got a good eye for good people. I spotted a good one, gave him some capital, and let him run with it," Ritchie told me. "If you are willing to take the time to build a human infrastructure, you can do things in this country that no one else can do."[2]

Other early ventures were set up by big-name companies intent mainly on supplying the Soviet oil industry—Combustion Engineering, Dresser Industries, and so on. Soon, oil companies themselves were lining up to negotiate joint ventures. But Western business became much more visible in Russia after Yeltsin freed prices, liberalized trade, and allowed the ruble to find its market rate against the dollar in 1992. Imports of food, beverages, and consumer goods like health products and detergents flooded in. When the government began privatizing state factories, some brave but farsighted Western companies leapt in.

Still, accumulated Western direct investment in Russia rose but slowly. From 1991 until the time of Yeltsin's reelection, it had increased to only about $6 billion. Only after Russia put the Communist threat to rest did the pace pick up. By the fall of 1997, investment levels topped $12 billion.[3]

Along the way, Western investors in Russia ran into countless problems, which intensified as the Soviet Union disintegrated and Yeltsin launched his economic reforms. The laws kept changing. Russian and Soviet laws contradicted each other. Taxes were ridiculously high, both for joint ventures and Russian enterprises. Property rights were not defined until 1996, when the Duma finally passed a law on joint-stock companies. And even then, rules on land ownership were unclear. Oil companies waited years for the Russian parliament to pass a production-sharing law that guaranteed their rights; when the legislation finally came in 1996, they still had concerns about its efficacy.

For Western partners eager to do business in Russia, the first hurdle was negotiating the deal. From the beginning, they did not know with whom to negotiate—a ministry in the Soviet government, a ministry in the Russian government, a local official, or simply the company officials themselves.

On top of that, Western (in particular, American) and Russian negotiating styles greatly differed. Russians believed that it was important to get to know their partners. They wanted to have "friendly relations" with the people with whom they did business, as Russian economist and consultant Rayr Simonyan told me. That meant spending time together, drinking vodka, getting to know each other's families, perhaps going on hunting trips—all of which could prove extremely time-consuming.[4] The American style, by contrast, was more rationalist. American businesspeople generally wanted negotiations and deals to be straight-forward and data-driven. They weren't used to the more intuitive style of Russian managers, who made business decisions based on instinct and friendship rather than on profit and loss.

And Americans didn't understand the Russians' lax attitude toward contracts. Americans wanted to know that when they had agreed, they had truly agreed. But to many Russian businesspeople, especially in the early 1990s, a contract simply represented what had been agreed *up to that point*. It could always be broken and renegotiated. A verbal promise was words—nothing more. A written agreement was stronger than a promise, especially if it was written up as a formal contract. But both could be broken.

Richard Dean, a partner at Coudert Brothers and one of the most ex-perienced American lawyers in dealings with Russia, put it this way: "Russia remains a long way from a 'rule of law' state; it remains a 'rule of relationships' state much like many developing countries."[5]

For potential investors in Russia, negotiating the deal was just the be-ginning. Registering the company, opening a bank account, hiring em-ployees—all the simple but necessary tasks involved in launching a business—often proved more time-consuming and arduous in Russia than in any Western country. Navigating the bureaucracy grew even harder in the 1990s, after the Soviet Union collapsed and official cor-ruption exploded.

Bureaucrats were scrambling to collect as many bribes as they could while the getting was still good. "With the breakup of the Soviet Union, the breakup of the whole system, we never know whom we have to ask to get the answer to this or that question. We always go to the wrong people," the Russian partner of one successful U.S.-Soviet joint venture told me in 1994. "The whole situation is so corrupt, everywhere you go people forget about the interests of the industry. They simply mind their own interests. Everybody wants to grab a buck. And they use their in-fluence not to improve the situation but to improve their own situa-tion."[6]

The same businessman also ran into serious problems with the mob. "Organized crime is a big problem. They say that maybe 70 to 80 percent of all businesses in Moscow and Russia are paying organized crime gangs. God knows, maybe it's much more. We were also approached by organized crime with the same intention. Not only to get the payoff but to get our own business," he explained.

The mobsters wanted to install their own people alongside this executive and demanded a cut of the venture's equity. They threatened to kill his family if he did not comply. Terrified, he sent his family outside the country and installed heavy security at the entrance of his office, while launching an investigation to track down the gang. The criminals were never found, he told me, but they did not return.

By 1994, both Western and Russian business executives freely admitted that they spent as much as 25 percent of their revenue on "security."[7] It was called paying for your *krisha,* or "roof," in the slang term. Armed, muscular men—former athletes, KGB agents, or Interior Ministry soldiers—hung around the entrances of offices, sometimes dressed in sport jackets and sometimes in military-style khakis. It was simply part of the cost of doing business in a state where the government and law were weak.

Occasionally foreign businesspeople were kidnapped or attacked. Only rarely were they killed, although it did happen. The most notorious incident was the 1996 murder of Oklahoma-born businessman Paul Tatum as he entered a metro station just a few steps from the popular Radisson Slavyanska Hotel in Moscow.[8] Tatum, president of a company called Americom Business Centers, was locked in a vicious battle with the city of Moscow over control of the joint venture that had built the Radisson Hotel and its adjoining business center. A proud, stubborn man, Tatum had engaged in a highly publicized crusade to maintain his stake in the venture, which had been negotiated before the Soviet Union's collapse.

It was a complicated tale, and the legal details were tangled. Tatum's case was in arbitration in Switzerland when he was killed, and the court later ruled against him. But it was too late. An assassin cut him down on a Sunday afternoon as he was walking into a metro station. No one else was even injured, including his bodyguards.

Tatum's case, however, was an extreme instance of failure and disaster in the market. There were failures for other reasons. IBM pulled the plug on plans to produce in Russia, citing the country's exorbitant taxes, but it continued to export to the market. Ben & Jerry's, the ice-cream makers, never overcame the transportation and distribution obstacles of producing ice cream in the northern republic of Karelia, not far from Finland, and shipping it to the rest of the country. The company had gone to Karelia to avoid problems with the mafia, but it lost money trying to get the ice cream to the cities in good shape and on time. It also faced tough competition from Russian-made ice cream.[9]

Volumes have been written on the failures of Western business in Russia. But what was the secret of success for those who stayed in the market? What kind of attitude was needed? What strategies worked?

By my observation, successful foreign businesspeople in Russia tended to be flexible, a little idealistic, dogged but not dogmatic. If they came across as arrogant know-it-alls preaching to the Russians, they were sure to fail sooner or later. Depending on their business, they might have to have deep pockets and be prepared to wait, possibly for years, for a return on their investment. They certainly had to be prepared to roll with the punches, from coups to elections to hyperinflation. It helped to be young and willing to take risks, although some of the longest-serving and most successful foreign executives in Russia were near retirement. It was important to have a sense of humor. For all these people, success might have to be defined in terms other than a set return-on-the-dollar earned within a set time period.

George Cohon was one of the most upbeat executives to invest in Russia. A gangling man with an irrepressible grin, he pursued his dream of bringing McDonald's hamburgers to the Russians for fourteen years. His first idea was to open a McDonald's in time for the 1980 Olympics in Moscow. Lengthy negotiations with the Soviet government ensued, but still the Communist Party's notables voted *nyet*. Only when Gorbachev permitted joint ventures did talks move forward. On January 31, 1990, Cohon finally greeted crowds of guests at his restaurant on Moscow's Pushkin Square, where hamburgers, French fries, and milkshakes sold for rubles, not hard currency. ("We put a sign up that said, 'Rubles only,'" Cohon explained, "because the only signs that were in evidence everywhere were 'Hard currency only.' So it was good to put up a sign that said, 'Rubles only.'") Although McDonald's had invested $50 million in the operation, Cohon declared that the restaurant was the "success of the Russian people."[10]

Cohon liked to tell the story of McDonald's push to open in Russia. "There were levels of pessimism," he said. "Legend Number One was that you'll never make your deal. Well, we made our deal. . . . Then people said, 'You won't be able to build to your standards.' And so, we did build to our standards." To do that, Cohon created a vertically integrated company. In the Solntseva region on the outskirts of town, a food-processing center and bakery churned out McDonald's hamburgers, French fries, and buns. He even brought in agricultural experts from Holland to help local farmers produce fatter beef cattle and better yields of potatoes.

Cohon continued: "Then people said, 'You won't be able to get a good crew. You'll never be able to hire people who will be willing to work properly.' My answer always was 'Who won the Olympics?' I couldn't believe that the former Soviet Union could win the medals and that we wouldn't be able to hire a good crew. I just couldn't believe that." And, indeed, when McDonald's placed just one want ad for employees, it received an astonishing twenty-seven thousand responses. After marathon interviews, the company hired six hundred workers and four top Russian managers for the restaurant.

Of course, Cohon was an expert at hyping his own creation. But the restaurant was an impressive achievement nevertheless, and when it opened in 1990, in the waning days of the Soviet Union, it stood out against the surrounding misery and grayness. The line of customers spilled out the doors and stretched all the way around the block, but even so, it took only twenty to thirty minutes for them to get inside. Not fast food American-style, but it was a phenomenon in Russia all the same.

One day, I joined the queue at McDonald's, standing in line for twenty minutes for a hamburger, fries, and shake. The store was clean. The young woman who served me smiled and wished me *priyatnogo appetita*—Russian for "bon appétit." As I sat down at a table, I smiled at the man next to me. He was an older gentleman, wearing a plaid shirt and gray sport coat. He said that he was an engineer from Vladivostok and was in Moscow on business. How did he like the food? Nodding as he swallowed, he said, "It's expensive, but it is tasty." After he finished, he slowly folded the paper wrappings and put them in his briefcase. "I'm going to bring them back to Vladivostok and give them to my daughter as a souvenir," he told me.

Moscow's McDonald's proved to be a national and even international sensation. The publicity benefited the company, but Cohon did not make money in Russia for several years. Still, McDonald's continued to expand slowly, unfazed by the coup in 1991, the attack on parliament in 1993, and the worries about the return of the Communists in 1996. By 1997, twenty-nine restaurants were dotted around Moscow and six other cities, serving tens of thousands of customers a day. This pace of growth was far slower than what the ambitious company had originally predicted in 1990, when it had boasted of plans to set up twenty restaurants in Moscow alone. But by 1997 the company was on a steady path of expansion, opening a restaurant every month or so.[11]

Cohon's huge investments in hamburger and French fry production underscored the lengths to which companies had to go to overcome Russia's underdeveloped infrastructure. Still, Cohon's experience held lessons for all potential investors in Russia: it could be done, even for rubles, but it took a long time, and it required a lot of money. Among key elements for success, his example showed, were perseverance and flexibility.

The details, of course, varied widely, but such lessons carried over from business to business. Probably the most seasoned American executive in Russia that I knew was Maxwell Asgari. In a decade of doing business first with the Soviet Union and then with Russia, he presided over both successes and failures. By 1997, his was a voice of wisdom on the ups and downs of doing business in a market like Russia.

I began hearing about Max Asgari in the late 1980s, when he negotiated the first U.S.-Soviet joint venture on behalf of his company, Combustion Engineering (CE). The venture was called Applied Engineering Systems, and it brought together CE and what was then called the Soviet Ministry for Oil and Petrochemicals. CE, which traded with the Soviet Union, had begun talking with contacts in the ministry in the mid-1980s, even before Gorbachev had announced that such joint ventures would be allowed. Referring to the Soviet ministry, Charles Hugel, then CE's chief executive officer, said that he wanted to deal with "the largest oil company in the world—probably bigger than Exxon and Shell put together."[12] And so Asgari worked behind the scenes to hammer out just such a deal. At the time, he was a senior executive for CE, which was based in Connecticut.

The agreement was announced in late 1987, timed to coincide with a summit between Presidents Gorbachev and Reagan. CE owned 49 percent and the Soviet ministry owned 51 percent of the joint venture. But according to Soviet joint-venture law, the general director had to be Soviet, and Vatslav Krotov was duly appointed; CE was allowed to hire a deputy director general. The aim of the joint venture was to boost output at Soviet oil refineries. CE was to be paid in the increased output, which it could then export. That allowed it to solve a crucial problem facing early Soviet-Western ventures: how to repatriate profits when the ruble wasn't convertible into dollars or other hard currencies.

It sounded like a reasonable deal, and CE executives were happy. Hugel made headlines for supporting and creating the first Soviet-American joint venture. It was the heyday of perestroika and the beginning of the end of the Cold War. Gorbachev and Reagan even blessed the deal in public pronouncements. But within three years, the joint venture foundered.

Cultural differences were to blame. The biggest problem, Asgari told me in 1990, was that Soviet law required that a Soviet be general director. Following in the tradition of most Soviet CEOs, Krotov had regularly made decisions without consulting other managers; he also often overrode the recommendations of his counterpart from CE. He didn't keep careful financial records, and he didn't show what records he did keep to executives from the U.S. company. By 1990, that company was the Swedish-Swiss conglomerate Asea Brown Boveri (ABB), which by then had acquired CE.[13]

But the Russians had their own side of the story. "I am doing business only with people who want to make profits, sign contracts, and have more money," complained Stanislav Kuzmin, general director of Nefteskimavtomatika, a Moscow oil refinery that the joint venture was revamping. He complained that ABB was denying the country the high technology that it had promised to transfer. Replied Asgari, "The venture must be run as a business."

ABB finally pulled out of the venture. But it did not pull out of Russia. Instead, it made Asgari head of its operations there. And when privatization auctions got under way in 1992, ABB began acquiring stakes in Russian power and engineering enterprises. A year later, in 1993, I met with Asgari in the new headquarters of ABB Russia on Tverskaya Ulitsa. (The headquarters were in a gleaming new office building built by McDonald's; on the ground floor was a new McDonald's restaurant. Moving into real estate was one way that Cohon covered his losses in the early years of building up his restaurant business in Russia.)

Asgari explained the company's strategy to me: "We have made a fundamental decision to be in this market for a long time. We also have convinced ourselves that it will probably take anywhere from five to ten years for this economy to turn around and really become a consumer economy. The third thing that we have accepted is that we should not try to base our investment condition on what the Russians might do this year or next year, or on what laws they might pass or what the Central Bank might do or might not do regarding the ruble."[14]

"In ABB's case," Asgari continued, "we have decided not to complain but find a way that we can still establish ourselves within the current laws, contradictions, and conflicts. We hope to be part of the organization that helps the economy turn around rather than say, 'Now that the economy has turned around, we'll show you our gadget.' We are a manufacturing company. Being a manufacturing company [means] you have to invest significantly every day, and it takes time to finally produce. It takes anywhere from one to two to three to sometimes four years from the time you make a decision and start your investment until you really start producing goods and services and supporting goods. For us and other people like us, if you want to be in the economy four years from now, you have to make the decision now. Our decision is yes. We are not going to wait for all the problems to be solved, because I don't think all the problems will be solved in such a short time."

ABB went on to buy or set up twenty companies which employed some three thousand people (including Russians). Located in St. Petersburg, Moscow, and Cheboksary, they produced gas turbines, control systems, pollution-control devices, meters, and other equipment for the energy business. They were serving customers in both Russia and the rest of the former Soviet Union and sometimes export customers. Like McDonald's in the consumer market, ABB soldiered on despite both political and economic instability in Russia.

I kept in touch with Asgari, speaking with him from time to time. When I went to see him again in 1996, he told me that ABB was selling about $500 million worth of goods and services in Russia. But the Russian unit still wasn't earning profits, because it was investing heavily in new technology and equipment for its acquisitions and in training six hundred people a year at a new center in Moscow. He was proud of the company's investment in the center, which had caught the attention of Russian officials. "Foreigners are seen by Russians as only being interested in increasing their profitability. That's why there's unfriendliness toward foreign investors. This demonstrates our commitment to contributing to the Russian economy," he said.[15]

I asked Asgari what he believed was the most important lesson for foreign investors in Russia. "Except for very few opportunities," he replied, "this is not a market where you can make fast money. This is a market where you really have to commit yourself. You have to want to run a business for a long time. The time framework is five, ten, fifteen years rather than six months, one year, or two years." He had some more advice: "It's very important that whatever agreement you sign with the Russians—whether it is a joint venture, joint-stock company, or a contract to provide supplies, you have to be sure that the deal is also good for the Russians on an ongoing basis. The day the Russian sees there's nothing in it for him, he will walk away from it. And there really is nothing you can do."

Asgari believed that the Russians had learned a great deal in the ten years he had been dealing with them. "There was euphoria under Gorbachev about foreign investment, and the Russians had very high expectations. Now they are more realistic," he observed. But in many ways, negotiating deals had grown tougher. "Before you were dealing with the general director and the government. Today there are shareholders. And in many enterprises, there are many shareholders. They have no common objective, no common agenda. Now as a foreign company you aren't just dealing with one person. You have to understand who are the key players and what kind of managers they are. The management of companies is more difficult." (On the other hand, Asgari added, respect for the law was growing. Westerners appealing to the courts for arbitration in contractual disputes had a greater chance of achieving a resolution than they did a few years before. Even so, personal relationships remained "an overriding consideration" in doing business in Russia, he acknowledged.)

Adapting to the Russian style of doing business remained a problem for less flexible companies. "Medium-sized companies are more aggressive than large companies. American companies are clearly much more cautious than European companies. And even with the Europeans, it depends on whether they are from Scandinavia, the Mediterranean, or Central Europe. The Americans tend to be more cautious because we are more legalistic in the United States. The more legalistic you are, the more difficult it is to do business [here]," Asgari said. Managing corruption, in other words, would continue to pose huge difficulties.

In 1997, Asgari retired from ABB after nearly twenty-five years with the company and its Connecticut-based unit, the former Combustion Engineering. But he did not retire from Russia. Instead, he joined Sun International, a group controlled by the Khenka family of India. It had acquired seven breweries in Russia through voucher auctions, and Asgari became chief executive officer of Sun Brewing Company. He also became chairman of a trading company called Sun Trading International, and he was helping to run a new private investment fund that the family had created to take stakes in Russian companies. The aim was to help them restructure, list their shares on the market, and sell out, at a profit.

Soon after Asgari joined Sun, I met with him in his new office in a park far from the center of Moscow, where the Khenkas had rented and renovated a two-story cottage. The setting was more casual than the one on Tverskaya Ulitsa in the center of Moscow. And Asgari was more relaxed as well. "The consumer business is different. It is very, very easy relative to the industrial business," he told me with a smile. He began to tick off the differences. In heavy industry, investors like ABB had to deal with the shortage of money at Russian enterprises. Because of the highly capital nature of the power industry, it took much longer to get products onto the market. But selling beer and other consumer goods was essentially a cash business, and Asgari had few problems with financing. "The consumer business is much more dynamic. It involves relatively low capital investment. You can get your product out onto the market in three months," he enthused.[16]

Sun was a tiny company compared to ABB. But it was thriving. Its beer sales had already topped $150 million a year, and the figure was growing. It had already created one national brand, Viking, and was planning to acquire more breweries. In the Soviet era, Asgari explained, the brewing business had been completely decentralized. Each region had its own brewery and its own labels. But as a type of business, breweries had one special characteristic: in contrast to enterprises in other industries, they paid heavy taxes to regional governments and just 15 percent of their tax take to Moscow. By running Sun, Asgari was gaining a keen insight into the differences among regional governments and how they treated foreign investors.

More and more, it was becoming crucial for foreign investors to understand these differences among Russia's regional governments. Russia was fast becoming a jumble of different economies, each with its own strengths and weaknesses. Some had moved quickly to spur industrial restructuring; others had tried to preserve the old ways. Some were more welcoming to foreign capital; others completely rejected it.

Although much had changed in a decade, Asgari found that disputes still arose over private property rights in many regions where he was working. "When you buy these breweries, they are in bad shape. But it doesn't take that much to improve them. Once you improve them, everyone wants to come and take them back," he told me. "Fundamentally it's an issue you always have to deal with here. Anytime a company is unprofitable, nobody is interested. The minute you make it profitable, there are people who want it back."

Who wanted it back? Sometimes the general director wanted to claim control, Asgari said. Sometimes the local beer distributor stepped forward. Sometimes the government did.

But Sun had taken cases to the Russian courts, and, to the surprise of some (including me), had won. "The concept of ownership is still not intimately understood here," Asgari continued. "If you bought something cheap three years ago and added value, they say, 'You bought it cheap.' The Russians are so paranoid about what you paid and what it is worth today. The fact that you've spent money on it and never taken money out is not considered. . . . When you buy something and it's unprofitable, you own 60 percent. Then suddenly they say you own 27 percent, and then suddenly you own nothing." He laughed.

To be successful in Russia, Asgari insisted, "you need the support of the regional government." Only with huge projects, such as those in oil and gas, could the central government overrule the decisions of the regional governments. "The regional governments are more powerful and influential than they used to be. They frankly now call the shots. They can make life miserable for you or easy for you."

A good deal of this power resided with the regional governors. "The governors as individuals are becoming more and more powerful. A lot of these governors run their regions as a one-man show. Nobody moves. Even the federal agencies within those regions take orders from the local governor. So that is a critical issue."

Although some governors, such as those in the Novgorod and Saratov regions, offered tax breaks to entice foreign investment, Asgari felt that "deep down" many regional governors opposed foreign investment. "They do not believe that foreign investment is a good thing for Russia," he told me. "They are happy to take your money, but deep down they don't really think that Russia needs foreign investment. They want foreign money, but they don't want foreign supervision. We disturb. Whether they are inefficient or counterbarter or bribe someone, they are content. And then we put in a few million [dollars] and start looking at the books. So we disturb, and that is what they don't want. In many cases they would rather have the situation as calm and tranquil as it was before, rather than to have someone come and shake things up. It's a matter of character and mentality—not economics."

Asgari felt that it would take a long time for the Russian business culture to change at its roots. "The reason many things don't take place is that these people have a tradition and culture: they are suspicious of foreigners. That has nothing to do with who is running the country. It will just take a long time to change. We almost have to wait until everyone who was involved in the decision-making process in the Soviet Union retires from business. We need a new generation to come."

Most of the new generation that Asgari longed for, however, was heading not into industry but into finance. Finance had zoomed ahead of the rest of the Russian economy. It suffered from its share of corruption and distortions, but it was dominated by young, energetic people who wanted to get ahead. I had spoken to a number of representatives of this tiny but growing class of young financiers. Most were in their twenties and early thirties. Most were men, but there were some women among them. All but a few were optimistic and ambitious and very well paid.

But in spite of his hopes for doing business with a younger generation, Asgari was somewhat skeptical of these financiers. He feared that they—whether Russian or Western—were promising too much to Russian industrialists and to Western investors. "Investment bankers have discovered Russia," Asgari said. "The bankers are telling the companies: 'Your problem is solved. We will take you to the international market. We will float you. We will raise international funds for you. The man on the white horse is here.'"

"And many of the Russians want the money," Asgari continued. "It's beautiful because when I go to buy a company, I talk about how I want a management change, I want people on the board. The investment bankers go and say: 'You don't have to do anything. You don't change. We are getting you money and you manage it.' It's a fantastic deal."

Were they setting themselves up for a giant fall? "Frankly," he said, "I think there are companies on the market that had no business being on the market. So investment bankers make money, a few million dollars, and the companies get money. But I think some of them are going to go down, and some investors will get burned."

Asgari had a point. There probably wasn't enough due diligence by investors of Russian enterprises eager to attract foreign money. Some companies probably would go down. But I thought that he was too negative. He had fought too many battles, perhaps. True, investment bankers were pouring into Russia. They ranged from individuals like Boris Jordan, the American of Russian ancestry who had set up his own Russian investment bank, to giant brokerage houses like Merrill Lynch. But those who caught my eye most often were the young Russian financiers, especially those who had gained a Western education or Western work experience. Some were Russians who had emigrated to the United States and returned. Others were Russians who managed to follow the path forged by Bakaleynik of the Vladimir Tractor Factory, gaining educations at top universities like Harvard and Columbia and then returning home.

All the new Russian brokerages were fighting to hire these young people. I happened to meet a group of them from Sector Capital, a Russian brokerage house headed by Jack Barbanel, an American financier. They included Leonard Tsomik, a Belarus native who had emigrated to the United States with his family in 1982 and later returned, and Yevgeny Ioffe, a native of St. Petersburg who had gone to the United States in 1989 and also returned.[17]

Tsomik, age thirty, was the senior player. "It is a very exciting time to be in Russia," he said. "You see a rather fast pace of development. Sometimes it goes backwards. But no matter how difficult it is or how uneven things might be, we still believe the direction will not change and it will go forward. You do have to have faith that the free market will reign in the country and that democracy will entrench itself firmly."

Referring to Ioffe and himself, he added: "We also feel that having certain skills and having prior experience working with the market, we bring to the problems an education and a mentality, and the ability to transfer between mentalities. We are a bridge between the two. We are fortunate to have a foot in both cultures. Business culture is very important here. It is one of the biggest barriers in instilling certain values. Certain values didn't have any place here—such as respect for contracts."

So the young Western-educated Russian financiers felt themselves to be almost ambassadors for the Western way of doing business. At the same time, though, they said that they could empathize with the socialist-era factory directors who liked to do things the old way.

There was no doubt in my mind that these young financiers, with experience, would make their mark. Ioffe, who was also thirty, put it this way: "We have a unique opportunity to rewrite the rules of the market. We can take this situation in our hands and shape the market. There is no precedent here, so it is an exciting opportunity for all of us. And at the same time there is a lot of responsibility to do the right thing."

Western investment in Russia was to go through many more twists and turns. But as small companies like Sun and huge multinationals like ABB, Procter & Gamble, and Coca-Cola overcame obstacles to doing business in the harsh Russian business climate, Russian consumption of foreign goods soared. Sometimes goods were produced inside the country. Often they came in from Europe or the United States. Indeed, by 1996, of all the goods that Russians purchased, imports accounted for at least half. Moscow made no secret of the fact that 80 percent of its food supply came from overseas.[18] The biggest winners in this market were producers of food, beverages, electronics, clothing, and household goods—all of which long-deprived Russians were generally glad to snap up, despite the occasional grumblings of a hard-liner about Western or American imperialism. Regions such as Novgorod, which offered tax breaks to lure such companies as Cadbury Schweppes, Korea's Goldstar Group, and the Danish producer of Stimorol gum to invest close to $500 million in 1995, also gained.

Russia was on its way to becoming a vibrant consumer society. As sometimes happens in the United States and other developed markets, certain products became so popular that their names and images seeped into the culture of everyday life. One joke that made the rounds in Moscow was about a schoolchild asked to name the planets. "Jupiter, Neptune, Mars, Snickers, . . ." the child replied. Even *Pravda* ran on its front page a cartoon that showed two workers reading newspapers, grimaces on their faces: "Only two people are worried about Russia these days," one fellow says to the other. "Johnson and Johnson." The second man replies: "No, four. There's also Procter and Gamble."[19]

Yet in all the tumult of transformation, it seemed to me, the westerners were always somehow peripheral to the main story—the Russians' battle for wealth and struggle to adapt. Westerners were advisers to reform and financiers of government projects like privatization, were merchandisers of consumer goods and investors in some industrial enterprises. Westerners were involved, increasingly, in the financial market. Westerners played a role. But far more important were the Russians—the reformers, the entrepreneurs, and the ordinary people.

Kapitalizm Reborn

We will manage to create a normal country. I have
no doubt. Yuri Levada, sociologist

"Let us not divide the country into victors and vanquished," Yeltsin told voters in a short, pretaped victory speech broadcast on television on July 4, 1996. He looked tired and spoke slowly. "We argued a great deal. Each of us asserted his position. You have resolved this dispute. I am sure that there will be room in the new team for all of those in whom you placed your trust."[1] The next day, campaign manager Anatoly Chubais was more exuberant at a packed press conference at the Interfax News Agency. Still looking boyish in spite of all his political battles, Chubais triumphantly proclaimed Yeltsin's victory a historical turning point for Russia.

Not since Peter the Great had Russia seen such a reformer, Chubais declared. "Neither Witte nor Stolypin nor Alexander II have done for Russian history what this man has done," he proclaimed. "July 3 showed that a return to the past is impossible in my country. No turn in democracy, in private property, in reform is possible, not in a year, not in ten years or one hundred years, not by anyone. Never."[2]

He sounded like a man looking for a job. Chubais insisted that he would be joining the private sector, probably as a consultant to privatized companies. But on July 15, Yeltsin appointed Chubais as his new chief of staff. The economist, privatization minister, campaign chief, and political survivor was back in his most influential position thus far. He would be gatekeeper to the president—a post that was to take on even more importance because of Yeltsin's failing health. A few days later, Yeltsin renamed Viktor Chernomyrdin as prime minister and, for the first time, brought a "new Russian" entrepreneur into the government: Vladimir Potanin, UnExim Bank chief and architect of the controversial loans-for-shares program, became first deputy prime minister in charge of the economy. He had been a leading financial backer of Yeltsin's campaign. The biznesmen were getting their rewards.

Yeltsin, looking sickly, took the oath of office in August. In September, he finally broke his silence and admitted that he was seriously ill. For the first time, he acknowledged publicly that he had suffered a heart attack between the two rounds of the elections and that he needed coronary bypass surgery. (The Communists and other members of the opposition condemned Yeltsin for his dishonesty, but much of the rest of the world, myself included, quietly breathed a sigh of relief. If Yeltsin had revealed the true state of his health in July, he would perhaps have handed victory to the Communists, essentially by default.)

A succession struggle—at the least a battle for power and influence—was already raging. Yeltsin retreated from daily work to prepare for his operation but refused to hand over the reins of power to anyone. (The constitution stipulated that the prime minister would become acting president if the president were incapacitated, but that the president himself had the power to decide whether he was capable of governing.) While Chernomyrdin continued to preside over the government, albeit unofficially, Chubais wielded extraordinary influence in the Kremlin. Consulting frequently with Yeltsin and his daughter, who had Yeltsin's ear, Chubais himself signed presidential decrees.

Both Chernomyrdin and Chubais vied to keep the populist and ambitious Alexander Lebed in check. His eye still on the presidency, Lebed was capturing headlines daily. As National Security chief and Yeltsin's envoy, he traveled to Chechnya to broker a peace deal, taking time off to play chess with rebel leaders. Lebed suggested that Russia restore the institution of the vice presidency and that he step into the job. But when he announced that he might become president before Yeltsin's term ended in 2000, the newly reelected president had had enough. On October 17, 1996, Yeltsin fired the National Security chief. "Everybody seems to be running for president. I cannot tolerate it any longer," Yeltsin said.[3]

Despite the uncertainty over Yeltsin's health, the Russian stock market boomed throughout the second half of 1996. Investors seemed reassured that democracy had won in Russia—and that even if Yeltsin were to disappear from the political scene, the market economy would remain. Foreign investment spiked upward for the first time since the market explosion in 1994. By year-end, it had risen 155 percent in dollar terms, and it was to continue to soar another 85 percent in 1997.[4] Of course, Russia's market was still small and illiquid compared to many emerging markets. But trading was picking up, especially for blue-chip companies, such as Lukoil, Mosenergo, and Vimpelcom, which had begun offering their shares (in the form of American Depositary Receipts) on the over-the-counter market in the United States. (Vimpelcom, a former military factory that had moved into the cellular phone business, managed to qualify for a full listing on the New York Stock Exchange, the first Russian company to do so.)

The real economy, however, continued to suffer. Although inflation stayed under control—despite Yeltsin's campaign spending promises— gross domestic product fell once again in 1996, by 6 percent in real terms.[5] The government still owed trillions of rubles in back wages and pensions. Industry was still starved for investment. Perhaps the biggest macroeconomic problem was the government's chronic inability to collect taxes. The government had partly created its own dilemma by awarding special tax exemptions to well-connected companies over the years. But scores of other companies underreported their income or simply paid no taxes at all.[6] Chernomyrdin said that he would force companies into bankruptcy if they did not begin to pay their taxes. The funds slowly started to flow, but the government was still desperately short of cash. Teachers, doctors, and coal miners once again threatened to strike.

Privatization also ground to a halt in the second half of 1996. But Potanin, as the new economic czar, made one crucial decision that marked another milestone on Russia's journey toward its own style of capitalist economy. According to the decrees that Yeltsin had signed for the 1995 loans-for-shares privatization program, the government had until September 1, 1996, to determine its position in the scheme. Either it had to pay back the loans that the banks had extended in exchange for shares or it had to allow the banks to keep the shares for eventual sale. Potanin himself had designed the program, and his bank was a leading participant in it. Chubais had lost his job as deputy prime minister in the public outcry over the program earlier in the year. Some opposition members of parliament even threatened to press criminal charges against its instigators.

Without fanfare or debate, Potanin managed to close the case on loans-for-shares in September 1996, just a few months after his appointment to the government. At Yeltsin's request, he later explained, he and Lebed wrote a letter setting out the government's position. "First of all, [the letter said] that this scheme of loans-for-shares was legally correct and there will be no administrative changes in it," Potanin told me in a quick interview in October, after he'd given a speech before an audience of American businesspeople in New York City. "The shareholders have the right to sell their shares, but under two conditions. First of all, it goes without saying that it should be done according to privatization law, which means by public auctions, et cetera. Secondly, the shareholders should coordinate their actions with the government and inform the government at least three months before they want to sell their shares."[7]

Through that letter, Potanin ensured that his UnExim Bank, Menatep, and other groups that had benefited from the loans-for-shares scheme could keep the oil companies, metals producers, and other lucrative assets that they had snapped up at bargain-basement prices. The decision underscored the growing power of financial-industrial groups. And it moved Russia a giant step closer to an oligarchical economic system, in which ownership was concentrated in the hands of a select, politically well connected elite.

Exactly how strong and influential was this elite? It was a matter of great debate. Surprisingly, some members of the club at the top of Russia's industrial hierarchy seemed to take pleasure in bragging about it. In October, Yeltsin appointed another of his campaign's key business backers, Boris Berezovsky, as deputy secretary of the National Security Council. It was Berezovsky who had first urged Chubais to jump into the presidential race, with the financial support of Russia's leading banks and business groups. In a controversial interview with the *Financial Times* a few weeks after his appointment, Berezovsky claimed that seven top bankers and businesspeople controlled half of the economy and that their economic power enabled them to influence or even call many of the shots in the government's policies. Berezovsky strongly believed that capital had replaced ideology as the driving force of Russian political and economic life.[8] "I think two types of power are possible," he said. "Either a power of ideology or a power of capital. Ideology is now dead, and today we have a period of transition from the power of ideology to the power of capital." Berezovsky added: "I think that if something is advantageous to capital, it goes without saying that it's advantageous to the nation. It's capital that is in a condition, to the greatest extent, to express the interests of the nation."[9]

Who were the members of the business elite? Berezovsky did not name those on his list of seven, but they undoubtedly included most or all of the group that had financed Yeltsin's campaign: Potanin, of UnExim Bank; Mikhail Khodorkovsky, founder of Menatep; Vladimir Vinogradov, founder and chief executive of Inkombank; Vladimir

Gusinsky, of Most Group; and Mikhail Fridman, president of Alfa Group. Vagit Alikperov, president of Lukoil, and Rem Vyakhirev, chairman of Gazprom, were also influential and had also backed Yeltsin's reelection.

Together, these businessmen controlled assets worth perhaps hundreds of billions of dollars. I asked several of them what percentage of the country's gross domestic product they estimated that they controlled, but all declined to cite a precise figure. And because of interlocking shareholdings, it was impossible for outside economists to come up with an accurate estimate, although several ventured to guess that the numbers could add up to as much as 50 percent.

Whatever the financial strength of the business elite, it was clear that their political influence was even greater, because they also controlled large chunks of the media. Most Group was the largest and most influential media company, with assets ranging from NTV and the newspaper *Segodnya* to *Itogi,* a newsmagazine published with *Newsweek,* and an arts and entertainment guide. Gusinsky was moving quickly into television broadcasting via satellite and fancied himself to be Russia's Rupert Murdoch. Nearly all the other leading banks, plus Lukoil and Gazprom, also owned newspapers, magazines, or television stations. In many cases, these were profitable businesses, but more important, they were a way to the hearts and minds of Russians. After all, it was through his savvy use of the media that Yeltsin won the election. The danger was that the new owners would begin to dictate editorial policy. (In May 1997, Lukoil would shake up *Izvestia,* taking control of the board of directors and firing its editor after the newspaper reprinted an article from *Le Monde* that was highly critical of Chernomyrdin. For journalists and believers in a free press, it would mark a worrying precedent.)

Mikhail Berger, *Izvestia*'s respected editor and commentator, downplayed the influence of the *semibankirshina*—the Rule of the Seven Bankers, as it was becoming known. "In my view, the level of influence that business has on economic policy and politics in general is greatly exaggerated," he wrote. "Even the biggest companies are much more dependent on political authorities than the other way around. Most big businesses are sustained by the government budget or with orders from the state."[10] (Because of the reorganization at *Izvestia,* Berger eventually left his job there to become deputy editor, and later editor, of *Segodnya.*)

But there is no doubt that the financial-industrial groups had accumulated wealth and strength on the back of the state. As authorized banks, they had been able to earn money on deposits from the government. Through the loans-for-shares program, they had gained privileged access to many of Russia's most lucrative industrial assets. Now they would have the chance to enhance their wealth by expanding their stakes in these holdings or by eventually selling their shares at a huge mark-up.

The leading bankers and businesspeople had united to reelect Yeltsin, but that was a special situation. That issue was black and white. Either back Yeltsin and keep their businesses, or allow Zyuganov to win and risk losing everything. But in everyday political and economic life in Russia, few if any issues were so cut-and-dried. And in the business world, these banks and businesses were rivals and competitors, in many cases fighting for the same customers or the same deals.

So I agreed with Berger and others who doubted that these business leaders could unite to form an unofficial, late twentieth-century politburo able to dictate policy to Yeltsin. Clearly they would—individually or collectively, depending on circumstances—continue to push the government for the best economic deals that they could get for their businesses. Some of them, like Berezovsky and Potanin, might get the chance to do it from inside the corridors of power, as ministers or as presidential advisers. Sometimes they would win, but sometimes they would lose.

I asked Menatep's Khodorkovsky what he thought of the Rule of the Seven Bankers and of his own role in particular. He laughed. "After Mr. Berezovsky came back to Moscow, many of the seven, myself included, promised him illegal actions—despite his bodyguards. I feel that he was completely incorrect in his statement of our role and what we are capable of."[11]

So what was the role of a Khodorkovsky or Berezovsky? "We are those young managers who will have to be the ones over the next ten or fifteen years to raise the economy of the country up," Khodorkovsky answered. "If the government doesn't pay attention to us, then it's not behaving properly. Not because we are politically influential. The reason the government should pay attention to us is because we will pull Russia out of the economic cul-de-sac that it is now in."

He gave an example. "If you want your factory to work well, you want to make sure that managers on the factory floor feel comfortable about doing their job right. We are those foremen in the big picture. If you look at us and see that we are in a situation where we can't do our jobs, then you'd better do something about it. Or tell us that you have other foremen who can do the job."

At the time that Khodorkovsky and I spoke, he was in New York City negotiating with bankers about long-term financing for Menatep's industrial projects. He had begun concentrating on Menatep's industrial assets—grouped together in a holding company called Rosprom—on a daily basis. Menatep had purchased 78 percent of Yukos, Russia's second-largest oil company, in the loans-for-shares auctions, and he wanted to borrow money and expand the company by investing in oil refineries and chemical companies. Interest rates in Russia were finally falling, but he thought that he could get the money more cheaply in the United States.

Khodorkovsky sighed when I asked him about industrial restructuring. Rosprom, he said, employed around 200,000 workers and had annual sales of about $5 billion—"a lot of people and not a lot of sales," as he put it. A U.S. consulting company had told Khodorkovsky that Rosprom could be compared to South Korea's Samsung in its structure. Yukos made up about 80 percent of Rosprom's sales; the rest included textiles, food processing, and equipment manufacturing. "But in Samsung, the sales are ten times more and the people are two times fewer," Khodorkovsky noted wryly.

What was Khodorkovsky going to do? "We don't have the possibility to reduce personnel that much. Most of our work is in [formerly] closed cities, where our factory is the only factory in the entire city. If we lay people off, the people go on the dole, which is paid for by the local government, and the local government dole fund comes out of our pocket anyway. Our company already has a little bit of experience in trying this, and it ended up being more expensive because the local authorities work very inefficiently. So it makes more sense for us to create a wholly-owned subsidiary within the larger company and give people jobs. All this is one reason why our banking arm right now is focusing on helping to finance small business ventures. But this is a long process."

Khodorkovsky's strategy was to spend about five years strengthening Rosprom as a conglomerate within Russia—"to diversify within Russia only," he explained. "Yukos we are going to clean up and make more of a standard, productive company, but Rosprom will soak up the people from the other companies as well as the social functions," such as housing, day care centers, and the health service. With Yukos, he hoped to invest in more oil fields and expand downstream, so to speak, into petrochemicals. "In ten years, we might try to go global based on the chemical industry. But ten years is a long time and many things can change." He said he was spending big money on getting the advice of Western consultants and would compare their vision with his own before taking decisive steps.

But Khodorkovsky seemed convinced that he was on the right track. "In the next five to ten years, we are planning to remain a broad-profile conglomerate for a very simple reason. In Russia, there aren't very many possibilities to accumulate big capital. In order to do that you have to be involved in everything. It is easier for us to do that than to go global now."

Of course, another reason Khodorkovsky couldn't go global was that he couldn't possibly compete. That was especially true if he had to hang on to employees for social and political reasons. "Mind you," he said, a little testily, "it would be a lot easier for me to work on the Western model. I know very clearly how this should be done. I've got articles and consultants that tell me how to do it. It's in the book. But I must proceed from the assumption that I carry a social burden. There's no way I can avoid it. I must deal with it."

Heavy burdens for a thirty-three-year-old. On the other hand, Khodorkovsky was possibly on his way to becoming a Rockefeller of his generation. Only Vagit Alikperov, president of Lukoil, was ahead of him in this respect. Alikperov had already succeeded in creating what most conceded was Russia's most progressive and successful oil company, and one that was already beginning to compete on a global scale. With a market value of $10.3 billion by 1997, Lukoil was becoming a force to be reckoned with in the energy business. Alikperov had started early, focusing on what he knew—oil. He had expanded rapidly and opened his company to the world, including the funds of a foreign partner, Atlantic Richfield Company. The race between these two entrepreneurs was to heat up as Khodorkovsky vied to become Russia's leading oil magnate. Khodorkovsky, for instance, later bought a medium-sized oil company known as Eastern when the government privatized it and also merged his Yukos with oil assets controlled by Berezovsky to create Yuksi, Russia's largest oil company in terms of production.[12]

UnExim Bank's Potanin agreed with Khodorkovsky's skeptical assessment of Berezovsky's Rule of the Seven Bankers. He explained: "The concentration of capital in the country of course is very high. If you take maybe thirty to thirty-five of the biggest companies, they really control more than half of the gross national product. But it's thirty to thirty-five, not seven. It's Gazprom, United Energy System, the Ministry of the Railways. Historically the concentration of capital in the country has been very high; that's why thirty to thirty-five companies control the economic situation. But in our country, the power of the president and the government is very big. If they have political will, they could do everything. The question is just political will."[13]

Potanin continued, making it clear that he thought Berezovsky's assessment was flawed in another way. "That's why when bankers and other private people think they have some kind of political power, they are mistaken. First, it's getting less and less. And then they are mistaken that it's good for the country when capital has such a direct influence on power. My personal opinion is that it's bad. Either you work as a businessman, or you leave business, you become a politician, and you are elected in the parliament, elected president or named prime minister. Then you become a politician and you have influence on the country. Either you do it for yourself, either you do it for the country. It's convertible, but it's not possible to do it at the same time. And people who think being in business, they could have direct influence on the government, they are not right." Without citing his name, Potanin was referring directly to Berezovsky.

Other entrepreneurs were clearly worried about the huge clout of the leading financial-industrial groups. Over breakfast one morning in March 1997, Kakha Bendukidze, who had been the first entrepreneur to tell me that he wanted to set up such a group, fretted about the power of his larger competitors.[14] He had come to New York City's Plaza Hotel to speak at an investment conference that had attracted perhaps one thousand fund managers, economists, bankers, and others newly intrigued by Russia. Suddenly, Russia had become hot. At receptions, brokers and investors exchanged tips even about Uralmash, the famous yet dilapidated heavy-equipment producer that Bendukidze had snapped up in 1993.

He was, of course, pleased that Uralmash was finding favor with investors. In the years since I had first visited the factory, Uralmash had changed dramatically. The company had halved its workforce, to sixteen thousand. It was producing far less now than it had in Soviet times, but it was recovering from its deep depression. Orders were on the rise from customers like Gazprom in Russia and others as far away as China and India. And Bendukidze hoped that the company would be able to raise money on the international financial markets to finance a further restructuring.

But Bendukidze was not so sanguine about Russia's overall picture. "We are definitely better off than we were under the Communists. There's no doubt about that. But it hasn't turned out in the best way." That was because "Russia has formed a market economy of a noncompetitive type. It is an oligarchical economy, an economy of privileges taking a more and more hidden form. They are not that clear. There's a desire to make the country more closed—to allow privileges, to curb internal competition. This will not work over the long term. Even though a company may be strong in Russia, it won't be able to compete with a strong global corporation."

In order for his own business to survive, Bendukidze admitted, he might have to unite his holding company, Bioprocess, with one of the larger financial-industrial groups. "It could turn out that I have no other choice but to become part of a bigger structure. About ten bankers control the greatest part of the [state] budget and the most important liquid layers of the economy. Maybe there will be others, but some are already very strong. No matter where you look in the market, they are there."

Bendukidze worried that the big groups would crowd out smaller groups like his, or even much smaller businesses, and keep them from operating. The financial-industrial giants already controlled a huge chunk of Russian exports. The service sector was falling under their influence. Small business needed to grow faster. Although close to a million new small businesses had sprung up and were operating (mostly in the black market), they found it tough to survive. (Economist Richard Layard has pointed out that companies with fewer than one hundred workers employ half of all workers in the West but only 13 percent of workers in Russia.)[15] Banks didn't offer loans to small companies. The raket skimmed off 20 to 30 percent in protection money. Russia's scenario would look better, Bendukidze argued, if the huge groups helped smaller companies to grow and compete as well.[16]

Others were even more harsh in their criticism of the financial-industrial groups. "They are very, very prominent and very, very influential. But as to the share of everything that they sometimes claim—it's ridiculous. They are nowhere near to the concentration of wealth that they claim," said banker and parliamentary deputy Boris Fyodorov, who had served as minister of finance in 1993.[17] (He was never one to mince words.)

"It's clear that there are quite a few people for whom a million dollars is nothing. Ten million—100, 200 million. There are quite a few people already who amassed this—mostly in not very nice ways, and they never declared it," said Fyodorov. "But in general it's still not the level of concentration that you hear about. And the division of property goes on."

"We are still in transition," Fyodorov continued. "It's clear that a lot of the mechanisms of the market economy started working—private property, property incentives, competition, and many others do work. At the same time, obviously not all mechanisms work, and it's clear that the role of the state has not been defined properly in the sense that the government has not separated itself from purely commercial activities. And obviously the corruption and very unscrupulous links to business—and profits—are at an incredible level. It has increased by one hundred times at least since I was in government in 1993."

"It's clear that most of the major privatization projects are very smelly," Fyodorov concluded. "And some of them stink."

What politician wouldn't say that things got worse after he left office? Still, I agreed with much of Fyodorov's analysis. Russia was too big for seven or ten businesspeople to control it. They weren't strong enough to monopolize the economy totally, and, as I expected, they soon began fighting with each other over assets up for grabs in privatizations and other market issues.

Indeed, it seemed sometimes that Russia was more like an overgrown Italy than a South Korea or a mafia-driven state like Colombia. In fact, a bigger share of property was in private hands in Russia than in Italy.[18] But, as in Italy, in Russia large conglomerates held leading places in industry, and they were made up of formerly state-owned structures that

had been privatized. Like Italy's, Russia's underground economy operated freely alongside the real economy, and people thought nothing of
simply not paying the state's exorbitantly high taxes. As in Italy, in Russia the mafia controlled important sectors of the economy. And, as in
Italy, in Russia the state was so weak that people had largely lost faith
in the idea that government would help them.

Yes, Russia was very much a giant, complicated state where private
industrial conglomerates, state-owned structures, small (often underground) businesses, and organized crime coexisted in an ever-changing yet somehow growing economic organism. But, as Bendukidze said,
Russia's future would depend heavily on how much competition would
drive growth within the country and on whether millions of new small
businesses would emerge to provide new goods and services and to ab-
sorb excess labor shed by dying industrial enterprises. Many of the people that I knew who were running small businesses were still engaged
in a constant battle against the Russian taxman, against corrupt bureaucrats who withheld licenses in exchange for bribes, and against
competition from much larger and better-financed trading houses
linked to banks or larger companies. "Soon I wonder whether any small
business will be left in Russia," one small-scale trader on the verge of
bankruptcy told me.

Much would still depend on the policies and, more immediately, on
the health of the president.

The country and indeed the world waited nervously as Yeltsin un-
derwent surgery on November 5, 1996. A team of surgeons operated
on the president for six hours, performing a quintuple coronary bypass
operation. Yeltsin not only survived; he seemed to recover quickly.
Within days he was walking, and within a month he was ready to return
to the Kremlin. Then more trouble: he came down with pneumonia and
was out for several more weeks. It was not until March 6, 1997, that
Yeltsin finally regained his health and truly reasserted his authority on
the political scene. The one-time boxer came back in fighting form,
sixty pounds lighter and far more energetic.

In his address to the nation that day, Yeltsin admitted that Russia was weighed down "with a heavy burden of problems," especially in the economy. Calling for the end of corruption, stronger state regulation of monopolies, tax reform, and a stronger focus on social policy, he declared: "In the year 2000, Russia will elect a new president. I want to hand over to my successor a country with a dynamically growing economy, with an effective and just system of social protection, a country whose citizens are confident of their future."[19]

A few days later, Yeltsin appointed Anatoly Chubais as first deputy prime minister in charge of the economy, ousting Potanin from that position. Then he shook up the rest of the cabinet, firing most of the other ministers as well. In a surprise move, he tapped Boris Nemtsov, the thirty-seven-year-old reformist governor of the Nizhny Novgorod region. His task: to oversee reform of Russia's social welfare system and to regulate Russia's so-called natural monopolies—Gazprom, the sprawling electrical utility known as RAO United Energy System, and the Russian railroads. Although Nemtsov called himself a "kamikaze" because he would have to take on some of the country's most powerful entrenched interests, many Russians also assumed that Yeltsin was grooming him as a possible successor.

By mid-1997, a new "liberal revolution," as Chubais called it, was under way. Nemtsov worked on getting Gazprom and the other natural-resource monopolies to forge agreements with the government on paying trillions in back taxes. Chernomyrdin went to the parliament and informed deputies that the government had no choice: it had to cut spending by about 20 percent, slicing subsidies for industry and agriculture and drastically cutting the military budget. Yeltsin announced a major reform of the military, which was in desperate shape (soldiers were literally going hungry); the goal was to create a professional army. And the government began pushing for tax reform, arguing for the abolition of many tax privileges and a reduction in the number of taxes.

But how liberal would the revolution really prove, and how long would it last? The financial-industrial groups continued to expand their power. In a new wave of privatization, the government sold off stakes in Tyumen Oil Company and in its giant telecommunications monopoly, Svyazinvest. This time, the government insisted, the tenders were fair: the bidder with the highest offer won the stakes. Alfa Group (together with Renova, owner of the Vladimir Tractor Factory) won a 40 percent stake in Tyumen Oil, owner of one of the country's largest oil fields in Nizhnevartovsk. And UnExim Bank bought the telecommunications company for $1.8 billion (with help from international investor George Soros and Deutsche Bank's investment banking arm).

At the same time, banks began selling shares that they had picked up in the loans-for-shares auctions. Predictably, they usually managed to sell the stakes to themselves or to affiliated companies. Monblan, a company believed to be a shell for Menatep, bought the bank's stake in Yukos. An UnExim Bank affiliate won the auction for Norilsk Nickel. On paper, the bankers could claim that the companies were separate organizations, independent units not directly linked to their banks. But few people were fooled by such nodding and winking.

Potanin's opponents—a group involving Vladimir Gusinsky's Most Group and, observers said, backed by Boris Berezovsky—immediately protested the Svyazinvest sale. They had expected to win the auction. (According to some sources, they had been given private assurances that they would be tapped.) And they were angry when Potanin outbid them and won, apparently fairly and squarely.

So much for Berezovsky's united front of capital willing to work together to determine Russia's future. UnExim Bank was consolidating its position as the country's most powerful conglomerate, and the other banks didn't like it one bit. The fight over Svyazinvest really boiled down to an argument over the rules of the game of Russian capitalism. Was the government favoring UnExim Bank, as Gusinsky and Berezovsky claimed in the Russian press, or had the top bidder in fact won? Would future privatizations and indeed future business dealings be done on a basis of fair and consistent rules that applied equally to everyone, or would insider deals remain the norm?

As was often the case in these situations, it was difficult to tell who was lying and who was telling the truth. The government and Potanin insisted that the tender was fair. And, on the surface, it did seem fair. Gusinsky's and Berezovsky's camp insisted that the government favored one bank—UnExim Bank—over all the others. Perhaps someday evidence that the auction was rigged will turn up. But in the meantime, their protests sounded to many (including me) like sour grapes.[20]

Throughout the summer of 1997, newspapers and television newscasts debated the Svyazinvest deal, the role of the bankers, and the question of whether the government was favoring Potanin. But this was not a straightforward example of a free press flushing out the truth. Gusinsky's and Berezovsky's media organs—*Segodnya,* NTV, and ORT (the Russian public television channel, partly owned by Berezovsky)—were defending their owners and attacking both Potanin and Chubais, who was in charge of economic policy. Finally, in late August, Alfred Kokh, the privatization minister who had conducted the Svyazinvest deal, resigned. Many speculated that, in doing so, he was taking responsibility for playing favorites with Potanin, with whom he happened to be friends. But there was another version of these events: Kokh had stepped down because he had promised Gusinsky and Berezovsky that their consortium would win. When Potanin bid highest, Kokh was forced to name him the winner. Gusinsky and Berezovsky, according to the story that circulated around Moscow, were angry that Kokh didn't live up to his pledge to do an insider deal with them.

Like the earlier loans-for-shares auctions, the Svyazinvest deal seemed like an important turning point, or at least an important marker of the government's intentions. I wanted to ask Chubais to explain his privatization strategy and his new push for "liberalization."

In an interview in the Russian White House, which the government had occupied since the violent events of October 1993, Chubais explained his view of the deteriorating relationships among the seven bankers and of the rift between some bankers and the government. "The relations between government and business are changing," he began. "My understanding is that until mid-1996, the major problem, the fundamental historical problem, for Russia was Communism versus capitalism. I think and I really believe that now this historical problem has been solved. I don't believe for any chance for a Communist to be elected as president in my country, ever. We won. What is the next stage? I think the next stage is strengthening the rules of the game—introducing rules of the game that are mandatory for everybody, regardless of the scale of the business or the role of the business leader in the political life of Russia. I believe that's the only way to civilized capitalism in Russia."

"It's not the easy way, and I couldn't say that every business leader in Russia is completely happy about this kind of understanding," he admitted. "But for me, that's the basic principle for which I, my whole team, Boris Nemtsov, Prime Minister Chernomyrdin, and President Yeltsin, will stand for."[21]

Chubais apparently had a new crusade. After years of struggles, he had defeated the Communists. He had brought private ownership to Russia. Now, it seemed, he did want to return to something closer to his original, liberal vision of a transparent, open economy. "What about the oligarchy?" I asked. "What about the Rule of the Seven Bankers?"

"I don't think it's bad that Russia has seven banks which are major banks," he replied. "I think it's bad that other businesses are not strong enough. We have to support the policy that will give any business a chance. It's a policy that will not give any special privileges for seven or six or ten businesses. It should be the same rules for everybody. And maybe in a year, maybe it will be seventy instead of seven, and not just banks. So it's just a stage. Two years ago, there weren't seven banks in Russia that could compete. In two years, we shall have seventy banks like the seven we have now.

"One of the major principles is to implement the single rules of the game. Implementing these single rules of the game, unfortunately we have to struggle at each stage with one or another bank."

Berezovsky had a different point of view and was tough in expressing it. We chatted one Saturday afternoon in the elegant business club that one of his companies, the Logovaz Group, had opened in a renovated prerevolutionary mansion. "I think that Chubais is making a principal mistake now," Berezovsky said. "And unfortunately, it has happened so that the first one that used this mistake was Potanin. But the problem is not in Potanin, the problem is with Chubais and his understanding of the nowadays situation in Russia. The problem is that we don't want to have more revolutions in Russia."[22]

"In one day, Chubais decided that he as first deputy prime minister and the representatives of capital do not have a basis for discussion. It means that he as a member of the government doesn't need to take into consideration the opinion of business," Berezovsky asserted. "No one insists that business should make decisions. But it is important to understand the position of business, the way that the business community thinks about the future. This is necessary for our current government. We don't want to have more revolutions in Russia. I think Chubais has another way of thinking."

"My understanding is that today we need to make another step, but I don't want to do it in a Bolshevik manner," he concluded. "It is impossible to change the rules in one day like Chubais tried to do it. Chubais doesn't have a real basis of support in Russia except Russian capital because society in general doesn't accept his privatization, doesn't accept the quick transformation. The only group that accepts it is real business.

"And today, whether Chubais likes it or not, it is the only basis for the power that exists. And it's very important that business understands well its responsibility for the future of the country. Business understands well that we need to move to a civil society—but not in one day."

Berezovsky seemed to want to have his cake and eat it too. He agreed with the need to change the rules, to make them fairer—"but not in one day." His words resembled those of the old industrial elite in 1990 and 1991, when they were trying to hold off price reform and privatization. Of course, they said, let us have reform. But only if we benefit and lose nothing.

Whether Berezovsky liked it or not, Potanin was building up his financial-industrial group. The three pillars would be Norilsk Nickel, the telecommunications company Svyazinvest, and oil holdings like the oil company Sidanko. Potanin was busy cutting costs, restructuring debts, and firing ineffectual managers. He brought in American managers from Shell Oil Company to reorganize Sidanko. He was determined to squeeze value from his industrial assets.

"This year will be the first year that Norilsk Nickel is without losses," Potanin said, quietly but proudly. "Last year, the old management planned 4 trillion rubles of losses, about $800 million. You can imagine it's not possible to work with a company that has such debts. By the way, the whole amount of debt is $2 billion. That's the reason for the low price [when we bought it.] Because it's easy to say theoretically that Norilsk Nickel is such an attractive thing, that everybody wants to buy it. But when it has $2 billion [in] debts, I don't know. . . . And it has $2.5 billion of cash flow per year. Can you imagine a company in the U.S. with such cash flow and such debts? You never know. Maybe it's easier to declare it bankrupt."[23]

I asked him about the flap over Svyazinvest. "You know it's very funny," he began. "Chubais said, 'Look, I like you, but please don't ask me for favors.' Just go to the auction and pay money. Everybody went to the auction and paid money. Afterwards, all those who lost started to say that Chubais has some preference. They asked for a favor, but they were refused. Very funny."

"The same thing with Kokh," Potanin said. "The fact that we are personal friends doesn't mean that this was the basis for us [to win]. If we could buy Svyazinvest at a cheaper price, you can imagine that this creates a basis for corruption. A commercial company gets something from the government cheaper than it costs on the market, it creates a basis for corruption. But when this possibility is eliminated, it's good for the government."

Potanin went on to say that his rivals, led by Gusinsky, had proposed that he not bid in the Svyazinvest deal. "When I was first deputy prime minister, they [told] Chubais that UnExim shouldn't participate when Potanin is in government." It wasn't fair, they argued. "I said, 'What's unfair?' If you consider that I am linked to UnExim, I should be eliminated from the government. If I'm not eliminated, it means that UnExim is free to do whatever it wants."

"But Chubais said maybe it's not crucial for UnExim to bid, and that maybe I could ask [my partner] Prokhorov to refrain from participating in order not to create a bad political situation. It was Chubais's request," Potanin explained. "I said, 'Okay, if it's your personal request, I will make a personal request to Prokhorov to refrain from participating in this case just as a friendly favor to me.' It was like this. But after that, I left the government. Of course I was free to participate. They continued to ask me to refrain. I said there was no basis for this."

All those informal talks underscored just how much business and government had grown accustomed to working together and how much they relied on favors from each other. In the end, Potanin argued, the fact that his bank had participated in the Svyazinvest auction meant that the government won a higher price for its 25 percent of the company.

On July 4, 1997, a year after his reelection to the presidency, Yeltsin announced that Russia's economy had hit bottom. "That is it. We have reached the point when it is possible for production to go up. The decline has been stopped."[24] It had been almost six years since Yeltsin had warned Russians, in October 1991, that they would have to suffer for six months as a result of price liberalization and radical economic reforms. In that time, inflation had been conquered. The ruble was stable. Most of the economy had been transferred to private hands. Private companies employed more than 70 percent of the workforce. A banking system had begun to take hold. The stock market was soaring. And, with Yeltsin cracking the whip, the government was at long last beginning to pay its wages and pensions on time.

Yet it would still turn out to be a very long haul. In an event hardly noticed in Russia, just a few days before Yeltsin's bold proclamation that the turnaround had begun, a financial crisis began to unfold in another emerging market—Thailand. When the government of Thailand was forced to devalue its currency, the baht, in the first days of July 1997, it was the start of a dangerous economic process that would, over the next several months, come to threaten the financial stability of emerging markets around the world, including Russia's. In what was to later seem a cruel irony (at least it seemed so to me), at that moment things were truly beginning to look up for Russia, for many Russians, and for long-struggling Russian enterprises. Interest rates for government bonds had fallen from more than 150 percent the year before to 20 percent by July 1997. And banks were at last beginning to lend to cash-starved industrial companies.

Like other troubled factories, the Vladimir Tractor Factory, which had been in such dire straits the year before, was moving forward again. Josef Bakaleynik, still CEO, was starting to spend some of his time at Tyumen Oil Company, which his partner Len Blavatnik's Renova had bought together with Alfa Group.

I went to talk to Bakaleynik at his Tyumen Oil office in a new, red-brick business complex in Moscow. The room was sparsely decorated, and there were few papers on his desk. It was clear that he was spending just part of his time there while he held down two jobs. Over tea and cookies, Bakaleynik expressed his hope that the Vladimir Tractor Factory was "finally getting out of the woods."[25]

Morale was desperately low at the plant, he admitted. Another 1,000 workers had left or been laid off, bringing the workforce down to 5,500—a shadow of its previous strength. And the factory owed the workers an average of four months' wages, Bakaleynik acknowledged. But orders were up, and because interest rates were falling, the bank had secured a credit line and was able to pick up production. "Before the banks were just playing games with the Ministry of Finance—lending to the government at outrageous rates and basically lending to the government what they got from it," he observed. "But now that game is over, so they have to look for real customers and real business. That certainly helps us."

Bakaleynik was revving up the assembly line to produce 350 to 400 tractors a month—nothing compared to the old days, but enough to break even and pay his workers. He had started negotiations with a European company about a partnership that would bring in new investment. Bakaleynik's goal remained the same: to raise money on the international markets for the factory. But he no longer dreamed of selling out and walking away with a few cool millions. "I may sell some, but all the improvements will come in another three, four, five years." And he admitted that his early expectations about turning around the plant had been unrealistic.

"My expectations have changed. If you remember, in 1993 and 1994, they were quite different. I was thinking about two or three years for the real change," Bakaleynik recalled. He laughed, a little ruefully. But he had not been alone in underestimating the challenges ahead, and through it all the Vladimir Tractor Factory had survived. "It looks like we've been able to muddle through the most difficult period. The company is still alive, and demand is picking up domestically."

Industrial production had begun to pick up not just in Vladimir but elsewhere around the country.[26] By the end of 1997, the economy was to grow 0.4 percent—the first year of growth since before Yeltsin launched his reforms in 1992. The government was forecasting that growth would pick up to hit 2 percent in 1998 and 4 to 5 percent in 1999 and 2000—just in time, in other words, for the next round of parliamentary and presidential elections.[27]

But as often was the case for Russia, reality would prove harsher than many expected or hoped. By late 1997, the financial crisis that had begun in Asia was affecting the financial markets in Russia, as it was those in Brazil, Mexico, and other countries. Around the world, top-ranking investors, funds, and brokerage houses began reassessing the economic strength and creditworthiness of countries wherein they had just recently been happy to pour millions. Also strapped for cash as they lost money in Asia, investors began pulling out of Russia's GKO, or Treasury bill, market, rushing to cash rubles into dollars and straining the Russian currency. The Central Bank hustled to defend the ruble, dipping into its reserves and jacking up interest rates to 40 percent and later much higher.

The financial crisis struck a mortal blow to Russia's long-delayed turnaround. Instead of watching their economy grow at 2 percent to 5 percent, as the government had hoped would occur, Russians seemed more likely to face a continued slump—no growth until 2000 or perhaps even later. For the government and for big oil companies like Lukoil and Yukos, the picture was darkened still further as world oil prices began to plunge. That meant not only lower profits for the companies but far fewer revenues for the government, since oil exports still contributed a huge percentage of Russia's foreign currency reserves and tax revenues.

It was to take several months for the true depth of the crisis to sink in. Meanwhile, other problems remained as well. Boris Nemtsov faced an extraordinary challenge in curbing the power of monopolies like Gazprom and forcing them to contribute their fair share to the government. Although Chernomyrdin publicly expressed his support for Yeltsin's and the reformers' new liberalization campaign, many Russians and Western observers began to believe that the prime minister was working behind the scenes to block the young reformers' efforts. As many companies and individuals ignored their tax bills, tax collection fell far short of the government's needs. One factor that contributed to the tax shortfall was the growing virtual industrial economy—the vast network of barter payments that allowed unproductive enterprises to keep functioning, if barely, even though they were not economically viable. The virtual economy had grown bigger and bigger as the government had delayed forcing companies into bankruptcy and closing them down. By the end of 1997, nearly 50 percent of all transactions between enterprises in Russia were done through barter rather than cash. This payment method represented one more way to evade taxes, yet the government itself also contributed to the problem. It allowed companies—such as Gazprom and the giant utility Unified Energy System—to pay its tax bill in goods rather than money.

All in all, Russia was still living far beyond its means. Its health, scientific, and educational infrastructures were creaking, if not crumbling, and the government didn't have the funds to finance them properly, let alone improve them. Millions of people—some 20 percent of the population—still lived in poverty.[28] Both state-funded organizations like schools and hospitals and many private enterprises still paid their wages months late. True, the middle class was growing—but slowly. The economy cried out for millions more small businesses to provide jobs and spur growth.

What was most striking about Russia's economy after five years of reform was how varied it was from place to place: Russia had become a patchwork of many different local and regional economies, all loosely sewn together. Some were growing, others were still struggling. Some were run by pro-market, pro-democracy leaders who wanted their regions to prosper. They worked to attract foreign investment to provide jobs. Other regions operated more like fiefdoms on behalf of their elite, who milked the economy for their own gain.

Moscow represented a unique swatch within this patchwork. Kept firmly in hand by its popular, authoritative mayor, Yuri Luzhkov, Moscow was booming by the fall of 1997. Luzhkov was an old-style apparatchik who had figured out how to turn the new market economy to the city's (and some said to his own) advantage. Partly through a financial-industrial group called Systema—The System—the city government was involved in hundreds of businesses, from hotels to fast-food chains to exhibition centers.

Construction cranes dotted the Moscow skyline. Luzhkov had fixed the potholes, repaved the ring road circling the city, and even revamped the zoo, where the animals had nearly starved just a few years before. And Luzhkov made sure that everyone knew who was behind all the positive changes in the city. He organized an enormous celebration to mark the city's 850th anniversary in September 1997. Every storefront in Moscow posted banners or posters congratulating the city on its birthday, while Luzhkov invited dignitaries and entertainers from all over the country and from abroad. He even seeded the clouds over Moscow to keep the sun shining.

Was Luzhkov laying the groundwork for a presidential bid in 2000, when Yeltsin's term would run out? Most people assumed so.

Whatever Luzhkov's motivations, his leadership had helped to ensure that no other Russian city could quite match Moscow as a center for business and wealth. Indeed, economists estimated that Moscow was a magnet for some 85 percent of the new capital flowing into Russia. Black spots of industrial decline still dotted the rest of the country, from the textile city of Ivanovo to the steel towns in the Urals, such as Magnitogorsk. In some areas, such as Vladivostok and the surrounding Primorski Krai, anti-Yeltsin politicians had stalled reforms, even provoking shortages of electricity and key supplies.

Yet it was possible to find areas of dynamism far from the capital. Novgorod was attracting billions in foreign investment. Although many of its old defense enterprises were still struggling, Nizhny Novgorod was managing to survive, after hustling to be in the vanguard of market experiments. Even within towns that still faced difficulties, such as Vladimir, it was possible to find pockets of prosperity.

To look at Russia at any one time was to have the possibility of seeing all these pluses and minuses, the good and the bad, all together. The vastness of Russia made it possible for observers to choose to see the glass as half-full or as half-empty—and at any given moment. Russia's situation after five years of transition was mixed. There were winners and losers. I had met both.

In the fall of 1997, I asked several of Russia's early reformers to look back and reflect on the ups and downs, the turning points and disappointments, of five years of Russia's transition to capitalism.

Yegor Gaidar, the architect of Yeltsin's initial shock therapy, was philosophical. "In some aspects, it generally is what we wanted to accomplish," he told me. "We wanted a working market: no shortages; an open, stable currency; a competitive economy with a big private sector; increased participation of foreign investors. In some aspects it is what we hoped we would achieve in 1991, when confronted with socialism that disintegrated every day. Just compare Moscow in 1991 to Moscow now," he challenged.[29]

"We thought from the beginning that it would be a difficult struggle. We hoped we could achieve financial stability already in 1993 instead of in 1997. At the beginning, we thought that the division of property and power would be the most difficult [task]. We generally understood the problems of our social heritage and its influence on the development of socialism. But we did not think it would be quite so difficult as it turned out to be."

Gaidar went on to say that what evolved was "the inevitable outcome of a society in change." The word he used to describe what was happening in Russia from 1991 to 1993 was "revolution." In any revolution, tragedies can happen, and what the government was struggling to do, he said, was prevent a "tragedy—especially a tragedy in a country of nuclear arms."

There were, he said, two choices: to destroy the elite by force, or to compromise. The first option risked fomenting a civil war. The second option, therefore, was the only choice. That's why the government decided to allow the elite to grab property in exchange for power. "Strategically, it was the only possible solution," Gaidar reflected. "Personally, I would have liked the compromise to have been cheaper for the country. But it was inevitable."

Gaidar considered Chernomyrdin's appointment to the government as the key turning point for Russia. The power of the "fuel and energy lobby," from which Chernomyrdin came, helped ensure the crucial compromise that Chubais made in the early stages of privatization: the deal allowing enterprise managers, together with their workers, to win control of their companies. As he analyzed the years of reform, Gaidar phrased his answers for me carefully, perhaps trying to avoid admitting that he had made mistakes. The oligarchical system that evolved in Russia, Gaidar argued, was an almost natural consequence of Chernomyrdin's appointments, first as fuel and energy minister and later as prime minister.

I wasn't so sure. Of course, Chernomyrdin had played an enormous role, although not always a positive one. But didn't Gaidar's first partner in reform—Anatoly Chubais—lose his principles somewhere along the road? Chubais had wanted an open, liberal market economy. He had wanted to break the influence that state planners, bureaucrats, and politicians had on enterprises. But to push through privatization, Chubais had compromised with the old industrial and bureaucratic elite. Surely he had failed to depoliticize the economy.

"I don't think that Chubais ever changed his views," Gaidar replied. "He worked in different governments and in different situations. In 1996, he stayed with his view and worked so that Russia would not return to the Communist experience. We were happy to make a big alliance to prevent that."

But, Gaidar added, there was no doubt that something far from liberal capitalism had evolved in Russia. "Russia never had liberal capitalism. It was a socialist dictatorship. We now have an oligarchical capitalism. The problem is how can we proceed." The oligarchy was "much, much deeper" than just seven banks, he explained. The oligarchy included representatives of former Communist structures and socialist-era enterprise directors in leading positions of power all across the country. Yet he felt that Russia still had a chance of developing a more liberal version of capitalism. It was on the road to developing a "civil society," he pointed out. And the middle class was rapidly developing.

I thought back to what Gaidar had said to me five years before, when he was just starting out. The goals he had articulated then had been modest. He had wanted to create the preconditions for economic growth in Russia: he mentioned specifically liberal prices, an open economy, a fairly strict budget, a relatively just distribution of goods. All these goals had been achieved, even though growth had not yet taken off. But the process had been much messier and more painful than most observers, back in 1991 and early 1992, had imagined that it would be. And the gains would prove to be so fragile.

Chubais also agreed to reflect on the successes and failures of the previous five years. How did Russia's market economy compare to his original vision?

In an interview at the White House, he replied: "I think some of it is much more optimistic than I could have predicted. And some of it is much more pessimistic. First of all, if you told me in 1992 that in five years we shall have 70 percent of GDP produced in the private sector, I wouldn't have believed you."[30]

"Even though you were planning the privatization program?" I interjected.

"Absolutely. Because at that time it looked politically absolutely impossible and unrealistic. I still believe that private property is the fundamental value and one of the major pillars not only of the economy in Russia but of freedom in Russia. And the outcome of the presidential elections is also the result of the private property spreading in Russia. That's positive."

But, Chubais continued, "if you would tell me in 1992 that our fight with inflation—which was at the center of our policy and was the most difficult fight—if you would tell me that in January 1995, we will have monthly inflation of 18 percent, I wouldn't believe you. Or I would say in 1992 that if we will still have in the beginning of 1995 such a high level of monthly inflation, it would mean that politically we will be completely anarchic.

"So it's two strange things—first that it was not nothing that we accomplished, and the second that it demanded such enormous efforts, such a huge battle to fight inflation in Russia. In 1995, it was achieved; inflation came down finally. Last August [1996] we had −0.1 percent of inflation."

Chubais had a bit more to say about the fallout from inflation. "But having the inflation later, longer, than we anticipated, than we would have liked to, we see the whole recovery of the Russian economy coming much later than it could have been. That is the greatest political burden that we bear today. That's why if we had been able to fight inflation not in 1995 but in 1993, I am sure that in 1996 we would have had economic growth in Russia.

"Now we can say that economic growth is the task for 1998. 1997 is the first year of no fall in Russian industry."

Chubais returned to the question that had prompted these thoughts, alluding to how today's Russia contrasted with his earlier vision for the country. "Now, if I discuss the standards of living in Russia, I have big misunderstandings. On the one hand, at $140 per month, the average wage in Russia now is very low. It is one of the major problems in Russia. But on the other hand, the average wage in Ukraine is about thirty-five dollars. Armenia is twenty dollars per month. So there is no single evaluation of this kind of situation. That's why I say that something is more optimistic and something more pessimistic than you could have predicted [in 1991]. And if you would ask me is it realistic that I would be in the government in 1997, I would laugh."

What about the oligarchical system? Did he think that would be a feature of Russian capitalism from the start?

"I didn't expect it. And in some way, it looks very positive because in 1993 and 1994, we had a number of former state-owned banks or state companies that were failing and that demanded money from the government and criticized our policy. But I didn't expect this level of concentration of the national economy that we have now. For me, it's not the result I would have liked to have."

I asked why the oligarchical system had come about. Was it the result, in his view, of his political compromises?

"The Russian economy is quite a complicated thing," he answered. "It's not just a car that you start and then drive left or right. There are a number of complicated factors and reasons moderating the whole thing."

He continued: "In my own activity in the government from 1991 until 1995, I always had to solve problems that looked like black and white, death and life. Will there be privatization, or will there not be privatization? Will the inflation go down, or will it never go down? Will Communists win? Or will they not win? That's the kind of problem I've had to solve during the whole time of my activity. It's not the best time for getting a very sophisticated compromise. If you are in a black-and-white position, you have to concentrate everything and everybody you can for reaching the goal. By doing it, you will be strongly criticized that your compromise was not very good. But you always have to weigh the problem you have and the means that you have to solve it. The final answer was June 1996, and that was the right answer."

I asked Chubais what he thought Russia's economy would look like in another five years—in 2002.

"We will have economic growth between 7 and 10 percent per year. The median wage will be between six hundred and one thousand dollars a month." And, he added, Russia would have a vibrant middle class.

I pondered the reformers' words. Gaidar had failed in the political game early on, but had remained closely in touch with the reform process. He had played an important role as an outsider, frequently conferring with Chubais and other pro-reform members of the Chernomyrdin government. Unlike the more academic Gaidar, Chubais had grown into a skilled political tactician. He had come up against fierce opponents of reform, and in the political-economic game that ensued he had not always played clean. But he had kept his eye on the prize. The prize was a non-Communist Russia in which private property dominated the economy. From his point of view, fine-tuning or improving the system could come later. That was the task he had set for himself and for the government by the end of 1997.

Freeing Russia's economy can be seen as the latest in a series of Russian reformations stretching back centuries. The story could be traced at least to Peter the Great and his efforts to build a proud and well-equipped Russian military in the early 1700s. There was Alexander II, who freed the serfs in 1861. Finance minister Sergei Witte guided Russia's industrial expansion in the last decade of the nineteenth century, and Peter Stolypin attempted to introduce private landownership into Russia's peasant communities between 1906 and 1911. (The plan was dropped after he was assassinated.) Vladimir Lenin, of course, turned fledgling Russian capitalism on its head with his Bolshevik Revolution. By combining fear, repression, and five-year plans, Joseph Stalin completed the industrialization of Russia as he centralized all economic decision-making, placing it in the hands of the Communist Party and state planners.

All these reforms represented supreme efforts to overcome Russia's backwardness compared to the rest of Europe. And, as historian Alexander Gerschenkron has written, all of them failed. The main reason, Gerschenkron explains, was that the harsh, top-down reforms held the seeds of their own failure. In almost every instance, the new programs were introduced in a bid to make Russia stronger militarily, which the state accomplished by developing its defense capabilities at the expense of the common people. In the end, these periods of economic growth accompanied by oppression—whether led by Peter the Great or by Stalin—were always followed by lapses into stagnation. The exhausted population could sacrifice no longer.[31]

Until the Gorbachev-Yeltsin era, the industrial boom of 1890–1914 seemed to be the only exception to this futile pattern. In those years Russia seemed to shed its deep-rooted ambivalence toward profit, business, industrial development, and capitalism. In the 1890s the government, led by Witte, pursued a "Germanization" (rather than an "Americanization") of the economy—a financial policy aimed at stimulating industrial expansion. Using state credits, Russia imported German and British technology, constructed huge textile plants, developed its oil and mining industries, and built railroads stretching from Europe to Asia. Instead of taxing the peasants to pay for this industrial boom, Stolypin took a radical, liberalizing move that made it possible for peasants to leave their farm collective or obschina by acquiring personal title to their share of the land and selling it. This controversial reform, made in 1906, opened the way for peasants to leave their farm and join the industrial labor force. By easing up on the peasants, Gerschenkron argues, the Russian leadership helped fuel a period of growth that was the most sustained of any in Russia's economic history.

Between 1906 and 1914, Russia's economy grew steadily. The general public's and the intelligentsia's attitudes toward entrepreneurs and industrialists became more favorable. Banks began to offer long-term credit to industrial companies, easing the state's financial burden. Workers' wages began to improve. Of course, there were problems. The state had failed to support small businesses. And a movement for a more democratic form of rule was growing among discontented intellectuals and workers. Still, as Gerschenkron writes, "one might surmise that in the absence of the war, Russia would have continued on the road of progressive westernization."[32] Unfortunately, World War I intervened.

Like Russia's spurt of industrialization in the late 1800s and early 1900s, Russia's transition to capitalism beginning in 1992 held great promise. Although the government once again imposed reform on the population, it did so in an era of relative political freedom. As they reacted to the shock of economic freedom or the opportunities presented to them by privatization, Russians were able to find their own economic solutions. The underground economy was a source of dynamism and a crucial safety valve, providing an outlet for workers put on extended vacations by factories that could no longer afford to pay them. By granting political and economic freedom to workers—even if the freedoms weren't complete or were marred by bureaucratic and mafia interference—the government gave itself a greater chance of success. There was one other crucial difference between Yeltsin's reforms and those of earlier decades and centuries: the goal was not to strengthen Russia militarily but to save and then improve its economy.

Throughout its five-year transition, Russia proved that the laws of market economics could also work in a country set back by seventy years of socialist experiments and an even longer intellectual tradition of anticapitalist attitudes. When Russians faced the opportunity or the necessity to make money, they worked to find ways to do so. Owners looked for ways to improve the value of their property and to defend it. And the macroeconomy responded similarly to market laws. When the Central Bank printed trillions of rubles (to cite just one example), inflation indeed went up.

Yet Russian capitalism could not but possess its own special characteristics. Russia's form of capitalism took shape as entrepreneurs, managers, and ordinary citizens sought opportunities for arbitrage in the distortions of the semistate, semiplanned, partially private economy as the government freed up the old state-controlled system. Most important, Russia's form of capitalism developed as a result of a massive redistribution of wealth—the vast property, industrial, and natural-resource assets, nearly 100 percent of which had been controlled by the state. This very fact set the Yeltsin era of Russian capitalism apart from early, prerevolutionary capitalism in Russia and from early capitalism in countries like the United States or Britain. In early capitalist America and Britain, the economies were less developed; the entrepreneurs began small, and they slowly built up whole industries—steel, railroads, oil, retailing, banking.

Central Europe was a different case. The economies of Poland, Hungary, and East Germany had been ruined by central planning, which had been imposed by Stalin after World War II. By contrast, in Russia (as Grigory Yavlinsky, the economist who became a presidential candidate in 1996, often remarked), the economy had been "*created*by central planning." Stalin had largely industrialized the country through brute force and five-year plans.[33] The task, then, was to dismantle the machine. Yeltsin and his government were trying to turn socialist industry into capitalist industry by dividing up the state's assets and hoping that the new owners would take steps needed to make their new enterprises competitive.

It was a big job—far bigger than the reform effort made by Poland a few years earlier. Although Gaidar and the early reformers modeled their initial shock therapy and price liberalization on the Polish experience, Russia's reforms proved to be far more complicated. Not only was Russia's economy larger and more heavily dominated by the state at the start of reforms; Russia also lacked the strong political consensus for change that Poland initially enjoyed. That slowed down the process of both political and economic renewal, allowing socialist-era managers and bureaucrats to block changes and even prevent economic growth. (Some economists argue that Poland's economy hit 7 percent growth long before Russia turned around precisely because the Polish government interfered much less with private businesses and was more supportive of a market economy, even though Poland's privatization program lagged behind Russia's.)[34]

So political realities proved just as important as specific economic measures in forging Russian capitalism. After Yeltsin freed prices and began preparing a privatization program, it didn't take long for opponents among enterprise managers and bureaucrats to start demanding a watering down of reforms and greater opportunities to hold onto or grab further power. A struggle erupted for state subsidies and cheap state credits. Prodded by Chubais, the government compromised on privatization, granting managers rights to easily acquire control of their state plants. He barely got privatization moving before the architect of reforms, Yegor Gaidar, was ousted by a Russian Congress of People's Deputies in December 1992.

Yeltsin's opponents in parliament kept pushing to roll back his reforms, to curb his powers, to impeach him. Time and again, Yeltsin took drastic measures to combat his opponents, won, and then failed to take advantage of the momentum. The referendum in April 1993—when the public, surprisingly, backed Yeltsin's harsh reforms—was one such instance. The bloody clash at the White House in October 1993, after Yeltsin suspended the parliament, was another. (Three months later, the opposition made tremendous gains in elections for the new parliament.) Politics and economics ticked along with periodic crises throughout 1994 and 1995, as Prime Minister Chernomyrdin strengthened the role of the government bureaucracy. In late 1995, when it looked as if the Communists had a chance of returning to power, Chubais again compromised on privatization—by selling off to banks the gems of Russia's state assets, which had been held back in early phases of the program—the oil, metals, and transport companies—in exchange for cheap loans to shore up the government budget. Said one source close to Chubais: "He looked around and realized that the Communists might be coming back. So he decided to dump the assets as quickly as possible, just as he had done in 1992."[35] But that compromise may have helped to secure Yeltsin's reelection. Banks and businesspeople nearly desperate to preserve their gains poured perhaps as much as $140 million into the president's reelection campaign. The giant energy companies joined them.

Could it have been done differently? Could Yeltsin have called an election in 1992 and swept away his political opponents in the Russian parliament? Could he have avoided violence? Could he have pushed through political reform much more quickly, thus paving the way for a more rapid stabilization of the ruble and faster industrial restructuring? It is tempting to echo some economists and political commentators and argue that, yes, he could have.[36] But Russia was in a state of tumult from August 1991 on. It was lurching through political, economic, and social revolution all at once. Its president was in questionable health. When Gaidar freed prices in January 1992, there were serious doubts about food supplies for the winter. It is hard to imagine Russia's beleaguered population welcoming an election at that time.

No doubt, the reformers made mistakes. Gaidar, for example, hugely underestimated his political opponents right from the start. Yeltsin often seemed distracted. But I am inclined to agree with the view of Yuri

Levada, the renowned sociologist who had pioneered public opinion studies during Gorbachev's time and who was one of the wisest observers of Russian political life I'd met. When we chatted in early 1994, shortly after hard-liners had scored major victories in parliamentary elections and Gaidar had left his government post for the second time, Levada expressed a philosophical, almost fatalistic outlook. "It is a sad course of events, but it became inevitable," Levada said. "The democratic reformers lost many possibilities—not today, not yesterday, but one year ago, maybe two years ago. Yet two years ago is far from here, and nobody may be sure that there really were such possibilities. There are many critics who ask, Why didn't Yeltsin start the real democratic development? Why he didn't he start when he was in favor, when he was a great person for the people? Why did he not form a new party, a new movement, new democratic institutions, a new constitution? Because the next two years, from 1991 to 1993, were the years of general disillusionment and disarray. If there were some possibilities, they were lost. But maybe we had no such possibilities even two years ago. It is understandable that people blame Gorbachev and Yeltsin, but maybe it is not true."[37]

Despite the long and difficult political road, by early 1997 privatization was nearly complete. Across the country, entrepreneurs, managers, and some foreign owners could consider themselves winners in the battle for Russian wealth. For now, the biggest winners of all were the new financial-industrial conglomerates led by UnExim Bank, Menatep, and their competitors. Other companies were playing a dominant role, too: Lukoil, Gazprom, United Energy System. Altogether, as some economists and businesspeople pointed out, about thirty Russian companies controlled around half of the economy. That was far too great a concentration for the economic health of the nation, but it was far from an oligarchy of seven banks.

I didn't find it surprising, given Russia's history, that the country had tilted toward a concentrated form of economic organization. Nothing was historically determined, of course, but Russia had always favored systems with high concentrations of wealth. Despite the initial hopes of Yegor Gaidar, Anatoly Chubais, Boris Fyodorov, and the liberalizers of 1991, the Russian bureaucracy had defended itself, just as it had in previous decades and centuries. The cleverest and quickest of the former state enterprise managers had also found a niche for themselves. Some were simply robbing their enterprises to build a nest egg for their retirement. Others shook up their companies to make them more productive. Others teamed up with the new Russian bankers and entrepreneurs. There was a whole new class of ruble barons, as I called them.

Having gained their stake of the state's former wealth, the new owners, enterprises, and financial-industrial conglomerates would have to be the ones to create wealth. Could they manage their newly acquired assets in such a way as to make them produce and compete more effectively? Would the owners of the giant corporations prove to be good managers as well? Or would the new era of concentrated wealth also turn out to be just a phase until a new battle for property and industrial shake-up began? For the smaller businesses—the traders and owners of smaller service and manufacturing businesses and banks—the days of easy money had ended with inflation. Now they, too, had to struggle harder to make their businesses profitable, especially in the face of onerous taxes, government corruption, and the demands of the raket. Together with the larger enterprises, would they be able to grow enough to create new jobs to make up for the still tremendous losses of work and output from heavy industry? By the end of 1997, five years after the reforms had started, the economy was just seeing the first signs of growth.

It wasn't up to just the businesspeople. To spur growth, Russia desperately needed a new surge of liberalization. At the least, the government needed to overhaul its tax system—to simplify it as well as to boost efforts at tax collection. And it needed to crack down on the mafia and corruption. Russia still had a long way to go in developing and strengthening the institutions necessary to regulate and support a market economy. It still had much to do in protecting the rights of shareholders and property owners and, perhaps most urgently, in being more aggressive in taking politics out of business, in breaking the ties between government and business from Moscow to provincial centers. Of course, it was impossible to do all this at once, and to do it well. At the same time, the government and the Central Bank also had to worry about the ominous financial cloud that was heading toward Russia, as the fallout from Asia's currency crisis began to rattle the investors that were buying Russian government bonds and Treasury bills, which were of crucial help in financing Russia's budget.

Still, by the end of 1997, Yeltsin and his new team, led by the survivor, Chubais, and a newcomer to the government, Nemtsov, were making a determined effort to push Russia farther down the path of radical reform. They were trying to rewrite the tax code, break up the monopolies, attack corruption, and pay attention to the poorer classes. They were trying to create a more liberal system in which the rules of competition applied equally to all participants in the game. Reformers, businesspeople, and westerners could only ask: how far would they be able to go?[38]

In fact, the country was already looking forward to the elections of 2000. The Russian constitution prohibited the president from running for a third term, and Yeltsin, aged sixty-six, had announced that he would step down at the end of his second term. It would be time for a younger generation of leaders to take over, he said. It was too early to know who the candidates would be. Luzhkov, Lebed, Nemtsov, Chernomyrdin, and Yavlinsky all held presidential ambitions, either privately or openly.

The key issue of the election, however, was already clear. If the 1996 election decided whether Russia would choose capitalism or Communism, the 2000 elections would determine what kind of capitalism Russia would embrace. "This is the next most serious question, and the most important political problem in Russia," Gaidar said. Would Russia have an open, liberal, democratic form of capitalism ruled by laws and competition? Or would it have a closed, tight, secretive oligarchy in which select people and organizations won favors from the government, at the expense of the people? Or would there be a government-business partnership, like the one that moved forward in Moscow? Would crony capitalism in Russia rule?

The next president, elected by the people, would largely decide the answer. As banker Boris Fyodorov put it, reminding me of the Russian expression, "the fish rots from the head."

I still hoped for the liberal alternative, or something as close to it as Russia's Russianness would allow. In the years that I had spent living in, visiting, and observing the country, millions of people had changed their way of thinking. Not only did they have to rely on themselves to survive, they could try to rely on themselves to get ahead. There was a new spirit of individualism. It was not the same as American-style individualism. There was still a stronger sense of shared experience, of community or collectivism in Russia. But there was more energetic self-reliance, both because it was necessary and because it was allowed.

One afternoon, I visited Moscow School Number 1076 in an industrial suburb on the outskirts of the city. Elena Albertovna, a tiny woman in her thirties, quizzed the students in her economics class. "What is most important in the economy? The material part or the spiritual part?"[39]

"What is most important to you," she repeated. "Your health, your family, making money, traveling abroad? What do you want?"

The group of fifteen- and sixteen-year-old students sat passively.

Finally, one big Russian boy, hair falling over his eyes, heaved himself up and stood beside his desk. "I want to be rich," he replied, as his classmates laughed.

"Of course, one's family and health are most important," countered one of his female classmates.

"In a recent poll of the Russian people," Elena Albertovna informed the class, "24 percent said they wanted to live in the richest sphere, while more than 50 percent said that *dukhovnost*—the spiritual or moral side—is most important. Our country is developing as a capitalistic economy, and this will remain a crucial issue."

A decade earlier, fifteen-year-old students and their teacher would never have dared to discuss private property, profits, and the positive aspects of kapitalizm in their classroom. Now this class seriously debated how their country was adapting to market economics. Such expressions as *risk tayker,* "risk-taker," and *yazyk rynka,* the "language of the market," crept into the conversation. Students voiced interest in becoming bankers and businesspeople as well as adopting the more traditional professions of lawyer, accountant, or teacher. What would be the balance between materialism and morality, wealth versus social goals?

Elena Albertovna and her students reached no conclusion on that cold winter day. That they were debating such issues was in itself an achievement for Russia. Despite the tumultuous events that had taken place in their country, most of the students still possessed the hope and optimism that come with being a teenager.

I left the class thinking that they had fewer obstacles to overcome than had many generations of students before them. I wished them well in finding the energy and ability to smash through the barriers remaining in their paths. And I hoped that when 2000 came along, they would head to the polls and vote for a president who would finish the job that Yeltsin and his liberal reformers had begun.

Postscript

Much more than a financial cloud cast its shadow over Russia in the spring and summer of 1998. An economic hurricane ripped through the country, destroying much in its wake. The backwash from the Asian currency collapse and a slump in global oil prices combined with Russia's still-unresolved structural economic problems to plunge the country into its own financial crisis.

All through the spring and summer of 1998, the Russian government had struggled to cope with its mounting short-term debt problems. Still living beyond its means, Russia had become hooked on borrowing through its GKO or Treasury bill market to finance its budget deficit. For much of 1997 and early 1998, foreign investors had provided about one-third of the money that the government needed. But in 1998, as foreigners reassessed all emerging markets, they began turning their backs on Russia. In a scramble to attract investors, the Central Bank kept raising interest rates—once doubling key rates to 150 percent overnight. At the same time, the bank had to dip into its shrinking foreign currency reserves to keep the value of the ruble from plunging. By July 1998, the government was begging the International Monetary Fund for a bailout to prevent a devaluation of the ruble. The IMF came through with a $22.6 billion package.

But it wasn't enough to avoid disaster. By mid-August the government had essentially run out of money. On August 17, 1998, it announced that it was defaulting on $40 billion in short-term debt and devaluing the ruble by 30 percent. This was a devastating step backward. Fearful that the ruble would again become worthless—as it had in 1991—panicky Russians raced to the stores to buy anything from washing machines to electronic equipment. Poor people, fearing food shortages, stocked up on macaroni, sugar, and salt. For the first time since the early 1990s, bare spots appeared on the shelves of Russian stores.

Meanwhile, the government's default hit not only foreign investors but Russian banks, which had invested billions in the previously lucrative GKOs. Suddenly the banks had no money to give clients who wished to withdraw their savings. In a matter of days, the banking system collapsed. Powerful financiers like Vladimir Potanin and Mikhail Khodorkovsky, who had recently dominated much of the economy, were scrambling to save their institutions. The stock market, which had reached its peak in October 1997, also plunged drastically. By August 1998, it was down more than 80 percent for the year.

How had everything unraveled so quickly? The Asian financial crisis and a plunge in oil prices had helped expose glaring weaknesses in Russia's new kapitalizm. In spite of the pledges of Anatoly Chubais, Boris Nemtsov, and other liberal reformers in 1997, the reformers had made only meager progress in fixing Russia's tax system, boosting tax collection, doing away with privileges for favored companies, and thus turning Russia into a stronger, fairer market economy with greater chances for long-term growth. The reformers' inability to force Russian companies and citizens to pay taxes left the government with little choice but to keep borrowing to finance its budget. Like anyone living beyond his means, Russia had simply dug itself into a financial hole. In August 1998, the walls of that hole came crashing in.

I returned to Moscow in September to gain firsthand impressions of "the crisis," as ordinary Russians were calling it. Yeltsin had installed a new prime minister, Yevgeny Primakov, sixty-eight, a former foreign minister and intelligence chief who had been a Communist Party apparatchik in Soviet times. (In April 1998 Yeltsin had stunned the world by replacing Prime Minister Viktor Chernomyrdin with a thirty-five-year-old banker, Sergei Kiriyenko. The hope was that Kiriyenko, a virtual political newcomer, had not yet been corrupted and would be able to smash opposition to liberal reforms, but he hadn't been able to cope with the deteriorating financial situation.) Now Primakov was groping for a policy that would restore Russia's banking system and bolster its industry while paying wages and pensions due Russians and debts due foreigners. It seemed an impossible task. Primakov asked Viktor Geraschenko—the central banker who was famous for printing rubles from 1992 to 1994—to help him as Central Bank chief. Walking along the streets, I heard Muscovites worriedly discussing the ruble and food prices, which had doubled or tripled for many goods. Would the winter of 1998 be remembered as one of hyperinflation and hardship? Was the era of reform over or was this another giant hook in the long, zigzag road from socialism to capitalism?

"It is a serious step backward," Yegor Gaidar admitted as we met at his economic institute in Moscow. Although he had been out of government for years, he had remained active behind the scenes as an adviser to Chubais and other reformers. Now he blamed himself for failing to take the role of the parliament seriously in Russia's fledgling democracy. The Duma had blocked many initiatives since Communists and nationalists had won a majority of seats in 1995. "I thought we could push through reforms even if we had a minority in parliament. We should have worked harder to make sure that didn't happen," Gaidar said. He was hoping that the middle class, which was facing big job losses, would rise up against the Primakov government.

In a press conference, Chubais also admitted to grave errors. He had been too upbeat about Russia's economic prospects, he said, even though he had been aware of the Asian financial crisis. "I thought 1998 would be a year of continued weak growth in Russia. I was mistaken," he said. "We also did not comprehend the enormity of the process we were dealing with. We thought it was a difficult transition that would last three years, five years, seven years. Now it's clear that the transition will last decades. It's also clear that Russia needs not billions but hundreds of billions of dollars of investment. Only that way can we modernize industry and make it competitive."

The country was in for a rough ride. Probably the economy would shrink by 5 percent in 1998 and that much again in 1999, economists said. Gaidar told me he was "disgusted" by the turn of events. I was rather sad. But some Russian businesspeople I had met over the years recognized opportunities in the tumult. With the power of the giant financial-industrial groups diminished, there could be room for other, well-managed companies to grow. Kakha Bendukidze, the entrepreneur and head of Uralmash, was hoping to market his group's small but still solvent bank, the Industrial and Trade Bank, as a trustworthy financial institution. Josef Bakaleynik, now chairman of the board of the Vladimir Tractor Factory and chief financial officer of Tyumen Oil Company, could see new prospects for both of his companies. Vladimir was pushing to increase its exports as a result of the weaker ruble. And Tyumen was hoping to buy oil assets from other companies that would have to raise money to pay back debts to foreign banks. Unlike Khodorkovsky's Yukos and others, Tyumen had not borrowed heavily. "It's a crisis. It's very difficult. But some companies have good management and they will gain," Bakaleynik told me.

However difficult the next few years would be, Russians were already looking forward to the next elections, debating the candidates' prospects. Boris Nemtsov, once a Yeltsin favorite, was out of the race. Would the economic slump in Moscow hurt the chances of Major Yuri Luzhkov? Would Grigory Yavlinsky, the pro-market economist who had long criticized Gaidar and Chubais, gain a stronger following? And what about the populist former general Alexander Lebed? He had recently been elected governor of Krasnoyarsk, a resource-rich region in Siberia. He was aiming to use that post as a springboard to the presidency.

I had interviewed Lebed in July 1998 in New York, a month after he started his term in Krasnoyarsk. Sipping orange juice in a hotel bar, he told me he wanted to make Krasnoyarsk "a model for all of Russia." His goal was to gain more "economic freedom" for the region and to "create new rules of the game" that all would have to follow. "We need to have people listen to the law," he said in his deep, gravelly voice.

I asked the general how he would treat private business, in particular businessmen like Potanin, who were active in his region. Would he crack down? Lebed paused before answering. "I am power," he said slowly. "Everyone will respect power. I welcome managers. I welcome everyone who wants to work and earn money. I do not intend to interfere with them. Let them earn as much as they want and they can. Let God give them health. But I am power. I am not going to be pushed to one side or the other. I am at the center." He traced a circle on the table to illustrate his point. "I can agree to whatever is necessary, but I am the arbiter. Everyone understands that."

How far Lebed would take his power wasn't clear. But his answer, to me, raised a key question still facing all of Russia: Could the country's power-hungry leaders, from Moscow to the regions, learn to regulate their unruly economy without quashing economic and political freedoms? As the crisis continued in September 1998, Lebed and other regional leaders began slapping price controls on goods—an almost desperate bid to hold down inflation. Meanwhile, the presidential race was getting under way. The crisis had ended another chapter in Russia's economic history. The next stage in the battle for Russia's wealth and power had begun.

Pozhivyom uvidim. We will live and see.

Appendix: A Statistical Portrait of Russia's Economy

Except where indicated, data are from *Russian Economic Trends,* a publication produced by the Working Centre for Economic Reform, Government of the Russian Federation, and Russian European Centre for Economic Policy; statistics come from the years 1993 (vol. 3), 1997 (vol. 4), and 1998 (vols. 1 and 2). The Russian Stock Trading System Index is from Bloomberg Business News.

Gross Domestic Product (GDP)

Year	GDP (Rubles, in Billions)	GDP (Dollars, in Billions)	Constant GDP (1995 = 100)
1992	19	71	130.8
1993	172	184	119.4
1994	611	277	104.3
1995	1,630	357	100.0
1996	2,256	440	95.1
1997	2,675	464	95.5

Note: Ruble figures are expressed as redenominated rubles, as of January 1, 1998, when the Central Bank knocked three zeros off the ruble exchange rate. For the actual figure in existence 1992–1997, add three zeros to all ruble figures.

Economic and Industrial Output

Year	Real GDP (%)	Industrial Production (%)
1992	−19.0	−18.8
1993	−8.7	−14.1
1994	−12.7	−20.9
1995	−4.1	−3.3
1996	−4.9	−4.0
1997	0.4	1.9

Inflation

Year	Average Monthly Rate (%)	Annual Rate (%)
1992	31.0	2,509.0
1993	20.5	839.9
1994	10.0	215.1
1995	7.2	131.3
1996	1.7	21.8
1997	0.9	11.0

Wages

Year	Average Monthly Wage		Real Wages (1995 = 100)	Rate of Growth (%)	Minimum Wage (Rubles)
	(Rubles)	(Dollars)			
1992	6.0	27	140	−34	0.8
1993	58.7	63	149	6	7.1
1994	220.4	100	136	−9	18.1
1995	472.4	104	100	−26	46.2
1996	805.9	157	113	13	72.7
1997	965.1	167	119	4	83.5

Poverty

Year	Subsistence Level, as Defined by Government (Rubles per Month)	Average Monthly Pension (% of Subsistence Level)	Population Below Subsistence Level (% of Total Population)
1992	2	85	32
1993	21	100	31
1994	87	89	23
1995	264	69	26
1996	370	80	21
1997	411	80	21

The Employed and the Unemployed

Year	Economically Active	Employed (in Millions)	Unemployed	Unemployment Rate (%)	Registered Unemployment Rate (%)
1992	75.7	72.1	3.6	4.8	0.6
1993	74.9	70.9	4.0	5.3	1.0
1994	73.7	68.5	5.2	7.1	1.7
1995	72.4	66.4	6.0	8.3	2.8
1996	72.6	66.0	6.7	9.1	3.5
1997	72.7	64.8	7.9	10.9	3.1
1998 Q1	72.7	64.4	8.3	11.4	2.7

Note: Percentages for column on unemployment rate were obtained using standards established by the International Labor Organization. In Russia those registered as unemployed represent a small subset of all unemployed, as many don't bother to register. Many also work unofficially in the underground economy.

Average Exchange Rates

Year	Rubles to the Dollar (as of Year-End)
1991	169.0
1992	414.5
1993	1,247.00
1994	3,550.00
1995	4,640.00
1996	5,483.00
1997	5,906.00

Note: Amounts are expressed in rubles before the 1998 redenomination. The ruble, effectively stabilized, traded in a band known as the ruble corridor, from 1995 on. On January 1, 1998, three zeros were taken off the ruble value; at the end of that month, the ruble-to-dollar rate was 6.048.

The Stock Market

Month	Year			
	1995	1996	1997	1998
January		80.71	274.68	284.35
February		71.31	329.97	325.50
March		75.63	301.30	325.50
April		103.97	321.19	312.37
May		146.91	355.64	191.29
June		204.13	418.63	151.34
July		152.15	506.45	
August		182.64	498.42	
September	86.09	165.93	474.80	
October	73.56	177.99	422.26	
November	70.47	187.90	328.49	
December	82.92	200.50	396.41	

Note: Values are in dollars, as measured by the Russian Stock Trading System Index.

Interest Rates

Date	Central Bank Refinancing Rates (%)	GKO Secondary Market Yield, All Maturities (%)
1993	144.2	121.0
1994	177.9	172.3
1995	185.4	161.8
1996	109.6	85.8
1997	32.0	26.0
1998 Q1	30.0	29.1
1998		
February 2	42.0	
February 17	39.0	
March 2	36.0	
March 16	30.0	
May 18	30.0	
May 19	50.0	
May 27	150.0	
June 5	60.0	

Note: Yearly figures are annual averages. Quarterly figures are period averages. All others are uncompounded.

Budget Deficit

Year	% of GDP
1992	21.6
1993	7.2
1994	10.4
1995	5.5
1996	8.3
1997	7.6

Note: Figures include federal and local deficits, import subsidies, and other off-budget expenses.

The Use of Barter in the Economy

Industry	% of Sales
Gas	91
Utilities	87
Steel	79
Oil	69
Autos	59
Alcoholic Beverages	37
Food Processing	10

Source: Patricia Kranz, "Who Needs Rubles?" *Business Week,* April 13, 1998 (European Edition), p. 18.

Household Income

Year	Rate of Growth of Real per Capita Income (%)	Sources of Income, as Percentage of Total			
		Wages and Salaries	Social Transfers	Property Income	Other Income
1992	−48	69.9	14	0	16.1
1993	16	58	17.2	0	24.8
1994	13	46.5	17.4	4.3	31.9
1995	−13	40.7	12.4	6.4	40.5
1996	−1	41.9	14.2	5.3	38.6
1997	3.5	42.9	14.8	6.2	36.1

Notes

This book is based largely on interviews with individual Russians, both the well known and the not so well known, and with Western economists and businesspeople. For these interviews, I have not referenced quotations in the text when it is clear who was speaking and when they spoke. Here follows a list of the most prominent and helpful businesspeople and officials whom I interviewed for this book between 1989 and 1997; others are mentioned in the text.

Among the Russian entrepreneurs, bankers, managers, and businesspeople whom I consulted were Vagit Alikperov, Elena Astapova, Josef Bakaleynik, Ilya Baskin, Kakha Bendukidze, Boris Berezovsky, Oleg Boiko, Konstantin Borovoi, Andrei Chuguevsky, Mikhail Fridman, Boris Fyodorov, Svyatoslav Fyodorov, Vladimir Gusinsky, Mikhail Khodorkovsky, Ivan Kivelidi (deceased), Viktor Korovin, Dmitri Lubinin, Igor Malashenko, Mark Massarsky, Alexander Panikin, Vladimir Potanin, Vladimir Scherbakov, Leonid Skoptsov, Sergei Solodov, Vladimir Vinogradov, and Sergei Zverev.

I interviewed a number of Russian politicians, economists, sociologists, journalists, and cultural figures. They included Leonid Abalkin, Vladislav Alexeev, Mikhail Berger, Anatoly Chubais, Yegor Gaidar, Viktor Geraschenko, Andrei Illarionov, Irina Khakulina, Yuri Levada, Vladimir Mau, Alexander Minakov, Igor Mintusov, Vitaly Naishul, Boris Nemtsov, Tatyana Paramonova, Vyacheslav Sheronin, Alexander Shokhin, Vladimir Shumeiko, Rayr Simonyan, Natalia Tikhonova, Svetlana Vasilenko, Dmitri Vasiliev, Sergei Vasiliev, Irina Yasina, and Grigory Yavlinsky.

I also consulted Western businesspeople, advisers, and economists, among them Max Asgari, Anders Åslund, Jack Barbanel, Bruce Bean, Len Blavatnik, Peter Charow, Richard Dean, Peter Derby, Anthony Doran, Jean Foglizzo, Roger Gale, Yevgeny Ioffe, Stephen Jennings, Boris Jordan, David Reuben, Joseph Ritchie, Charlie Ryan, Robert Strauss, and Leonard Tsomik.

In addition, throughout the book I draw on statistics from *Russian Economic Trends,* a quarterly report on the Russian economy produced by the Working Centre for Economic Reforms, Government of the Russian Federation, with the assistance of the London School of Economics team working within the Russian European Centre for Economic Policy. For more information, see their site on the World Wide Web, at http://cep.lse.ac.uk.

Preface

1. Chubais press conference, attended by author, July 5, 1996.
2. *Moskovsky Komsomolets,* October 20, 1994.
3. The Russian European Centre for Economic Policy, which helps to produce the journal *Russian Economic Trends,* worked hard to amend that problem.

Chapter 1: Images, Voices

Most of the interviews on which this chapter is based took place between June and December 1994. I met the woman who was picking through the garbage in the summer of 1993.

1. I am indebted to financier Michael Pocalyko, a longtime observer of Russia, for the expression "conga line" of babushki.

Chapter 2: The Shock of Economic Freedom

Note to epigraph: Jeffrey Sachs, comments made at a press conference attended by the author, at the USSR Foreign Ministry in November 1991.

1. For this example, I am indebted to Deborah Stead, Moscow correspondent for *Business Week,* who interviewed Lyudmila Rukova for the magazine in November 1991.
2. Åslund, *Gorbachev's Struggle for Economic Reform.*
3. Quoted in Åslund, *How Russia Became a Market Economy,* pp. 63 – 65. The author also attended this session.
4. Anders Åslund and Jean Foglizzo, interviews with author, November 1991.
5. Interview with author, May 1992.
6. Alexander Shokhin, interview with author, November 1991.
7. Until July 1, 1992, Russia had separate exchange rates for tourist and commercial transactions, and a black market in dollars flourished as well. The tourist and commercial rates were unified on July 1, when regular auctions began setting the unified rate.
8. Yegor Gaidar, interview with author, February 10, 1992.
9. Svetlana Vasilenko, interview with author, June 1993.
10. The liberal Russian economist Vitaly Naishul developed an entire school of thought based on his observations of the Soviet barter economy. See Chapter 3.
11. Andrei and Vera, interview with author, July 1994.
12. Elena Antonenko, conversation with author, February 1993.
13. Natalia Tikhonova, sociologist at the Center for Economic and Political History of Russia, interview with author, October 1994.
14. Nadezhda Yakovleva Kojikova, interview with author, November 1992.
15. Yegor Gaidar was quoted making these points at press conferences and on Russian television in February 1992.
16. Åslund, *How Russia Became a Market Economy,* p. 208; statistics from *Russian Economic Trends.* Some economists have pointed out that Russia's interenterprise arrears were a disguised form of government credit at a time when banks were not lending to enterprises and were not unusual for an economy in transition. It still struck me as an extraordinarily widespread and significant phenomenon, lasting for years.
17. Viktor Korovin, Uralmash general director, interview with author, March 1992.

18. Stephen Handelman's *Comrade Criminal,* published in 1995, is the classic work on the post-Soviet mafia in Russia.
19. Yegor Gaidar, press conference, April 16, 1992.
20. Yegor Gaidar, interview with author, June 1992.
21. Viktor Geraschenko, interview with author, September 1997.
22. Sachs repeated this view on numerous occasions in press conferences and interviews, a fact that he confirmed in a telephone interview with the author in July 1998.
23. Peter Derby, interview with author, October 1992.
24. Andrei Illarionov, interview with author, November 1994.

Chapter 3: The Rise of the New Russians

Note to epigraph: Sergei Zverev, interview with author, August 1993.
1. Much of this chapter is based on the many excellent works on the history of Russian entrepreneurship, including those by Blackwell, Owen, Rieber, and Ruckman. The figures on millionaires are from Blackwell, *Beginnings of Russian Industrialization,* p. 190.
2. Heinrich Storch, quoted in Blackwell, *Beginnings of Russian Industrialization,* p. 197.
3. Alexander Herzen and Vissarion Belinsky are quoted in Riasanovsky, *Russia and the West.*
4. P. M. Tretiakov, cited in Ruckman, *Moscow Business Elite,* p. 96.
5. Owen, *The Corporation Under Russian Law,* p. 1.
6. Nove, *Economic History of the USSR,* pp. 78–114.
7. Alan Ball, "Private Trade and Traders During NEP," in Fitzpatrick, Rabinowitz, and Stites, *Russia in the Era of NEP,* p. 97.
8. Smith, *The Russians,* is a good source on the Russian black market.
9. Naishul, *Last Stage of Socialism,* p. 26.
10. Ilya Baskin, interview with author, August 1993. In 1990 Leningrad's former name, St. Petersburg, was reinstated.
11. Andrei Chuguevsky, interview with author, April 1993.
12. Ivan Kivelidi, interview with author, November 1994.
13. *Sovietskaya Kultura,* October 4, 1988, p. 1.
14. Gimpelson, "Russia's New Independent Entrepreneurs," pp. 44–48.
15. Mikhail Khodorkovsky, interview with author, January 1990.
16. Vagit Alikperov, interview with author, November 1994.
17. Alexander Panikin, interview with author, July 1993.

18. Alexander Minakov, interview with author, August 1993.
19. Sergei Zverev, interview with author, August 1993.

Chapter 4: The Battle for Russia's Wealth

Note to epigraph: Yegor Gaidar, interview with author, September 1997.
 1. Anatoly Chubais, interview with author and *Business Week* senior writer Karen Pennar, May 1992.
 2. Yuri Levada, Russian Center for Public Opinion and Market Research, interview with author, spring 1992.
 3. Vladimir Shumeiko, interview with author, June 1992.
 4. Boycko, Shleifer, and Vishny, *Privatizing Russia,* p. 15.
 5. Boris Nemtsov, interview with author, June 1992.
 6. Anthony Doran and Anatoly Chubais, press conferences attended by author, spring 1992.
 7. Yegor Gaidar, interview with author, June 1993.
 8. *Pravda* and *Dyen,* quoted in Celestine Bohlen, "Citizens of Russia to Be Given Share of State's Wealth," *New York Times,* October 2, 1992.
 9. Boris Jordan, interview with author, April 1997.
10. Stephen Jennings, interview with author, April 1997.
11. Chubais press conference, attended by author, January 1993.
12. Kakha Bendukidze, interview with author, July 1993.
13. Kakha Bendukidze, interview with author, July 1996.
14. Uralmash manager, interview with author, November 1994.
15. Josef Bakaleynik, interview with author, July 1994.
16. Len Blavatnik, interview with author, October 1994.
17. The author attended the meeting.
18. Boris Fyodorov, press conference, spring 1993, attended by author.
19. Viktor Geraschenko, interview with author, September 1997.
20. See Margaret Shapiro, "Russian Congress Acts Against Yeltsin's Ministers, Targets Media," *Washington Post,* March 14, 1993; and Serge Schmemann, "Yeltsin Suffers Final Rout as Russian Congress Ends," *New York Times,* March 14, 1993. The author attended the congressional session.
21. The author attended the rallies and the Congress, which were also covered by other Russian and Western media. See Margaret Shapiro, "Moscow Has Biggest Demonstration Since 1991 Coup Attempt," *Washington Post,* March 29, 1993.

22. Yeltsin's statement was widely quoted in both the Russian and the Western press, including in Serge Schmemann, "Yeltsin and Legislature Act to Oust Each Other," *New York Times,* September 22, 1993.

23. This account is a composite of a variety of reports in newspapers and magazines and on television (including the *New York Times, Washington Post,* and Cable News Network) as well as interviews with journalists and others who observed the events. See also Yeltsin, *Zapiski Prezidenta.* The author was not present.

24. Kakha Bendukidze, interview with author, November 1993.

25. *Russian Economic Trends* 2 (1996): 171–175.

26. See William Safire, "Who Lost Russia?" *New York Times,* January 31, 1994.

27. "Yuri," interview with author, August 1994.

28. Ivan Kivelidi, interview with author, November 1994.

29. In October 1994 I visited Cyprus, where real estate brokers did indeed tell of selling houses for cash.

30. In *Resurrection,* David Remnick writes that Most, although its name means "bridge," was really named after a decal that Gusinsky saw near an automatic teller machine in the United States.

31. Vladimir Gusinsky, interview with author, November 1994.

32. Interview with author, March 1993.

33. Mikhail Fridman, interview with author and Patricia Kranz, Moscow bureau chief for *Business Week,* June 1996.

34. Jordan interview, April 1997. The later comments by Jennings also come from an April 1997 interview.

35. *Russian Economic Trends* 4 (1994).

36. *Argumenti i Fakti,* no. 42, 1994.

37. *Izvestia,* March 27, 1996.

38. Åslund, *How Russia Became a Market Economy,* p. 286.

39. Natalia Tikhonova, interview with author, October 1994.

40. Vladimir Vinogradov, president of Inkombank, press conference, December 4, 1994, attended by author.

41. *Russian Economic Trends* 2 (1995): 36.

42. Josef Bakaleynik, interview with author, August 1994.

43. Blasi, Kroumova, and Kruse, *Kremlin Capitalism,* deals thoroughly with the issue of Red Directors and inside ownership.

44. Sergei I. Postnov, interview with author, August 1994.

45. *Russian Economic Trends* 2 (1995): 37. See also Blasi, Kroumova, and Kruse, *Kremlin Capitalism,* p. 190.

46. Kakha Bendukidze, interview with author, November 1994.
47. Viktor Geraschenko, conversation with author, January 1997.
48. Mikhail Berger, quoted in "Who Will Become the Chairman of the Central Bank?" *Kommersant Weekly,* July 11, 1995, p. 7.
49. Tatiana Paramonova, interview with author, September 1997.
50. Foreigners were largely excluded from the GKO market then. They were allowed to buy only up to 10 percent of an issue, and profits were not allowed to be repatriated.
51. Geraschenko interview, September 1997.
52. Tatiana Paramonova, quoted in Alexei Putintsev, "Tatiana Paramonova: 'We Won't Allow a Banking Crisis in Russia,'" *Segodnya,* June 8, 1995.
53. Peter Derby, quoted in Claudia Rosett, "Banking Crisis Erupts in Russia amid Rumors of Unsoundness," *Wall Street Journal,* August 25, 1995.
54. Yeltsin, quoted in "Yeltsin Blasts Top Bankers for Credit Crisis," *Moscow Times,* September 1, 1995. For an interesting assessment of why financial stabilization occurred when it did, see Schleifer and Treisman, *Transition to an Open Market Economy.* According to their analysis, both the commercial banks and the Central Bank shifted from opposing stabilization to supporting stabilization largely as a result of the high returns that could be had from the GKO market. GKOs replaced currency trading as a means of profit for commercial banks.
55. Mikhail Berger, "Banking Crisis: The Prelude to Much Worse?" *Moscow Times,* August 29, 1995.
56. Boris Fyodorov, interview with author, September 1997.
57. Vladimir Potanin, interview with author and Patricia Kranz, Moscow bureau chief for *Business Week,* September 1997.
58. Kakha Bendukidze, quoted in Chrystia Freeland and John Thornhill, "Russia Set for Pact with Banks on Sell-Offs," *Financial Times,* April 2, 1995.
59. Anatoly Chubais, press conference, quoted in "Russian Loans Plan Under Fire," *Financial Times,* September 6, 1995.
60. Quoted in Michael Gulyayer, "Menatep Sets Sights on Yukos Takeover," *Moscow Times,* November 10, 1995. Source for auction results is AIOC Capital, "Auctions and Events Calendar," no. 1, November 1, 1995–January 31, 1996.
61. Boris Yeltsin, quoted in Jean MacKenzie, "Yeltsin to Voters: Don't Turn Back to Past," *Moscow Times,* December 16, 1995.
62. See *Moscow Times,* December 18, 1995, and Michael Specter, "Oppo-

sition Gains as Russians Elect New Parliament," *New York Times,* December 18, 1996.
63. Maxim, conversation with author and Elena Antonenko, November 1994. My conversation with his mother also took place in November 1994.
64. Alexander Minakov, interview with author, August 1993.
65. Murray Feshbach discussed these figures and the suicide problem at a seminar on Russia sponsored by the Council on Foreign Relations, Washington, D.C., May 1994. See also Feshbach and Friendly, *Ecocide in the USSR.*
66. "Viktor," interview with author, summer 1994.
67. Ivan Kivelidi, interview with author, November 1994. See also Handelman's *Comrade Criminal* for details on the Russian mob.

Chapter 5: Capitalism Versus Communism

Note to epigraph: Serafim Ivanovna, conversation with author, June 1996.
1. Yuri Levada, "Ten Weeks Are Remaining Until the Elections," *Segodnya,* April 4, 1996.
2. Sergei Kovalev, "The Case Against Yeltsin," *Washington Post,* January 29, 1996.
3. The government later reported that $811 million fled the country, although outside analysts, including Deutsche Morgan Grenfell, estimated that as much as $22.3 billion was transferred to banks in places like Switzerland and Cyprus. See "The Flow of Capital from Russia in 1996 Was Ten Times Higher than Foreign Investment," *Finansovaya Izvestia,* April 1, 1997.
4. Boris Nemtsov, interview with author, April 1996.
5. Claudia Rosett, "Russian Communists Target Privatizers," *Wall Street Journal,* February 13, 1996.
6. Chubais press conference at Davos, quoted from Reuters in Jim Kennett, "Chubais, Zyuganov Skirmish in Davos," *Moscow Times,* February 6, 1996.
7. Boris Berezovsky, interview with author and Patricia Kranz, Moscow bureau chief for *Business Week,* September 1997.
8. Boris Yeltsin, quoted in Robin Lodge, "President: I Must Run to Stop Red Revanche," *Moscow Times,* February 17, 1996.
9. Itogi television poll, cited in Robin Lodge, "Democrats Mend Fences with Yeltsin," *Moscow Times,* February 22, 1996.

10. Alessandra Stanley, "With Campaign Staff in Disarray, Yeltsin Depends on Perks of Office," *New York Times,* May 13, 1996.
11. Leonid Skoptsov, interview with author, November 1995.
12. "Businessmen Demand That Politicians Make Mutual Concessions," *Nezavisimaya Gazeta,* English-language edition, vol. 3, 1996.
13. Andranik Migrayan, "The Appeal of the 'Group of Thirteen,'" *Nezavisimaya Gazeta,* May 6, 1996, p. 2.
14. Berezovsky interview, September 1997.
15. "The Communists Want to Return Gosplan, Gosnab, and Empty Shelves!" and "Can Zyuganov Be Trusted?" *Izvestia,* March 20, 1996.
16. Igor Malashenko, Freedom Forum, New York, December 9, 1996.
17. In *Resurrection,* David Remnick covers Korzhakov extensively.
18. Letter quoted in Alexander Gubski, "On Whose Side Is Business?" *Kapital,* June 11–18, 1996.
19. See Jim Kennett, "Stock Markets Soar in Buying Frenzy," *Moscow Times,* May 25, 1996. See also *Russian Economic Trends* 3 (1997): 118.
20. This joke was also printed in Thomas de Waal, "Voters Get a Helping Hand," *Moscow Times,* April 26, 1996.
21. *Nezavisimaya Gazeta,* June 18, 1996.
22. Josef Bakaleynik, interview with author, June 1996.
23. Vladislav Alexeev, interview with author and consultant Grace Kennan Warnecke, June 1996.
24. Alexey Gorenkov, interview with author, June 1996.
25. Zoya Ivanovna Pronina, interview with author, June 1996.
26. For more on this episode, see Remnick, *Resurrection.*
27. Viktor Chernomyrdin, quoted in *Izvestia,* July 1, 1996.

Chapter 6: The Wary Westerners

Note to epigraph: Leonard Tsomik, interview with author, April 1997.
1. Robert Strauss, interview with author, June 1992.
2. Joseph Ritchie, interview with author, March 1993.
3. *Russian Economic Trends* 1 (1998).
4. Rayr Simonyan, interview with author, July 1993.
5. Richard Dean, "The Russian Legal System: Ten Years Later," in-house document produced by Coudert Brothers, 1996.
6. Background interview with author, November 1994.
7. A number of sources cited this figure.
8. This account of Tatum's troubles is a compilation of common knowl-

edge, press reports, and interviews with members of the American business community in Moscow. I never interviewed Tatum. See Nick Allen, "Tatum Shot Dead by Eleven Bullets," *Moscow Times,* November 5, 1996; Erin Arvedlund, "Murder in Moscow," *Fortune,* March 3, 1997, p. 128; and Lee Hockstader, "American Slain in Moscow," *Washington Post,* November 5, 1996.

9. *Moscow Times,* April 30, 1996.

10. George Cohon, press conference, Moscow, January 31, 1990. In Toronto, Cohon also granted an interview to Todd Mason, then a correspondent for *Business Week,* who kindly shared his notes. *Business Week* stringer Rosemarie Boyle interviewed Redmond J. Langan, marketing director of McDonald's, and Terry Williams, manager of the company's food-processing plant, in January 1990. See also Cohon, *To Russia with Fries.*

11. Telephone interview with spokesperson from McDonald's of Canada, March 1998.

12. This account comes from reporting done for *Business Week* in 1988.

13. Maxwell Asgari, interview with author, October 1990. For an account of CE's joint-venture troubles, see Rose Brady and Rosemarie Boyle, "Combustion Engineering's Dislocated Joint Venture," *Business Week,* October 22, 1990, p. 50.

14. Maxwell Asgari, interview with author, July 1993.

15. Maxwell Asgari, interview with author, July 1996.

16. Maxwell Asgari, interview with author, April 1997.

17. Leonard Tsomik, interview with author, April 1997.

18. Liam Halligan, "Import Goods Go Native," *Moscow Times,* April 30, 1996; *Russian Economic Trends* 3 (1997): 65.

19. Cartoon appeared on the front page of *Pravda* on October 15, 1995. See also "Selling in Russia: The March on Moscow," *The Economist,* March 18, 1995, p. 65.

Chapter 7: Kapitalizm Reborn

Note to epigraph: Yuri Levada, interview with author, September 1997.

1. Boris Yeltsin, quoted in *Moscow Times,* July 5, 1996.

2. Anatoly Chubais, press conference attended by author, July 5, 1996.

3. Boris Yeltsin, quoted in Michael Specter, "Shake-Up in Russia," *New York Times,* October 18, 1996.

4. See *Russian Economic Trends* 3 (1997): 118. The Russian Stock Trading System Index and the *Moscow Times* Index are cited in Bloomberg Business News. See Appendix.

5. *Russian Economic Trends* 1 (1997): 94; in its first volume of 1998, the journal adjusted the figure to 4.9 percent.

6. The State Tax Service estimated that 34 percent of all firms failed to submit tax returns, according to *Russian Economic Trends* 1 (1997): 142.

7. Vladimir Potanin, conversation with author, October 1996.

8. Boris Berezovsky, quoted in Chrystia Freeland, John Thornhill, and Andrew Gowers, "Moscow's Group of Seven," *Financial Times,* November 1, 1996. See also Jonas Bernstein, "Business Clique Claims to Rule," *Moscow Times,* November 2, 1996.

9. Boris Berezovsky, quoted in David Hoffman, "'Workers State' Renovated as Plutocrats Club," *Washington Post,* January 10, 1997.

10. Mikhail Berger, "Seven Bankers Not All That Magnificent," *Moscow Times,* January 5, 1997.

11. Mikhail Khodorkovsky, interview with author, March 1997.

12. The merger of Yukos and Sibneft to create Yuksi was announced in a press release by the companies on January 19, 1998. By then, Khodorkovsky was already talking publicly about selling off Rosprom's other industrial assets, which were holding back his growth plans.

13. Vladimir Potanin, interview with author and Patricia Kranz, Moscow bureau chief for *Business Week,* September 1997.

14. Kakha Bendukidze, interview with author, March 1997.

15. Richard Layard, press conference in Moscow, April 14, 1997, quoted in Federal News Service, Bloomberg Business News.

16. A year later, in March 1998, Bendukidze announced that his Uralmash was acquiring Izhorsky Zavod of St. Petersburg to create a machinery manufacturing giant that would dominate its market in Russia.

17. Boris Fyodorov, interview with author, September 1997.

18. In Italy, about 50 percent of the gross domestic product was produced by the private sector versus 70 percent in Russia by 1997.

19. Boris Yeltsin, speech quoted on Bloomberg Business News wire, March 6, 1997.

20. See Chrystia Freeland, "Soros 'Lent Millions' to Bail Out Kremlin," *Financial Times,* March 5, 1998, which reports that George Soros, who joined Potanin in the Svyazinvest tender, had extended a "secret loan" to the Kremlin to finance the payment of back wages to Russian work-

ers. There was no evidence that the loan at all influenced the Svyazinvest deal, but the news provided further ammunition for Potanin's opponents.

21. Anatoly Chubais, interview with author and Patricia Kranz, Moscow
bureau chief for *Business Week,* September 1997.

22. Boris Berezovsky, interview with author and Patricia Kranz, Moscow
bureau chief for *Business Week*, September 1997.

23. Potanin interview, September 1997.

24. Boris Yeltsin, quoted in Michael Specter, "Yeltsin Declares Economic
Decline Has Been Stopped," *New York Times,* July 5, 1997.

25. Josef Bakaleynik, interview with author, September 1997.

26. According to *Russian Economic Trends* 1 (1998), the figure for industrial
production growth was 2.8 percent in the third quarter and 3.4 percent
in the fourth quarter of 1997.

27. Until the Asian financial crisis, the government had forecast at least 2
percent growth in 1998. That looked unachievable once the government
hiked interest rates. Still, in January 1998, the economy grew 1.3 percent, according to *Russian Economic Trends,* March 1998. But the financial picture was soon to worsen.

28. *Russian Economic Trends* 1 (1998).

29. Yegor Gaidar, interview with author, September 1997.

30. Anatoly Chubais, interview with author and Patricia Kranz, Moscow
bureau chief for *Business Week,* September 1997.

31. This section draws on Gerschenkron, *Economic Backwardness in Historical Perspective;* and Snyder, "Russian Backwardness and the Future
of Europe."

32. Gerschenkron, *Economic Backwardness,* pp. 138, 142. See also Snyder,
"Russian Backwardness and the Future of Europe," p. 184.

33. Yavlinsky told me this in a 1993 interview. But he often repeated it publicly.

34. Economist Andrei Shleifer has argued that Russia has lagged behind
Poland in the transition of its government to "an institution supporting
a market economy." That may be one reason for Russia's poor growth
record so far. See Andrei Shleifer, "Government in Transition," *European Economic Review* 41 (1997).

35. Interview with author, October 1996.

36. Jeffrey Sachs has argued that the reformers failed to make a breakthrough quickly enough and so became lost in a "vicious cycle" of failed

reforms. See Sachs, "It Could Have Been So Much Better: Reflections on Russian Economic Reform," *Moscow Times,* May 6, 1996; and Sachs and Pistor, *The Rule of Law and Economic Reform in Russia.*

37. Yuri Levada, interview with author, February 16, 1994.
38. See *Russian Economic Trends* 1 (1998); and Patricia Kranz, "Who Needs Rubles?" *Business Week,* European edition, April 13, 1998, pp. 16–18.
39. I recorded the following exchange during my visit to Moscow School Number 1076 in December 1994.

Recommended Reading

In addition to the works cited here, I referred to news reports in numerous Russian and Western newspapers, including *Izvestia, Moskovsky Komsomolets, Komsomolskaya Pravda, Kommersant* (daily and weekly), *Itogi, Literaturnaya Gazeta,* the *Moscow Times,* the *New York Times,* the *Washington Post,* and *Business Week;* the annual reports of companies, including Lukoil, UnExim Bank, Dialog Bank, and Inkombank; and the research reports of financial firms like MFK-Renaissance, Brunswick International, AIOC Capital, Merrill Lynch, and Price Waterhouse.

Åslund, Anders. *Gorbachev's Struggle for Economic Reform: The Soviet Reform Process, 1985–1988.* Ithaca, N.Y.: Cornell University Press, 1989.
———. *How Russia Became a Market Economy.* Washington, D.C.: Brookings Institution, 1995.
Berdyaev, Nikolai. *The Russian Idea.* Translated by R. M. French. Hudson, N.Y.: Lindisfarne Press, 1992.
Billington, James H. *The Icon and the Axe: An Interpretive History of Russian Culture.* New York: Vintage, 1970.

Blackwell, William L. *The Beginnings of Russian Industrialization, 1800–1860.* Princeton: Princeton University Press, 1968.

Blasi, Joseph R., Maya Kroumova, and Douglas Kruse. *Kremlin Capitalism: The Privatization of the Russian Economy.* Ithaca, N.Y.: ILR Press, 1997.

Boycko, Maxim, Andrei Shleifer, and Robert Vishny. *Privatizing Russia.* Cambridge: MIT Press, 1995.

Bunin, I. *Biznesmeni Rossii* (Businessmen of Russia). Moscow: AO OKO, 1994.

Clowes, Edith W., Samuel D. Kassow, and James L. West, eds. *Between Tsar and People: Educated Society and the Quest for Public Identity in Late Imperial Russia.* Princeton: Princeton University Press, 1991.

Cohon, George. *To Russia with Fries.* Toronto: McClelland and Stewart, 1997.

Feshbach, Murray, and Alfred Friendly, Jr. *Ecocide in the USSR: Health and Nature Under Siege.* New York: Basic Books, 1991.

Fitzpatrick, Sheila, Alexander Rabinowitz, and Richard Stites, eds. *Russia in the Era of NEP: Explorations in Soviet Society and Culture.* Bloomington: Indiana University Press, 1991.

Frye, Timothy, and Andrei Shleifer. "The Invisible Hand and the Grabbing Hand." *AEA Papers and Proceedings,* May 1997.

Gaidar, Yegor. *Gosudarstvo i Evolutsia* (State and Evolution). St. Petersburg: Norma, 1997.

Galuszka, Peter, and Rose Brady. "The Battle for Russia's Wealth." *Business Week,* April 1, 1996.

Gerschenkron, Alexander. *Economic Backwardness in Historical Perspective: A Book of Essays.* Cambridge: Belknap Press of Harvard University Press, 1962.

Gimpelson, Vladimir. "Russia's New Independent Entrepreneurs." In *RFE/RL Research Report,* September 10, 1993, pp. 44–48.

Guroff, Gregory, and Fred V. Carstensen, eds. *Entrepreneurship in Imperial Russia and the Soviet Union.* Princeton: Princeton University Press, 1983.

Handelman, Stephen. *Comrade Criminal: Russia's New Mafiya.* New Haven: Yale University Press, 1995.

Johnson, Simon, Daniel Kaufman, and Andrei Shleifer. "The Unofficial Economy in Transition." *Brookings Papers on Economic Activity* 2 (1997): 159–239.

Josephson, Matthew. *The Robber Barons: The Great American Capitalists.* New York: Harcourt Brace, 1962.

Khakhulina, Lyudmilla. "Managers on the Economic Situation at Their Enterprises." *Russian Centre for Public Opinion Research (VCIOM) Bulletin of Information* 2 (March–April 1994).

Klimaschevskaya, O. L., and Y. N. Korolev. *Vozvrozhdenaya Elita Ruskovo Biznesa* (The Renaissance of the Elite of Russian Business). Moscow: Institute of the Study of Reform, 1994.

Korzhakov, Aleksandr. *Boris Eltsin: Ot Rasveta do Zakata* (Boris Yeltsin: From Dawn to Dusk). Moscow: Interbrook, 1997.

Layard, Richard, and John Parker. *The Coming Russian Boom*. New York: Free Press, 1996.

Lenin, V. I. *The Development of Capitalism in Russia*. Translation of vol. 3 of Lenin's *Collected Works*. Moscow: Progress Publishers, 1974.

Mosse, W. E. *An Economic History of Russia, 1856–1914*. London: I. B. Tauris, 1996.

Naishul, Vitaly. *The Supreme and Last Stage of Socialism*. London: Centre for Research into Communist Economies, 1991.

Nove, Alec. *An Economic History of the USSR, 1917–1991*. 3d ed. London: Penguin Books, 1992.

———. *The Soviet System in Retrospect: An Obituary Notice*. New York: Harriman Institute, Columbia University, 1993.

Owen, Thomas C. *Capitalism and Politics in Russia: A Social History of the Moscow Merchants, 1855–1905*. Cambridge: Cambridge University Press, 1981.

———. *The Corporation Under Russian Law, 1800–1917: A Study in Tsarist Economic Policy*. Cambridge: Cambridge University Press, 1991.

Pipes, Richard. *Russia Under the Old Regime*. 2d ed. New York: Penguin, 1995.

Proskurov, V. S. *Azbyka Predprinimatelstva* (Alphabet of Entrepreneurship). Moscow: Pallada, 1993.

Remnick, David. *Resurrection: The Struggle for a New Russia*. New York: Random House, 1997.

Riasanovsky, Nicholas V. *Russia and the West in the Teaching of the Slavophiles*. Cambridge: Harvard University Press, 1952.

Rieber, Alfred J. *Merchants and Entrepreneurs in Imperial Russia*. Chapel Hill: University of North Carolina Press, 1982.

Ruckman, Jo Ann. *The Moscow Business Elite: A Social and Cultural Portrait of Two Generations, 1840–1905*. DeKalb: Northern Illinois University Press, 1984.

Russian Economic Trends. Working Centre for Economic Reform Government of Russian Federation, Russian European Centre for Economic Policy, various issues, 1994–1998.

Russian Economy in 1996. Moscow: Institute for the Economy in Transition, March 1997.

Sachs, Jeffrey D., and Katharina Pistor, eds. *The Rule of Law and Economic Reform in Russia.* Boulder, Colo.: Westview Press, 1997.

Safire, William. "Who Lost Russia?" *New York Times,* January 31, 1994.

Scott, John. *Behind the Urals.* Bloomington: Indiana University Press, 1989.

Shleifer, Andrei. "Government in Transition." *European Economic Review* 41 (1997).

Shleifer, Andrei, and Daniel Treisman. *The Economics and Politics of Transition to an Open Market Economy: Russia.* Paris: OECD, 1998.

Smith, Hedrick. *The Russians.* Rev. ed. London: Sphere Books, 1985.

———. *The New Russians.* New York: Random House, 1990.

Snyder, Jack. "Russian Backwardness and the Future of Europe." *Daedalus* 123, no. 2 (spring 1994).

Wedel, Janine R. "Clique-Run Organizations and U.S. Economic Aid: An Institutional Analysis." *Demokratizatsiya* 4, no. 4 (fall 1996).

Yeltsin, Boris. *Against the Grain: An Autobiography.* Translated by Michael Glenny. London: Jonathan Cape, 1990.

———. *The Struggle for Russia.* New York: Random House, 1994.

———. *Zapiski Prezidenta* (Notes of the President). Moscow: Ogonyek, 1994.

Yergin, Daniel, and Thane Gustafson. *Russia 2010 and What It Means for the World.* New York: Vintage, 1995.

Index

Abalkin, Leonid, 12
Aganbegyan, Abel, 9
Agriculture: government credits to,
    40–41, 112
Aid, economic, 27
Albertovna, Elena, 242–43
Alexander II, 234
Alexeev, Vladislav, 176
Alfa Group: loans-for-shares pro-
    gram criticized by, 140; as part of
    the business elite, 208; Tyumen
    Oil Company acquired by, 218,
    224; voucher investment fund of,
    104–6
Alikperov, Vagit, 56–58, 128, 208,
    212
Americanization, xii–xiii
Americom Business Centers, 188

Andrei (shuttler), 22–24
Antonenko, Elena, 25, 144, 149
A/O Chasprom, 133–34
"Appeal of the Thirteen," 162–64
Applied Engineering Systems,
    192–93
Asea Brown Boveri (ABB), 193–96
Asgari, Maxwell, 192–200
Asian financial crisis, 224, 244, 247
Åslund, Anders, 10, 12, 13
Athletes, racketeering by, 152
Atlantic Richfield Company, 212
Attali, Jacques, 73
Auctions: loans-for-shares, 139–43,
    158, 206–7; of stores and service
    businesses, 67–68; voucher, of
    state enterprises, 73–76, 79–80,
    85, 107–8

August *1991* coup attempt, x, 8, 13, 18, 40
Authorized banks, 100–103
Azerbaijan, 57

Babushki traders, 1–3
Bakaleynik, Josef, 247; control of the Vladimir Tractor Factory assumed by, 117–26; on the difficulties faced by the factory, 170–72, 175, 224–25; proxy battle with Grishin, 83–91; workers' opinion of, 174; Yeltsin supported by, 172
Baltic States, 9
Bank for Foreign Trade, 136
Banking system, 223; crises of, 113–14, 129–35, 244–48; interest rates in, 99, 102, 117, 134; privatization of, 40. *See also* Commercial banks
Bankruptcy, 29–30, 116
Barbanel, Jack, 200
Bartering, 21, 53, 226–27, 255, 259*n*10
Bashkir, 57
Bashneft, 57
Baskin, Ilya, 51
Belinsky, Vissarion, 46–47
Belorussia, 8
Ben & Jerry's, 189
Bendukidze, Kakha, 76–81, 106, 151, 247; on democracy in Russia, 97; on industrial policy, 127–28; on the power of financial-industrial groups, 139, 213–14, 216
Berezovsky, Boris, 159–60, 162–64, 166, 167; on the "liberal revolution" plan, 220–22; as a member of the business elite, 207, 209, 210, 213; and the Svyazinvest deal, 218–19; Yuksi formed by, 212
Berger, Mikhail, 130, 134, 208–9
Bioprocess, 76–78, 80, 214
Biznesmen. *See* Entrepreneurs
Black market, 49–50, 216, 235
Black Tuesday, 112–14, 129
Blagovest, 85
Blavatnik, Len, 84–85, 120, 224
Boiko, Oleg, 53, 132
Bolshevik Biscuit Company, 75
Bonds. *See* GKOs
Bonner, Yelena, 67
Borovoi, Konstantin, 51
Boys, street, 144–46
Brezhnev, Leonid, 2, 9, 49, 148, 155
Bribes, xiii, 60–61, 148, 187, 216; Soviet era, 49, 54, 58, 148
Brokerages, Russian, 200–201
Brunswick International, 108
Budget deficits, 37, 95, 131, 254
Burbulis, Gennady, 10
Bureaucrats: acquisition of state enterprises by, 65; corruption among, 26, 54, 58, 60–61, 148, 187, 216; opposition to reform of, 54; trading system of, 50
Bush, George, 27
Business Roundtable, 151

Capitalism, Russian, 4, 8, 235–37; characteristics of, 100; and the elections of *2000,* 241–42, 247–48; optimism about, 5–6

Capitalists, 6, 44–45; "collective" of, 58; cooperatives of, 51–54, 56–58; in prerevolutionary Russia, 45–48; deal-making practices of, 59–60, 186–87, 195–96; KGB targeting of, 54; Lebed's campaign supported by, 170; money game of, 98–104; power of business elites, 207–19, 229–33; public hatred of, 54; rush for money among, 60; security forces of, 61; in Soviet Russia, 48–58; support for Yeltsin in the 1996 elections, 160–64, 166–67, 209, 238

Carnegie, Dale, 178

Central Bank: Dubinin's tenure at, 134–35; Geraschenko's tenure at, 39–42, 91–92, 95, 100, 112–13, 129, 135; interest rates fixed by, 17, 102, 117; Matyukhin's resignation from, 39, 40; Paramonova's tenure at, 129–35; regulation of lending practices by, 99; response to the world financial crisis, 226, 244–45

Central planning, 20–21, 49, 234, 236

Chara Bank, 114

Chechen war, x, 31, 130, 161, 205

Chekhov, Anton, 46

Chelnoki (shuttlers), 22–24

Chernadski, Arkady, 35

Chernomyrdin, Viktor, 37, 91, 171, 241; appointed prime minister, 43, 73, 204–5, 229–30, 238; at Gazprom, 128; at the Group of Seven summit, 182; on the "lib-eral revolution" plan, 217, 226; in the parliamentary elections of 1995, 143; replaced as prime minister, 246; at the siege of the White House, 96

Chevron, 57

Chubais, Anatoly, ix–x, 131, 240; appointed first deputy prime minister, 217; auctions of stores and service businesses by, 67–68; as chief of staff, 204–5; dismissed as first deputy prime minister, 158; dissolution of his privatization committee, 95; and financial crisis of 1997–98, 245–47; "liberal revolution" plan of, 217–23; loans-for-shares plan, 135, 139–43, 158, 238; privatization programs of, 63–67, 70–72, 141, 229–33; "ruble corridor" plan, 132, 171; voucher auctions planned by, 73–76; at the World Economic Forum, 158–60; in Yeltsin's 1996 election campaign, 160, 164–66, 170, 181–82, 203

Chuguevsky, Andrei, 52, 58

City governments: social service burdens on, 33

Civic Union, 66

Civil society, 230

Clinton, Bill, 96

Cohon, George, 185, 189–92, 193

Cold War, xii, 185

Combustion Engineering (CE), 185, 192–93

COMECON, 136

Commercial banks, 5, 54–56; as "authorized banks," 100–103;

Commercial banks (*continued*)
bond market for, 103; contract
killings of bankers, 114–15, 151;
effect of the Black Tuesday ruble
collapse on, 113–14, 129–35; financial-industrial conglomerates, 79, 80, 105, 207–19,
239–40; interbank lending, 103,
133–34; interest rates of, 99, 102,
117, 134; investment banking,
199–201; loans-for-shares consortium of, 135–43; power of,
207–19; security forces of, 114
Commonwealth of Independent
States, 8
Communist Party: cooperatives
criticized by, 54; disbanding of,
x, 8; economic advantage of former members, 25–26; entrepreneurship promoted by, 55–56;
gains in the *1995* parliamentary
elections, 143; in joint ventures,
56; Soviet economy controlled
by, 49, 234; threatened revival of
in the *1996* elections, 157–60,
238
Computers, trading of, 52–53
Conglomerates, financial-industrial, 79–81, 105, 207–19, 239–40
Congress of People's Deputies, 11;
economic reform stymied by,
94–95; Gaidar's compromises
with, 36–38; Gaidar's resignation
forced by, 42–43, 76, 237; motion to impeach Yeltsin, 93–94
Constitution, Russian, 94, 95, 97
Consumerism, x, 24
Contract killings, xiii, 146, 150–54;
of bankers, 114–15, 151

Contracts: Russians' lax attitude to-
ward, 59, 187
Cooperatives, 44, 50–54, 56–58
Corruption, xii, 26, 60–61, 99, 129,
146, 148–49, 187, 216–17, 240
Coudert Brothers, 187
Council for Mutual Economic As-
sistance. *See* COMECON
Credit cards, 178
Credits, government issues of, 34,
37, 40–41, 92, 100, 112, 116
Credit Suisse First Boston (CSFB),
73–74, 81, 106–9, 112
Crime, 3–4, 146, 174. *See also* Con-
tract killings; Organized crime

Dean, Richard, 187
Debt, interenterprise, 29–30, 39,
116, 259n16
Democracy, Russian, x, 97; and am-
bivalence about the rule of law,
147; Yeltsin's version of, 157
Derby, Peter, 41–42, 134
Dialog Bank Group, 41, 108, 134
Dialog joint venture, 185
Dollars, 11, 72, 131. *See also* Ex-
change rates
Doran, Tony, 70
Dresser Industries, 185
Dubinin, Sergei, 113, 129, 134–35
Duma, 158–60
Dyachenko, Tatyana (Yeltsin's
daughter), 166, 204
Dyen, 72
Dzerzhinsky, Felix, 12, 22

Economic freedom, 20; as free-for-
all for state assets, 26; and moral
crisis, 25; public criticism of,

26–28; and shuttle trading, 22–24; unequal opportunity in, 25–26

Economic growth, 225, 268*n*27

Economic reforms, x–xiii, 8–11, 223; in czarist Russia, 234–35; Gaidar's compromises on, 36–38; Geraschenko's attempt at financial stabilization, 40–42, 91–92, 246; kamikaze theme of, 14; "liberal revolution" plan, 217–23, 226; mixed success of, 227–42; in Poland, 10, 237; and poverty, 143–46, 227; public response to, 12–17, 26–28; Russian parliament's opposition to, 94–95, 237–38; in Soviet Russia, 234; state enterprise managers' opposition to, 33, 34, 36–37; Western advisers' response to, 12–14; Yeltsin's presentation to the Congress of People's Deputies, 11. *See also* Industrial restructuring; Price liberalization; Privatization

Elections: in *1993*, 97; in *1995*, 139, 143, 155; in *2000*, 241–42, 247–248

—elections of *1996:* advertising in, 182–83; capitalists' support for Yeltsin in, 160–64, 166–67, 209, 238; delay of, debated, 165–66; first round of balloting, 167–70; journalists' support for Yeltsin in, 164; opposition to Yeltsin in, 156–57, 173–76; second round of balloting, 180–83; threat of Communist Party revival in, 157–60, 238; Vladimir Tractor Factory's response to, 170–76; Yeltsin's campaign, ix, 155–57, 160–62, 164–67

Energy prices, 29, 30, 36–38

Enterprises: auctions of stores and service businesses, 67–68; bankruptcies of, 116; debt between, 29–30, 39, 116; factory directors' control of, 65, 70, 71, 73, 229–30, 237; financial-industrial conglomerates, 79, 80, 105, 207–19, 239–40; investors' proxy battles with factory directors, 81–91; loans-for-shares program for, 135–43, 158, 206–7, 238; privatization plans for, 63–67; shell companies, 99; voucher auctions of, 70–76, 79–80, 85, 107–8; worker-controlled, 65

Entrepreneurs, 6, 44–45; "collective" of, 58; Communist Party promotion of, 55–56; cooperatives, 51–54, 56–58; in czarist Russia, 45–48; deal-making practices of, 59–60, 186–87, 195–96; KGB targeting of, 54; Lebed's campaign supported by, 170; money game of, 98–104; power of business elites, 207–19, 229–33; public hatred of, 54; rush for money among, 60; security forces of, 61; in Soviet Russia, 48–58; support for Yeltsin in the *1996* elections, 160–64, 166–67, 209, 238

European Bank for Reconstruction and Development, 73, 108

Exchange rates, 17–18, 21, 72, 253, 259*n*7; Black Tuesday collapse

Exchange rates (*continued*) of, 112, 129; "ruble corridor" plan for, 132

Exhibition of Economic Achievements, 185

Factory directors: acquisition of state enterprises by, 65, 70, 71, 73, 229–30, 237; adaptation to reforms by, 240; "bureaucratic market" of, 50; foreign investors' conflicts with, 121, 140–43; investors' proxy battles with, 81–91; opposition to privatization by, 33, 34, 36–37, 66, 69, 120–21; shell companies established by, 99

Fedorov, Andrei, 51

Finance, 199–201

Financial crisis, 224, 225–27, 244–48

Financial-industrial groups, 79, 80, 105, 207–19, 239–40

Financial stabilization, 40–42

Five Hundred Days program, 12

Foglizzo, Jean, 13, 30

Food shortages, 7–8, 12, 14–15, 17, 238, 245

Foreign investment: factory directors' opposition to, 121, 140–42; in the loans-for-shares auctions, 139–42; in Novgorod, 176–77, 228; and organized crime, 188–89; problems encountered by, 186–89; in Russia's regional economies, 197–99; reduced during financial crisis of *1997–98,* 244; success stories of,

189–200; in vouchers, 106–9. *See also* U.S. investments

Forward, Russia! movement, 161

Fridman, Mikhail, 105, 162, 208

Fyodorov, Boris, 240, 242; Central Bank policy criticized by, 92, 135; financial-industrial groups criticized by, 214–15; resigns as finance minister, 97; support for Yeltsin in the *1996* elections, 161

Fyodorov, Svyatoslov, 161

Fyodorov Eye Institute, 65

Gaidar, Yegor, 8–12, 63, 229–31, 233, 240, 246–47; compromises on crucial reforms, 36–38, 229; economic aid requested by, 27; forced resignation as deputy prime minister, 42–43, 76, 237; and Geraschenko's tenure at the Central Bank, 39–42; and industrial restructuring, 29–36; and the interenterprise debt crisis, 30; on privatization of state enterprises, 71; public response to his economic reform program, 17–20; resigns from government, 97, 239; returns as deputy prime minister, 95; on the siege of parliament, 96; on the strengthening ruble, 21; support for Yeltsin in the *1996* elections, 161

Gangs, 3–4, 26. *See also* Organized crime

Gazprom, 37, 128, 208, 212, 217, 226, 239

Geraschenko, Viktor: in the Black

Tuesday debacle, 112–13, 129; Central Bank tenure of, 39–42, 91–92, 95, 100, 112–13, 135, 246; on Paramonova's rejection, 132

Gerschenkron, Alexander, 234–35

GKI (State Committee on Privatization), 63, 67, 68, 140

GKOs (short-term bonds), 103, 114, 131, 138, 226, 263n50, 244, 245

Glasnost, 9, 20

Golubkov, Lyonya, 110–11

Gorbachev, Mikhail S.: August *1991* coup attempt against, x, 8, 13, 18, 40; Brezhnev's son-in-law jailed by, 148; cooperatives permitted by, 44, 50; in the elections of *1996,* 161; and glasnost reforms, 9, 20; joint ventures permitted by, 50, 64, 185, 190; and perestroika reforms, 3, 9, 83; resignation of, 11; summit with Reagan, 192–93

Gorenkov, Alexey, 178

Gosudarstvennye kratkosrochnye obligatsii. *See* GKOs

Graborski, Alexander, 178

Grachev, Pavel, xii, 96

Grigorievna, Antonina, 2

Grishin, Anatoly, 82–83, 104, 116–17; proxy battle with Bakaleynik, 83–91

Gross Domestic Product (GDP), 249

Group of Seven economic summit (*1996*), 182

Gusinsky, Vladimir, 51; in "The Appeal of the Thirteen," 162; authorized banks invented by,

100–102; as a member of the business elite, 208; NTV founded by, 164; security guards for, 114; in the Svyazinvest deal, 218–19, 222–23; at the World Economic Forum, 159; Zyuganov criticized by, 167

Hammer, Armand, 48

Hay, Jonathan, 73

Herzen, Alexander, 46

Hugel, Charles, 192, 193

Hyperinflation, 40–42, 92, 131

IBEC. *See* International Bank for Economic Cooperation

IBM, 189

IFC. *See* International Finance Corporation

Illarionov, Andrei, 42

IMF. *See* International Monetary Fund

Imperial Bank, 135

Income, household, 255

Individualism, Russian style of, 242–43

Industrial and Trade Bank, 78, 247

Industrial restructuring, 29–36, 63–66, 116–20, 171; Communist Party attack on, 158–60; factory directors' opposition to, 66, 69, 70, 73, 139–42; investors' proxy battles with factory directors, 81–91; loans-for-shares program for, 135–43, 158, 206–7; in Nizhny Novgorod, 66–70; voucher auctions for, 73–76, 79–80, 85

Industry: credits issued to, 34, 37, 40–41, 92, 116; in czarist Russia, 45–48, 234–35; in Soviet Russia, 48–54; tax breaks for, 128–29. *See also* Enterprises

Inflation, 34, 39, 109, 112, 116, 158, 250; hyperinflation, 40–42, 92, 131; legalization of the term, 9; stabilization of, 223, 231–32

Inkombank, 115; liquidity crisis of, 134; in the loans-for-shares program, 135, 140; as part of the business elite, 207

Institute for the Study of the Economy in Transition, 9

Institute of Foreign Languages, 4

Institute of Microeconomics, 76

Interest rates, 17, 99, 102, 117, 125, 134, 171–72, 224, 254; rise of in the world financial crisis, 226, 244–245

International Bank for Economic Cooperation (IBEC), 136–37

International Finance Company, 140

International Finance Corporation (IFC), 67, 68, 73, 119

International Monetary Fund (IMF), 12, 27, 131, 245

Interros, 136, 137

Ioffe, Yevgeny, 200–201

Irish House, 16

Ivanovna, Serafima, 155, 179–81

Izvestia, 164, 208–9

Jennings, Stephen, 74, 75, 81, 106–8

Jews: as entrepreneurs, 46, 47

Joint ventures, 64; of the Communist Party, 56; in oil companies, 57–58, 192–93; U.S.-Soviet, 41, 50, 57–58, 185, 190, 192–93

Jordan, Boris, 73–76, 81, 106–9, 200

Judicial system, 148, 156

Julia (Moscow student), 4

Kamaz factory, 28

Karelia, 189

Kazakhstan, 10, 57

Kazyanov, Nikolai, 174

KGB, 22, 35; entrepreneurs scrutinized by, 54; joint ventures and cooperatives of, 56; and Menatep, 56; reform of, 8

Khasbulatov, Ruslan, 96

Khenka family, 196

Khisa, Georgy, 37, 73

Khodorkovsky, Mikhail, 55–56, 162, 207, 209–12, 267n12, 245, 247

Kholodov, Dmitri, 164

Kiosks, 24, 181

Kiriyenko, Sergei, 246

Kivelidi, Ivan, 53, 99, 151

Kogalym, 57

Kojikova, Nadezhda Yakovleva, 27

Kokh, Alfred, 219

Kommunist, 9

Komsomol, 23, 26, 44, 55

Korovin, Viktor, 31–35

Korzhakov, Alexander: attacks on bankers orchestrated by, 114–15; delay of the *1996* elections sought by, 165; fired by Yeltsin, 181–82

Kovalev, Sergei, 156–57
Kozyrev, Andrei, 42
Krotov, Vatslav, 192–93
Kuzmin, Stanislav, 193

Laguna Company, 140
Law, Russians' ambivalent attitude toward, 146–48, 187
Layard, Richard, 214
Layoffs, 25, 32, 170–75, 177, 224
Lebed, Alexander, 161, 169, 170, 174, 205, 241, 248
Lenin, V. I., 48–49, 185, 234
Levada, Yuri, 65–66, 203, 238–39
Liberal Democratic Party, 97, 143
Lipetsk Tractor Factory, 82, 117
Lisovsky, Sergei, 182
Loans-for-shares program, 135–43, 206–7, 238; Communist Party investigation of, 158
Logovaz Group, 221
Lukoil, 56–58, 128, 135, 205; as part of the business elite, 208, 212, 239
Luzhkov, Yuri, 61, 101–2, 227–28, 241, 247; Korzhakov's intimidation of, 114–15; support for Yeltsin in the 1996 elections, 161, 169

Mafia, xii, 149–54, 174, 216, 240; attacks on bankers, 114; Western investors' encounters with, 188–89
Magnitogorsk, 177–81, 228
Magnitogorsk Metallurgical Kombinat, 177–78
Makarova, Tatyana, 123

Malashenko, Igor, 164–66
Market reform, 54
Martisyanov, Alexander, 4–5
Matyukhin, Georgy, 39, 40
Mavrodi, Sergei, 110
Maxim (street boy), 144–46, 149
McDonald's Restaurants of Canada, 185, 189–92, 193
Media: in the 1996 elections, 164; power of media conglomerates, 208
Menatep, 55–56, 62; as authorized bank for Moscow, 101–3; liquidity crisis of, 134; in the loans-for-shares program, 135, 140, 143, 207; as part of the business elite, 207, 209, 210, 239; security force of, 61
Migrayan, Andranik, 163
Mikhailova, Natalia, 177
Military, reform of, xii, 217
Military industrial complex, 20
Militia, 33, 146, 149–50
Minakov, Alexander, 59, 147–48, 150
MMM fund, 110–11
Monblan, 218
Monetary policy, disputes over, 91–92. *See also* Central Bank
Money, xii; frenzy attitude toward, 109; hard currency, 16, 53, 100, 131–32; and moral crisis, 25; new importance of, 21, 23–24; non-cash money, 30. *See also* Exchange rates; Rubles
Money game, 98–104
Moscow: authorized commercial banks in, 101–2; boom in,

Moscow (*continued*)
227–28; McDonald's restaurant
in, 185, 189–92; real estate market in, 78, 150
Moscow Arts Theater, 47
Moscow Institute of High Temperature, 55
Moscow Institute of Metals and Alloys, 104–5
Moscow Interbank Currency Exchange, 131
Moscow State University, 9
Moscow Taxi Park, 65
Moscow Times stock index, 112
Mosenergo, 205
Most Group, 51, 60–62, 101–3, 114; Korzhakov's attack on, 114–15; as part of the business elite, 208; in the Svyazinvest deal, 218
Multinational companies, 6, 176, 201–2

Naberezhnye Chelny, 28
Naishul, Vitaly, 50, 259n10
Nationalny Kredit, 132, 134
National Salvation Front, 42
National Security Council, 207
Natural resource enterprises, privatization of, 135–43, 217–19
Nemtsov, Boris, 67, 68–70, 157–58, 217, 226, 241, 245, 247
NEP-men, 48–49
New Economic Policy (NEP), 48–49, 60, 185
New Russians. *See* Entrepreneurs
Nikiferovna, Vera, 2
NIPEK (People's Oil Industrial Investment Euro-Asian Corporation), 76, 78
Nizhny Novgorod, 157; pilot auction in, 67–68; privatized stores in, 68–70
Norilsk Nickel, 121, 135, 137, 140, 218, 222
North West Shipping, 140
Novgorod, 176–77, 228
NTTMS, 55
NTV, 164, 208, 219

Oil companies, 53, 56–58, 135, 140; U.S.-Soviet joint ventures, 57–58, 192–93
Oil prices, 53, 99; deregulation of, 128; plunge of, 226
OLBI Investments, 53
Old Believer faith, 46
Oligarchic economic system, 207–19, 229–33
Organized crime, xii, 33, 149–54, 156, 174, 216, 240; attacks on bankers, 114; Western investors' encounters with, 188–89
Ostrovsky, Alexander, 46
Our Home Is Russia party, 143

Panikin, Alexander, 58–59
Paramonova, Tatiana, 129–35
Pavlov, Valentin, 12, 40
Payment system crisis, 39
Perestroika, 3, 9, 83, 136, 193
Peter the Great, 234
Petrovna, Nadezhda, 2
Pinochet Ugarte, Augusto, 134
Poland: economic reform in, 10, 236–37

Police forces. *See* Militia
Political freedom, 13, 20, 235
Postnov, Sergei I., 121–23
Potanin, Vladimir: in "The Appeal of the Thirteen," 162; appointed first deputy prime minister, 204; dismissed as first deputy prime minister, 217; in the financial crisis of *1997–98,* 245; loans-for-shares program of, 135–39; as a member of the business elite, 206–7, 209, 212–13; in the Svyazinvest deal, 218–19, 221, 222–23; Zyuganov criticized by, 167
Poverty, 143–46, 148, 227, 251
Pravda, 9, 54, 72
Price liberalization, xii, 9, 39, 223, 237, 238; entrepreneurs' use of, 44; public response to, 14–17; Western advisers' response to, 12
Primakov, Yevgeny, 246
Privatization, 235–39; auctions of stores and service businesses, 67–68; of the banking system, 40; Chubais's plan for, 63–67; Communist Party attack on, 158–60; and factory directors' control of enterprises, 65, 70, 71, 229–30, 237; investors' proxy battles with factory directors, 81–91; loans-for-shares program for, 135–43, 158, 206–7; in Nizhny Novgorod, 66–70; opposition to, 36, 64, 65–66, 69, 70, 74; public views of, 65–66. *See also* Vouchers
Production, industrial, 29, 124, 225, 250

Prokhorov, Mikhail, 136
Pronina, Zoya Ivanovna, 179
Property, privatization of, xii, 9, 63–64, 231, 233, 234
Pyramid schemes, 110–12

Railroad reform, 217
RAO United Energy System, 217
Reagan, Ronald, 166, 192–93
Real estate market, 78, 101, 150
Red Directors. *See* Factory directors
Red Proletariat Machine Tool Factory, 65
Referendum of April *1993,* 93–94, 237
Regional economies, 197–99, 227
Renova, 224
Ritchie, Joseph, 185
Rosprom, 210–11, 267*n*12
Rossisky Kredit, 5–6, 115, 140
Rubles: Black Tuesday collapse of, 112–14, 129; declines in value of, 10–11, 97, 109; devaluation in the world financial crisis, 226, 245; gains in purchasing power of, 17–18, 109; Geraschenko's invalidation of old notes, 95; Geraschenko's mass printing of, 40–42, 246; movement abroad of, 100, 157, 264*n*3; "ruble corridor" plan, 132, 171; scarcity of, 21, 131; slang terms for, 109; strengthening of against the dollar, 17–18, 131. *See also* Exchange rates
Rudloff, Hans George, 73
Rukova, Lyudmila, 7

Rule of the Seven Bankers, 207–16, 220
Russian Center for Public Opinion and Market Research, 65–66
Russian Orthodox church, 46, 128
Russian Raw Materials and Commodities Exchange, 51; MMM fund in, 110–11; voucher trading in, 72, 79–80, 103–4
Russian Union of Industrialists and Entrepreneurs, 66, 166
Rutskoi, Alexander, 14, 95–97
Ryzhkov, Nikolai, 12, 31, 54

Sachs, Jeffrey, 10, 27, 41, 260n22, 268n36
Sakharov, Andrei, 67
Sberbank, 72, 136
Sector Capital, 200
Security forces, private, 61, 114, 188
Segodnya, 164, 208, 219
Serf-capitalists, 45–48
Shalin, Yuri, 124
Shareholding societies, 64–65
Shary, Alexander, 173
Shatalin, Stanislav, 9, 12, 83
Shell companies, 99
Shevardnadze, Eduard, 14
Shleifer, Andrei, 73, 268n34
Shokhin, Alexander, 14
Shumeiko, Vladimir, 37, 66, 73
Shuttle traders, 22–24
Sidanko Oil Holding, 135, 140, 222
Simonyan, Rayr, 186
Small business: cooperatives, 44, 50–54, 56–58; in Novgorod, 176–77; scarcity of, 215–16

Sobchak, Anatoly, 64
Social welfare system, 33, 217
Solodov, Sergei, 5–6
Soros, George, 218, 267n20
Soviet State Bank for Foreign Economic Deals, 8, 41
Soviet Union: August 1991 coup attempt in, x, 8, 13, 18, 40; black-market entrepreneurs in, 48–50; breakup of, x, 8, 13–14; central planning in, 20–21, 49, 234, 236; Communist Party's economic control of, 40, 234; cooperatives in, 44, 48–54, 56–58; economic reforms in, 234; industrialization of, 30–31, 234; New Economic Policy in, 48–49, 60, 185; U.S. joint ventures with, 41, 50, 57–58, 185, 190, 192–93
Stack, Jack, 119
Stalin, Joseph, 30–31, 48–49, 60, 185, 234, 236
Stanislavsky, Konstantin, 47
State Committee for Science and Technology, 55
State Committee on Privatization. See GKI
State enterprises, privatization of, 64–65; auctions of stores and service businesses, 67–68; loans-for-shares programs, 135–43, 158, 206–7, 238; natural resource enterprises, 135–43, 217–19; voucher auctions, 73–76, 79–80, 85, 107–8
Stock market, Russian, 253; Black Tuesday, 112–14, 129; boom of 1996, 205, 223; support for

Yeltsin evidenced in, 167;
  voucher trading in, 108–9
Stolichny Bank, 135
Stolypin, Peter, 234
Storch, Heinrich, 46
Strauss, Robert, 184
Subsidies, food, 7
Suicide, 149, 264n65
Sun International, 196–98
Surgutneftegaz, 137
Svyazinvest deal, 218–19, 222–23,
  268n20
Systema, 227

Tatum, Paul, 188–89, 265n8
Taxes: ambivalent Russian attitude
  toward, 146–47; as a barrier for
  foreign investment, 186, 189;
  breaks for industry, 128–29; col-
  lection problems, 205–6, 240;
  evasion of, xiii, 58, 146, 151,
  216, 226–27, 245–46; reforms of,
  217, 245–46; value-added tax
  cuts, 36
Thailand, financial crisis in, 224
Tikhonova, Natalia, 25, 26, 113,
  147
Traders: babushki traders, 1–3;
  NEP-men, 48–49; shuttle traders,
  22–24. See also Entrepreneurs
Traktor Export, 82
Transport industry, 69
Treasury bills. See GKOs
Tretiakov, Pavel, 47
Troika Dialog, 108
Tsomik, Leonard, 184, 200–201
Tyumen Oil Company, 218, 224,
  247

Ukraine, 8
Underground economy, 49–50,
  216, 235
Unemployment, 19, 29, 32, 35, 36,
  125–26, 252
UnExim Bank: creation of, 136,
  137–38; in the loans-for-shares
  program, 135, 140, 207; as part
  of the business elite, 207, 212,
  239; Svyazinvest acquired by,
  218–19, 222–23
Union of Industrialists and Entrepreneurs, 30, 42
United Energy System, 239
Uralmash, 31–35, 213; Bendukidze's investment in, 80–81;
  difficulties faced by, 127–28
U.S. investments: and corruption,
  187; early post-Soviet ventures,
  185–86; and organized crime,
  188–89; problems encountered
  by, 186–89; and Russian negotiating styles, 186–87, 195–96; in
  Russian regional economies,
  197–99; U.S.-Soviet joint ventures, 41, 50, 57–58, 185, 190,
  192–93. See also McDonald's
  Restaurants of Canada

Vasilenko, Svetlana, 20
Vasiliev, Dmitri, 67, 75
Vasyukov, Valery, 35
Vera (shuttler), 22–24
Video International, 166
Viktor (Moscow gang member),
  3–4, 150, 151–53
Vimpelcom, 205
Vinogradov, Vladimir, 115, 207

Virtual industrial economy, 30, 116, 178, 226–27
Vladimir (town), 81, 83, 121–23, 170, 228
Vladimir Tractor Factory, 81–83, 247; Bakaleynik's battle with Grishin for control of, 83–91; difficulties faced by, 116–26, 170–76; recovery beginning in, 224–25
Vladislavlev, Alexander, 66
Vladivostok, 228
Volsky, Arkady, 30, 42
Vouchers: auctions of state enterprises with, 73–76, 79–80, 85, 107–8; First Central Depository for, 108; foreign purchasers of, 106–9; privatization plan using, 70–72, 141; street trading of, 103–4; voucher investment funds, 104–6
Vyakhirev, Rem, 208

Wages, 30, 42, 251
White House: attack on, 95–97, 238
Witte, Sergei, 45, 234
Worker-controlled enterprises, 65
World Bank, 12; International Finance Corporation, 67, 68, 73, 119
World Economic Forum, 159–60

Yavlinsky, Grigory, 12, 64, 143, 161, 236, 241, 247
Yekaterinburg, 31, 33
Yeltsin, Boris N.: acts as own prime minister, 11; auction system de-

cree, 74; cabinet shakeups by, 217, 246; campaign for reelection, ix, 155–57, 160–62, 164–67; capitalists' support for, 160–64, 166–67, 209, 238; constitutional reforms of, 94, 95, 97; economic decree powers stripped from, 42–43; economic reform team appointed by, 8–9; economic turnaround proclaimed by, 223; health problems of, x, 165, 181, 204–5, 216; impeachment called for, 93–94; Kovalev's harsh letter to, 156–57; loans-for-shares auctions decree, 139; opposition to, 74, 157–60, 173–76, 238; parliament suspended by, 95–97; promises improvement within one year, xii, 11, 19; public criticism of, 27–28, 42, 173–76; re-election of, 170, 183, 238; referendum on his presidency, 93–94, 237–38; response to Black Tuesday by, 113, 129; "special powers" assumed by, 93; support for in Magnitorgorsk, 178–81; support for in Novgorod, 177; trade-authorizing decree, 21–22; victory speech, 203; Vladimir Tractor Factory workers' support for, 173
Yevstafiev, Arkady, 182
Young Communists. See Komsomol
Yukos Oil Holding, 135, 140, 210–12, 218, 247
Yuksi, 212, 267n12
Yuroshova, Raya, 16

Zhdanov, A. A., 122
Zhilsotsbank, 55
Zhirinovsky, Vladimir, 97, 132, 143,
    161, 170
Zverev, Sergei, 44, 60–61
Zyuganov, Gennady, ix, 143, 155,
    170; defeat conceded by, 183; en-
trepreneurs' distrust of, 164,
166–67; journalists' criticism of,
164–65; Vladimir Tractor Factory workers' support for,
173–76; at the World Economic
Forum, 159